GAZA CONFLICT 2021

With sincere
thanks and
gratitude.

FOUNDATION FOR
DEFENSE OF DEMOCRACIES

GAZA CONFLICT 2021

Hamas, Israel and Eleven Days of War

JONATHAN SCHANZER

CONTENTS

INTRODUCTION

I first visited the Gaza Strip in 1998. Back then, I was a dark-haired graduate student at the Hebrew University of Jerusalem. After seven years in the workforce, I had decided to devote my career to the study of the Middle East. As I set about learning the languages, history, and culture of the region, I felt compelled to visit as much of it as I could. Gaza was remarkably close to my apartment — perhaps two hours away. Yet it felt like another world. Despite the US-led peace process, the territory had become a stronghold of the terrorist group Hamas. In large part, that was what drew me to the place.

It was not long before I met a Palestinian man from eastern Jerusalem who said he could take me and a few classmates to Gaza from an agreed upon spot just outside the Damascus Gate of the Old City. We met him there early on a Sunday morning, boarded a minibus, and started off. Before we had even left Jerusalem, he warned our small group not to stray, not to mention Israel, and not ever to speak a word of Hebrew — one of the two languages most of us were studying at the time. We all nodded in agreement, then looked at one another, wondering exactly what we had just gotten ourselves into.

As the minibus entered Gaza, there was an immediate change in scenery. The signs changed from Hebrew to Arabic. It was dustier. It was poorer. The streets were crowded. I distinctly recall Hamas graffiti on the walls. One spray-painted message featured a large Israeli flag with a knife lodged in it. That prompted more nervous glances inside the minibus.

The day was both memorable and enjoyable. We took turns taking photos next to a sign that said, "Welcome to Gaza." We walked the streets of Gaza City. Children descended upon our small group, imploring us to take their pictures. We went to a school operated by the United Nations Works and Relief Agency, where children once again jostled to get into the middle of the photos we snapped. We went shopping. We went to a church. We visited an association that cared for Gazans injured during the First Intifada — the Palestinian uprising of 1987 that ultimately paved the road for the establishment of the semi-independent Palestinian Authority (PA), which at the time of our visit could barely control the Gaza Strip. Of course, one would not know that based on the ubiquitous signs featuring the smiling face of then-PA President Yasser Arafat.

We drove by the sea — the same sea in which Israelis were swimming just a few miles north. Our guide took us to Israeli settlements, which were roundly derided by the Gazans we met nearby. The Israeli buildings, considerably better built than the surrounding structures and guarded by Israeli soldiers, would seven years later be uprooted as part of a unilateral Israeli withdrawal that would open the political and security vacuum that enabled Hamas to conquer the Gaza Strip in 2007.

By the time I completed my studies and returned home to America, Gaza was no longer a place I could visit. The Second Intifada had erupted. Launched in 2000, this was less of a popular uprising and more of a war. Gaza had become a hotbed of Hamas terrorist activity.

In the years since, I have thought often about that trip to Gaza. The territory has come under the complete control of Hamas. In fact, one can argue that Hamas is the sovereign. It controls the borders, at least in terms of determining who can enter and exit (imports and exports are still controlled by Israel and Egypt). It has a functioning government with a monopoly on the use of force; other terrorist groups operate openly in Gaza, but with Hamas' permission. Gaza is a breakaway republic, no longer part of the PA. For Israel, Gaza has become a problem from hell.

Though Israel is a far superior military power, there is no clear military solution to the Hamas threat. Israelis have no appetite for retaking the enclave or for utterly vanquishing the group. Yet wars continue to erupt between Israel and Hamas on a regular basis. Hamas starts them. Israel finishes them. The skirmishes draw intense attention from the international media and from zealous partisans on both sides of the Palestinian-Israeli divide.

Writing a book in this crowded space is never easy. I have written several over the years, and they have received equal parts praise and criticism. Yet after the most recent war between Hamas and Israel in May of 2021, I felt compelled to write another.

This is not a book about whether Hamas is or is not a terrorist organization. According to US law, it is.[1] Many other governments around the world agree with that assessment.

Nor is this book about whether Israel is a valuable, democratic ally of the United States. It is. Every US president since Israel's founding has attested to this. So have most legislators. This reflects a broad consensus among the American people, too.[2]

This book will also avoid the unproductive debates about whether Israel is justified in its military control over the West Bank or in its *de facto* control over the borders surrounding the Gaza Strip. There are hundreds, even thousands, of analyses on this topic. It is unclear whether any of them will ever settle the dispute. A solution to the conflict is ultimately up to the Palestinians and Israelis themselves. This is not to imply that Israel doesn't have important choices to make about its policy toward the Palestinians and their national project. It does. But that is another book for another time.

This book is about the 2021 conflict between Israel and Hamas. That war was the fourth between these two bitter foes. The Israelis called it Operation Guardian of the Walls. Hamas called it The Battle of the Sword of Jerusalem. The conflict lasted for 11 days during the month of May. This book aims to explain that war, with the benefit of hindsight, better than it was explained at the time.

After the war concluded, it dawned on me that I monitored this conflict more closely than any of the previous ones during my career. This was not a reflection of greater interest. Rather, it was a matter of available technology. Thanks to smartphone and smart television technology, I was able to track a flood of news updates in several languages and watch multiple Middle Eastern television broadcasts in real time from my home in suburban Washington, DC. Thankfully, over the previous year of isolation during the COVID-19 crisis, I had decided to brush up on the Middle Eastern languages I learned in graduate school.

During those 11 days, I worked the phones, talking to officials in the United States, Israel, and several Arab governments. They invariably offered interesting insights not covered by the media. I also talked to journalists who were digesting off-the-record statements by Biden administration officials. Those conversations often helped me better understand the daily reports churned out by newspapers and websites the world over.

Perhaps it goes without saying, but I did not sleep much during those 11 days. By the time I would have normally gone to bed, Israelis and Gazans were starting their days anew, with fresh news from the front. These reports usually started to air around midnight Eastern Standard Time. For some reason, I felt compelled to understand the current state of play before trying to catch a few winks. After that, I often laid awake in bed, scrolling in the dark through my Twitter feed, watching the war unfold thousands of miles way.

What stayed with me after those 11 days of war were not the scenes of conflict. Over the years, I have sadly become accustomed to jarring images of violence and mayhem. Rather, it was the disconnect between American news reporting versus what I was watching, reading, and hearing from the region itself.

The term "fake news" is not helpful here. I am not sure it is helpful anywhere. There was no clear attempt to mislead on the part of most reporters. Admittedly, there are always observers of this conflict with an axe to grind. There were plenty of pundits who appeared on television or wrote op-eds in America's top papers who missed the mark. But those people were being asked for their opinions. It was their right to share those opinions, even when they were remarkably wrong.

For me, the disconnect between reporting and reality was more fundamental. It ignored the history. While Hamas' leadership undeniably makes its decisions independently, the group is the product of its patrons over the years. The Islamic Republic in Iran, the world's leading state sponsor of terrorism, remains the most influential among them. The Arab-Israeli conflict has retracted over the years. Israel has made peace with several Arab neighbors. Others have simply grown to understand that after multiple costly wars, efforts to destroy Israel are futile. Not the Islamic Republic. The regime in Iran has worked overtime to keep the conflict burning through its proxies. Tehran controls some directly. Others simply enjoy Iran's financial, political, and military support, with the understanding that they share a common goal: the destruction of the Jewish state. Hamas is more the latter than the former. Yet Iran's role failed to register headlines during the recent war.

Nor was there much Western interest in noting that, even as the war raged, the White House was openly pursuing a return to the highly controversial 2015 nuclear deal with Iran, formally known as the Joint Comprehensive Plan of Action (JCPOA). Returning to the JCPOA would likely grant Iran, Hamas' top sponsor, a significant financial boon. This would compromise America's role as peacemaker, to say the least.

Furthermore, most American commentators failed to tie the conflict to very recent events preceding the war. Here, I am referring to Israel and Iran's ongoing shadow war across the Middle East. Tehran has for years sought to surround Israel with proxies and to arm them with advanced weapons. Israel has recently started to fight back — and not just against the proxies. That shadow war continues to intensify, and it influenced the Gaza battlefield more than most observers noted.

Admittedly, Tehran is not alone in its support for Hamas. The Islamist-leaning governments of Qatar, Turkey, and even Malaysia also exercise influence over Hamas. While these governments purport to support the Gazan people, it has become glaringly obvious that their assistance has military dimensions. This, too, was barely noted during the 2021 conflict.

Equally mystifying, if not more so, was that media reporting during the 2021 conflict often ignored the clear patterns from the previous rounds of conflict between Hamas and Israel. There is plenty of material from which to draw. The Gaza wars of 2008, 2012, and 2014 offer a clear and rather predictable template. Each time, Hamas tested Israel with provocative attacks. Each time, Israel responded. And each time, Israel emerged the stronger party. There was never any doubt that it would. This was, after all, a conflict between a non-state actor and a powerful regional state.

Here in America, the reporting and analysis on the 2021 Gaza war also ignored the brutality of Hamas. The group had clearly diverted huge amounts of international aid to build military structures that a superior military power would predictably destroy. The group's fighters were guilty of war crimes, as well. The most obvious sign of this was the fact that the unguided rockets they fired were aimed at civilian areas. Human Rights Watch, a group not typically sympathetic to Israel, concluded months after the battle that Hamas had committed war crimes through these indiscriminate launches.[3] It was also clear during the war that Hamas was using human shields to protect their fighters and military infrastructure, which is also a war crime.

The reporting often focused on the death toll. Remarkably, numbers produced by the Hamas-controlled "Gaza Ministry of Health" were reported frequently and without caveats. Few reports bothered to note that it was Hamas that started the war. Moreover, the significant lengths to which Israel went to minimize civilian casualties, with its emphasis on precision strikes against military targets, went largely undocumented. Without question, any loss of civilian life is a tragedy. However, the relatively low death toll — 212 people, most of them combatants — over the course of an intense 11-day conflict,[4] while thousands of projectiles darkened the skies over Israel, was an undeniable indication of Israeli restraint. Had Israel simply returned fire to the exact spot of every rocket launch, regardless of its surroundings, there would have been an unspeakable bloodbath.

Nor did Western media acknowledge how far Israel went to protect its own people from terrorist attacks intended to cause widespread death and destruction. During the conflict, Israel spent about as much on missile defense to deflect Hamas rockets (at least $340 million, assuming Israel expended on average one $100,000 interceptor for each of the roughly 3,400 Hamas rockets fired into Israeli territory)[5] as the World Bank estimates Gaza requires for reconstruction (between $290 to $380 million).[6] This does not include the cost of damage to Israeli property caused by the rockets that managed to get through. Rather than noting this, a remarkably large number of media reports pointed to the uneven death counts as an indication that Israel was fighting an offensive war.

In attributing the Gaza war's causes, Western coverage also largely ignored the April 2021 decision by PA President Mahmoud Abbas to cancel upcoming Palestinian elections. Hamas likely would have won those elections but was ultimately (and probably justifiably) denied the chance to compete. Looking back, it seems clear that Hamas tried to win the hearts and minds of the Palestinian people by other means — namely, by fomenting conflict with Israel.

Finally, Western reporting paid virtually no attention to Hamas' many contradictions. On the one hand, it is a religious Islamist group. Yet it also employs nationalist symbols and ideology. Hamas asserts its independence, yet it relies heavily on financial and political patrons. It controls a defined territory in Gaza, which the group nevertheless claims is under Israeli occupation. Hamas holds elections for its leadership, yet it rules Gaza with an iron fist. It engages in terrorist tactics such as suicide bombing, but it insists that it is fighting a legal war of resistance. Few news organizations grappled with these complex notions prior to the May 2021 war, let alone during it.

The result was a mountain of flawed news and thin analysis that framed the war as just one more battle between Israelis and Palestinians. Never mind that the Israelis did not want it. Never mind that Gaza's population did not want it, either.

To be fair, the Israeli government deserves some blame here. It failed spectacularly in its efforts to explain the war. One would think that after more than seven decades of conflict, the government would be better at this. Of course, there may be a good reason why they are not: When war erupts, Israel's primary goal is to deter other threat actors in the region from joining the fray. In other words, Israeli officials are typically focused more on baring their teeth at their enemies than on discrediting false reports or disinformation. Israel's more concerted efforts to set the record straight usually come later, when the military crisis has passed. That is typically when a diplomatic pile-on is already well underway, with the UN Human Rights Council, an Orwellian organization whose members include some of the world's worst human rights abusers, almost always leading the charge.

I wrote the first draft of this book in the days and weeks that followed the war. Remarkably, the writing was not particularly difficult. I had previously written extensively on Hamas, Israel, and the Palestinians — including books and congressional testimony. During the conflict itself, I also wrote several articles, either solo or with colleagues, that formed the basis of several chapters herein. In short, I had a lot of material at my fingertips.

The editing of the book took a bit longer. I took a trip to Israel — my first international travel since the COVID-19 crisis began — to fill in a few gaps. After that, I needed a few more weeks to wrestle my prose to the ground. From there, I solicited feedback from trusted friends and colleagues. But I worked quickly for a reason. I wanted to see this book come out sooner rather than later.

My hope is that the following short chapters will help novice and experienced Middle East watchers alike better understand Hamas' history, how it rules Gaza and fights wars, and the role of Iran and other foreign patrons. I further hope to foster a better understanding of the 2021 war itself by examining the conflict through a wider aperture than the reporting at the time allowed.

The narrative of this book bounces back and forth between the distant past and the recent war. My intention here is to ensure that the reader can more easily draw straight lines between history and current events. The book concludes with a look to the future. There is, of course, no predicting what comes next in this patch of land on the Mediterranean coast. One can only hope for a better understanding of this recurring conflict that has vexed policymakers for decades. The 2021 conflict was the fourth Gaza war. There will be a fifth.

ONE
NO SINGLE SPARK

When the 2021 conflict began, it was not immediately apparent that it would be the fourth Gaza war. Hamas has fired thousands of rockets into Israel over the years, and Israel does not always choose to respond. Judging by the sheer number of rockets fired in the early hours of the May 2021 war, however, Hamas was not simply looking to make a statement.[1] Hamas was looking for a fight; militants fired 470 rockets in the first 24 hours.[2] With millions of civilians under threat, Israel had no choice but to respond.

When the conflict erupted, a great many news reports pointed to a legal matter as the reason for the war. Israel's Supreme Court was set to hear a case that had the potential to lead to the eviction of six families in the East Jerusalem neighborhood of Sheikh Jarrah. The hearing was scheduled during the Muslim holy month of Ramadan, when tensions typically run higher in Jerusalem. Simply put, Muslim Palestinians during Ramadan are often on edge because they fast from sunup to sundown. Many are already less than pleased about Israeli security restrictions in Jerusalem, home to the Al-Aqsa Mosque, often described as the "third holiest" city in the Islamic faith, after Mecca and Medina in Saudi Arabia. In early May 2021, some of the Palestinian faithful took to the streets of Jerusalem to protest the Sheikh Jarrah case. Some even clashed with Israeli police and right-wing Israeli activists.

The historical context surrounding the Sheikh Jarrah homes is important to briefly review. The neighborhood itself is well-known to observers of the region. It is a short walk from the Damascus Gate of the Old City. Nestled within the neighborhood is the American Colony Hotel, where journalists often stay and swap stories during times of conflict. It is also the neighborhood where the US consulate in Jerusalem, essentially the US embassy for the Palestinians, was located — until President Trump shuttered it in 2019.[3]

The specific property dispute requires a somewhat long view of history to fully grasp. The homes in question were originally bought by Jewish families in 1875. During the first Arab-Israeli war of 1948, after Jordan occupied the eastern half of Jerusalem, the Jewish inhabitants were expelled. This was the status quo until the 1967 Six-Day War, during which Israel captured eastern Jerusalem. (Israelis say they "reunited" their capital.) After 1967, Israel did not eject the inhabitants of the homes. The descendants of the original owners subsequently sued to recover their family property.

The legal battle lasted four decades. The Israeli legal system found in favor of the original Jewish families in several rulings. However, the courts also endeavored to protect those who were seen as legal tenants, ruling that they would not be evicted if they paid rent. The Palestinian families refused, with Palestinian activists claiming that Israel was attempting to "Judaize" Jerusalem, leading to the standoff that grabbed headlines in early May 2021.[4]

Elsewhere in Jerusalem, trouble had been brewing since April, at the start of Ramadan, when Israeli police erected barriers to prevent youth from congregating on the steps of Damascus Gate.[5] There were sporadic reports of violence between Jews and Arabs. Then, on May 7, at least 205 Palestinians and 17 Israeli police officers were wounded in clashes at the Temple Mount.[6] That was three days before Israel's Supreme Court was expected to issue its decision on the Sheikh Jarrah case.

Then there was the drama of Jerusalem Day on May 10. Israelis celebrated the religious and historical significance of their political capital at the Western Wall, the holiest site open to Jewish prayer. Meanwhile, Palestinians atop the Temple Mount launched fireworks at Israeli police, igniting a tree in the process.[7] The visuals, devoid of context, were infuriating for Palestinians watching from home: Jews dancing and singing as a fire raged at the Al-Aqsa Mosque. Violence began after Israeli police entered the compound that evening in response to stone-throwing Palestinians, firing rubber bullets and stun grenades. In the end, more than 330 Palestinians were injured. At least three were in critical condition. *The New York Times* reported that 21 Israeli police officers were injured, too.[8]

Watching from Gaza, roughly 50 miles from the Temple Mount, Hamas decided to enter the fray. The group had been threatening for weeks to respond to what its leaders described as Israeli provocations. "Tampering with Jerusalem will burn the heads of the occupiers," said senior Hamas official Saleh al-Arouri.[9] After demanding that Israel remove its security forces from the Temple Mount — a demand Israel would never accept — Hamas unleashed an estimated 150 rockets toward Israel.[10] The rockets rained down on the southern and central sectors of the country. One struck just west of Jerusalem, causing some damage.[11] The war was underway.

War is a chaotic thing to cover. During the opening stanza of this conflict, hundreds of rockets were hurtling into Israel. Israel's

Iron Dome air defense system knocked down many of them. The Israel Defense Forces (IDF) soon mobilized and struck back at its "target bank" of Hamas military assets throughout the Gaza Strip, aiming to stymie the rocket fire.

The early reporting on the war conveyed these basic facts well enough. However, in explaining the conflict's outbreak, a great many reporters focused on the Sheikh Jarrah controversy. Some reports cited observers who claimed that the legal dispute "caused" the war.[12]

Blaming the war on legal issues or political tensions is an odd interpretation of the events. Wars begin when the first shots are fired. In May 2021, those shots (rockets) were fired by Hamas, some 50 miles from the political controversy in question. More than 3,400 rocket attacks on Israel followed — many in large salvos prepared months in advance. Hamas readied its commando fighters for tunnel warfare. Hamas also prepared drones for attacks against Israel by air and sea.

More broadly, conflict erupts between Israel and Hamas on a regular basis. Hamas usually picks these fights every few years, and it does not need a particular reason. Fighting the Jewish state is the group's *raison d'être*. Recent history suggests that a conflict was overdue.

But if one was searching for events that might have precipitated the 2021 war, one obvious episode was the PA's April 29 cancelation of its long-awaited May 22 elections. This blocked Hamas from re-entering Palestinian politics. The terrorist group was set to win a considerable number of seats in the Palestinian legislature. Hamas' leadership was seething and sought to reassert itself among the Palestinian population.

Finally, Hamas' top patron, Iran, and Israel were fighting a shadow war across the Middle East. The Islamic Republic threatened to attack Israel just weeks before the Gaza conflict erupted.[13] It is also worth noting here that the regime, having already helped the group build up its military capabilities, openly cheered on Hamas attacks throughout the war.[14]

For all these reasons, which are explained in greater detail throughout this book, the system was blinking red. Israeli officers on the country's southern border confirmed this to me just one month after the conflict subsided. "We could see that Hamas was mobilizing weeks before the war. Something was happening," said a young female IDF soldier dressed in fatigues, standing in front of a matrix of monitors at Israel's Southern Command headquarters.[15]

As my colleague David May and I explained during the war, in an article we penned for *The Jerusalem Post*, this was certainly not the first time that the "single point of failure" narrative had been wielded to explain organized Palestinian or Arab-Israeli violence.[16]

Take, for example, the reporting surrounding the outbreak of the Second Intifada in 2000. Israeli opposition leader Ariel Sharon's visit to the Temple Mount was the purported catalyst. The former general, accompanied by a security entourage, walked on the Temple Mount on September 28, 2000, in what was widely deemed a provocative act. Palestinians responded with violent protests.[17] Those protests rapidly gave way to a coordinated campaign that included suicide bombings and other gruesome acts of violence specifically designed to target civilians inside Israel. The violence lasted until 2005.

Did Sharon single-handedly provoke a five-year conflict? *Wikipedia* says so, reflecting the broad consensus of countless journalists at the time.[18] However, according to senior Hamas officials and Palestinian President Yasser Arafat's widow,[19] the Palestinian leader had already decided to launch an intifada when he walked away from US-led negotiations with Israel at Camp David in July 2000.[20] What we now know as the "Second Intifada" may well have been intended to be smaller in scope. It was most likely pre-arranged to gain the Palestinians leverage at the negotiating table. To be clear, Sharon's stroll was not the cause. It was a convenient pretext. The unrest was the coordinated decision of the Palestinian leadership.

The 1929 riots, one of the first serious bouts of Arab violence against Jews in the Holy Land, is also falsely blamed on a single provocation. On August 15, 1929, after Jews asserted their right to pray at the Western Wall, Arab leaders warned that Jews planned to overtake Al-Aqsa Mosque. Nine days later, Arab mobs butchered nearly 70 Jews in the city of Hebron. More massacres followed.[21] The event, even today, is blamed on Jews crossing a religious red line. However, the cause of the violence was a coordinated decision by the Palestinian leadership. Chief among them was Haj Amin al-Husseini, the grand mufti of Jerusalem who subsequently forged ties with Adolf Hitler during World War II.[22]

More recently, the Palestinian leadership pushed the single spark narrative when the PA acceded to the International Criminal Court (ICC). The Palestinians accepted ICC jurisdiction over the West Bank and Gaza starting on June 13, 2014, which marked the start of Israeli raids on Hamas and other Palestinian terrorists in the West Bank.[23] According to the PA, this was the spark for the 2014 Gaza war. That narrative, focusing on the specific IDF operations, conveniently excludes the Hamas kidnapping and murder of three Israeli teens on June 12 — one event among several that ultimately gave way to the third major Israel-Hamas conflagration.

The Palestinian reliance on individual events to justify violence has been mimicked by the Lebanese terrorist group Hezbollah. When Israel ended its military presence in southern Lebanon in May 2000, it retained a small territory known as Mount Dov (also known as Shebaa Farms). Israel had seized it from Syria (not Lebanon) during the 1967 Six-Day War. Despite Israel's withdrawal from the rest of southern Lebanon, Hezbollah pointed to Israel's control over this small patch of earth — which officials from the Lebanese state had never even mentioned until 2000 — as a grave provocation. Ever since, Hezbollah has wielded it as justification for violence against Israel.[24] Curiously, many observers of the region appear to take this claim at face value.

In the Palestinian context today, very few things occur in a vacuum. Sometimes tensions run high. Sometimes a false sense of calm prevails. But the flame is always burning, susceptible to anything combustible. More importantly, the preparations for conflict against Israel are a constant, and usually with help from state sponsors. There is rarely one single spark that ignites a conflict. There is no single point of failure — except, perhaps, in the reporting that follows.

TWO
THE ORIGINS OF HAMAS

There is one notable exception to the single-spark fiction: the First Intifada. History shows that this was indeed a spontaneous expression of Palestinian discontent. This uprising gave birth to Hamas.

On December 8, 1987, an IDF truck collided with a car filled with Gazans returning home after working that day in Israel. The accident killed four and injured others. That night, the funerals in the Gaza Strip devolved into tense demonstrations, which quickly spread across the coastal enclave. Thus began the *intifada*,[1] a nationalist-inspired campaign of violent and nonviolent protests against Israel. The unrest quickly spread to the West Bank.[2]

At the time, the Palestine Liberation Organization (PLO) was widely recognized as the sole representative of the Palestinian people. The group had for years grabbed sensational headlines for its terrorist attacks against Israel and Western nations. However, the PLO watched the intifada unfold from its headquarters in Tunisia after the Israelis drove the group out of Lebanon in the early 1980s. The group's leaders watched helplessly as Palestinian grassroots organizers advanced the Palestinian nationalist agenda.

Amidst the unrest, a new group called Hamas assumed center stage. Hamas was born of an ideological debate within the Palestinian Muslim Brotherhood movement. Steeped in anti-Western ideology, the Brotherhood had been anti-Israel (and still is) since its inception in Egypt in 1928. However, it was during the intifada that Brotherhood figures who embraced violence against the Jewish state decided to splinter from the rest of the movement. They created a new organization in December 1987 or January 1988. The group was called *Harakat al-Muqawamma al-Islamiyya*, which in Arabic means "Islamic Resistance Movement." The acronym is HAMAS, or "zeal" in Arabic.

Some historians say the first leaflet issued by Hamas appeared on February 11, 1988, calling the group the "powerful arm of the Association of Muslim Brothers."[3] However, Hamas leaders today insist that the first leaflet dropped in Gaza on December 14, 1987, just days after the uprising began.[4] Regardless, Hamas undeniably inspired Palestinians to take to the streets during the intifada. In so doing, Hamas imbued the population with a greater appreciation for the group's violent Islamist ideology.[5]

The influence of Hamas in those early days was remarkable for a nascent organization. By one estimate, Hamas in the late 1980s enjoyed significant influence in some 40 percent of Gaza's mosques, thanks to previous religious outreach efforts of the group's founder and spiritual guide, Ahmed Yassin.[6] Hamas further asserted its leadership through the provision of social services. The group reportedly also wielded its security and intelligence arm, *Majed*, to punish those who did not participate in intifada activities.[7]

With Hamas on the rise in the Palestinian territories, the exiled PLO leadership in Tunisia quickly understood that it was losing stature among the people. Simply put, the PLO was not standing shoulder to shoulder with the population. PLO leader Yasser Arafat, who had recklessly alienated his people from the West by throwing in his lot with Saddam Hussein in the 1991 Gulf War, understood that he needed to solidify his stature quickly among Palestinians and in the international community. If he did not, the PLO would become a casualty of the intifada.

In a bid to re-establish the PLO as the sole, legitimate representative of the Palestinian people, Arafat accepted UN General Assembly Resolution 181. Passed in November 1947, the resolution called for partitioning the British Mandate of Palestine into a Jewish and an Arab state. The United States and Israel immediately viewed Arafat's move as both a tacit recognition of Israel and an opportunity to quell the intifada. The West began to test the theory that the PLO (or the Fatah faction, a terror group founded in the 1950s, composed of many of the same figures) was willing to accept Israel's existence. Despite his prolific résumé as an arch-terrorist, Arafat was rapidly on his way to becoming a world leader.

Back in the West Bank and Gaza, the intifada continued, and Hamas led the way. On August 18, 1988, the group published its charter calling for an independent Palestinian state run according to *Sharia* — that is, Islamic law. The document asserted that Palestinians should not cede an inch of Palestinian land. The organization declared *jihad* (holy war) and asked regional states to open their borders to Hamas *mujahideen* (jihadi fighters) as part of this war.[8]

Admittedly, the PLO's charter was not much different in tone or substance.[9] But Arafat refused to be eclipsed. In November 1988, he called for an international peace conference based upon the PLO's formal acceptance of UN Security Council resolutions 242 and 338, which were issued after the 1967 and 1973 Arab-Israeli wars, respectively. Both resolutions acknowledged Israel's right to exist within internationally recognized borders. After having terrorized Israelis around the world, Arafat's move was nothing short of historic. He overtly signaled the PLO's acceptance of Israel's existence. Within weeks, more than 50 countries recognized the PLO.[10] A new diplomatic construct was born.

While the international community pursued a new era in Palestinian-Israeli relations, Hamas launched a violent campaign against Israel. Hamas kidnapped soldiers, stabbed others, and even commandeered an Israeli bus and crashed it, killing 16 people.[11] Deeply alarmed, Israeli authorities arrested hundreds of the group's members, including Hamas founder Ahmad Yassin,[12] and declared Hamas an illegal organization.[13]

In late 1989 and early 1990, Hamas formed an alliance with the Islamic Republic in Iran, following what Hamas spokesman Ibrahim Goshi called "meetings at the highest level."[14] Until then, Tehran had devoted most of its resources to the Lebanese terrorist group Hezbollah and, to a lesser extent, to Palestinian Islamic Jihad (PIJ), a smaller group that conducted attacks against Israel. The Islamic Republic's goals were twofold: to continue to erase the ties that had existed between the Shah and Israel before the Islamic Revolution of 1979, and to "Islamize" the Arab-Israeli conflict. The regime's supreme leader, Ali Khamenei, thus declared that "the usurper and racist regime ruling over occupied Palestine must be destroyed and eliminated."[15]

The sectarian differences between Iran's Shiite regime and Hamas, Tehran's Sunni client, were not insignificant. The struggle between Sunnis (85 percent of the Islamic world) and Shiites (15 percent), continues to figure prominently in regional turmoil. Yet, Hamas and Iran shared a common goal in "the liberation of Palestine." Thus began a patron-client relationship that would serve

Hamas well into the future. According to reports, Iran initially provided Hamas with an estimated $30 million annually along with military training abroad.[16]

Financing was only part of the Islamic Republic's patronage. In 1991, Hamas opened an office in Tehran.[17] Later that year, Tehran invited Hamas to attend a conference with other Iranian clients to promote the "Islamic intifada." The conference produced a communiqué opposing the PLO's peace talks with Israel.[18]

With assistance from Iran, as well as Arab states that rejected Israel's very existence, Hamas began enforcing professional standards. In 1991, Hamas announced the formation of its military wing, the Izz al-Din al-Qassam Brigades, named after a well-known Muslim guerilla fighter who was killed fighting the British in 1935.[19] The group also created a politburo that mirrored the structure of its PLO rival.[20]

In 1992, Tehran secured an agreement with the Sudanese government to provide a safe haven for Islamists in the country, including Hamas. Iran subsequently trained numerous Hamas and other terrorists on Sudanese soil.[21] In October 1992, a Hamas delegation led by Politburo chief Mousa Abu Marzouk visited Tehran for meetings with key Iranian figures, reportedly including Supreme Leader Khamenei.[22] Hamas also announced it would increase its ties with the Iran-backed Hezbollah.[23]

By December 1992, mounting fears over Hamas violence led Israel to deport more than 400 suspected Hamas members to Lebanon.[24] But these deportations achieved little. In fact, many of those Hamas members established close ties with Hezbollah and Iran. Some received training and indoctrination.[25] Moreover, Hamas took the opportunity to create a presence in Lebanon's lawless Palestinian refugee camps, establishing social programs and religious organizations.[26] In 1993, Egyptian intelligence reported that Iran was training up to 3,000 Hamas militants.[27] Khamenei, meanwhile, was urging preachers back in the West Bank and Gaza to "fill their sermons with slogans against Israel and the White House and the treasonous PLO leaders."[28]

Looking to counter Iran and Hamas through the pursuit of peace, Prime Minister Yitzhak Rabin made a strategic decision to recognize the PLO.[29] On September 13, 1993, Rabin and Arafat signed an historic peace agreement and shook hands on the White House lawn. As the diplomatic process kicked into high gear, Hamas remained adamantly opposed to recognition, negotiations, or peace with Israel.[30]

In December 1993, Marzouk, Hamas' Politburo chief, returned to Iran and met with President Ali Rafsanjani, who at the time was widely hailed as a moderate — an overly optimistic assessment that would become common in the West as other politicians came and went in the Islamic Republic.[31] By 1994, the intifada was over. Yet, Hamas began to prepare for its first wave of suicide bombings against Israel — a tactic previously employed only by Hezbollah.[32] The goal was to derail the peace process. The first successful Hamas suicide attack occurred in the northern Israeli town of Afula in April 1994. The bomber detonated his explosives in a car positioned near a bus, killing eight and wounding many more. By autumn, Hamas had launched three more suicide attacks.[33]

Hamas sometimes framed its suiciding bombings as a response to Israeli settler Baruch Goldstein's 1994 massacre of 29 Muslims in Hebron. However, the violence undoubtedly represented Hamas' strategy to torpedo the ongoing Israeli-Palestinian negotiations. Iran's influence was hugely significant in this regard. Amidst the uptick in violence, Osama Hamdan, the group's representative to Tehran, boasted of flourishing ties with the Islamic Republic.[34]

On October 14, 1994, the Nobel Committee announced that Yizhak Rabin, Shimon Peres, and Yasir Arafat would win its coveted peace prize.[35] Five days later, a Hamas suicide bus bombing killed 22 Israelis and wounded 56. Over the next year, the group carried out attacks in Hebron, Jerusalem, Ramat Gan, and elsewhere.[36] In 1995, with the death toll mounting, the United States designated Hamas pursuant to Executive Order 12947, which targeted terrorist groups that disrupted the Middle East peace process.[37]

It was clear that two things had to happen if peace was to prevail: Iranian support for Hamas would need to cease, and the PLO would require political legitimacy. Both would likely come only at Hamas' expense. The group's leaders seemed to grasp this and rejected PLO political overtures. Mohammed Dahlan, then Arafat's right hand in Gaza, accused Hamas of acting on behalf of foreign interests — a clear reference to Iran.[38]

On January 5, 1996, Israel assassinated Yahya Ayyash, widely known as "the engineer" who planned multiple Hamas attacks against Israel. The Israeli Shin Bet felled him by detonating a small explosive device placed in his mobile phone. Hamas struck back with a series of revenge attacks. Regional players soon met in Egypt to address the escalating violence. Hamas sympathizer Azzam Tamimi described the summit as a "declaration of war on Hamas."[39]

Hamas would not be deterred, however. The group's violent attacks continued, and it refused to take part in the 1996 elections. The result was a politically brittle PA, weakened consistently by terrorist attacks that undermined diplomacy. One could even argue that Hamas, with significant assistance from the regime in Tehran, contributed to the election of right-wing politician Benjamin Netanyahu, an avowed skeptic of the Oslo process, as prime minister of Israel in 1996.[40] Netanyahu would only serve three years in that position, but he would later return in 2009 as the foremost opponent of Iran's nuclear program and its regional hegemonic designs.

In 1997, Iran hosted conferences with Hamas, PIJ, and other militant groups, during which the regime pledged money, training, arms, and operational guidance.[41] That support helped fuel continued terrorism in Israel. Seeking to weaken the group's leadership, Israel attempted to poison Khaled Meshal, the Jordan-based head of the Hamas Politburo. Jordanian authorities, however, arrested two Israeli agents involved in the plot. The Israelis had little choice but to provide the antidote. Meshal survived, and the Hashemite Kingdom later released the two spies in exchange for Hamas founder Ahmed Yassin, who had been languishing in an Israeli jail.[42]

By the late 1990s, Hamas was conducting terror attacks inside Israel with relative impunity, earning the group a US Foreign Terrorist Organization designation in 1997 — a move that compounded the pressure on Hamas from previous US sanctions.[43] Hamas clearly represented a significant and persistent threat to the peace process. In October 1998, President Bill Clinton pressed forward with the Wye Plantation Accords, an additional framework for peace. In its continued opposition, Hamas conducted at least three attacks against Israelis that month, killing at least one person and wounding more than 80. After that, Hamas attacks slowed. This may have been a result of cooperative efforts by the PA security apparatus, Israel's Shin Bet, and the CIA.[44]

In 1998, Ahmed Yassin arrived in Tehran for what was essentially a state visit. While meeting with the regime's top leaders, Yassin lauded "Iran's support for the Palestinians' struggle against Israel."[45]

In 1999, Iranian Foreign Minister Ali Akbar Vilayati declared, "Iran is the main supporter of Hamas and Hezbollah and their struggle against Israel."[46] Canadian intelligence assessed that in 1999 alone the regime had transferred $35 million to Hamas.[47]

In the summer of 1999, Hamas initiated a rash of shootings and ambushes in the West Bank. Hamas terrorists wounded six in two different car rammings near the West Bank that August. The following month, Hamas recruited Israeli Arabs for two bus bombings in Israel's north.[48] In November, the group exploded three pipe bombs in the coastal town of Netanya.[49]

Hamas continued to refine its lethal terror tactics with Iranian help. Hamas fighters were training in places such as Iran and Sudan before returning to the West Bank and Gaza Strip for commando or suicide operations.[50] By 2000, Iran was likely providing Hamas with as much as $50 million annually.[51]

In the summer of 2000, with the end of President Bill Clinton's second term in sight, a Nobel Prize beckoned. The White House made its final push for peace. Clinton hosted Arafat and Israeli Prime Minister Ehud Barak for final-status peace talks — an attempt to reach a diplomatic agreement that would end all claims on both sides. The talks collapsed in July after Arafat rejected an Israeli offer of full Palestinian sovereignty over the Gaza Strip and an estimated 95 percent of the West Bank.

After several months of simmering tensions, the Palestinians launched the Al-Aqsa Intifada, also known as the Second Intifada, in September 2000. The campaign of violence that followed was both bloody and soul-crushing. It was a string of gruesome suicide bombings on Israeli buses, hotels, restaurants, shopping areas, and nightclubs. Some were carried out by Hamas. Others were conducted by Fatah or Iran-backed PIJ. Still others were carried out in tandem. The "National and Islamic Forces," a 13-member coalition of violent factions, was even formed to coordinate attacks.[52] In 2001, Hamas and other militant groups also began the firing of mortars and rockets into Israel, sowing terror among the Israeli communities within range of these crude and unguided projectiles. Nobody knew when they would be fired or where they would land. Within a few years, this would become the preferred tactic of Hamas.

THREE
THE HAMAS UNDERGROUND

With the notable exception of a few short years during the "Arab Spring," Iranian support for Hamas has been a constant. It has come in the form of financial assistance, as well as training and weapons. In some cases, Tehran also helps the group build military infrastructure.

The Gaza war of 2021 revealed a huge Hamas undertaking. The group had diverted massive amounts of building material, contributed to Gaza as part of an ongoing international assistance effort, to construct a deadly underground tunnel network designed to give Hamas an edge against Israel in close-quarter combat. The project required years of construction and enormous amounts of material and cash. There can be little doubt that this project was funded, at least in part, by Iran. Israeli military officers say that Iranian engineers were likely involved, too.[1]

On May 13, amidst the flying rockets, Iron Dome interceptions, chaotic media coverage, and rising tensions across the region, the Israeli military made an announcement that few expected. At a little past midnight, in both Hebrew and English, the IDF announced on Twitter that "IDF air and ground troops are currently attacking in the Gaza Strip."[2]

The announcement was somewhat shocking for several reasons. First, Prime Minister Benjamin Netanyahu was far more risk-averse than most observers give him credit for. While he had built a reputation as a right-wing politician who took a hard line against Iran and its terrorist proxies, he had also become Israel's longest-serving leader in part by avoiding messy military entanglements. As a student of Israeli and Jewish history, Netanyahu seemed to grasp instinctively that quagmires had been the undoing of many politicians before him.

For Israel, the risks of a ground war in Gaza were well-known. In 2006, Hamas abducted a 19-year-old Israeli soldier named Gilad Shalit during an operation near the Israel-Gaza border. The terrorists had infiltrated through a tunnel that snaked into Israel from Gaza. As the group fired rockets and mortars into Israel, Hamas commandos grabbed Shalit, and took him back to Gaza,[3] where he was held in captivity until 2011. Two other Israeli soldiers died in the attack. Hamas finally released Shalit in exchange for no fewer than 1,027 Palestinian prisoners held in Israeli jails — most of whom were incarcerated for politically motivated violent crimes.[4]

The Shalit swap was a lopsided one, but it was par for the course. For the Israelis, every soldier holds immense value. Politicians are always willing to make great concessions for their return — even if it means only receiving remains. Even today, Israel seeks a prisoner deal with Hamas that would return home two prisoners and two fallen Israeli soldiers, Hadar Goldin and Oron Shaul, who were killed and taken by Hamas during the 2014 war.[5]

In Israel, the stories of these soldiers, not to mention the many others wounded in close-quarters combat, serve as caution against ground wars. Nevertheless, the IDF's May 13 statements indicated that ground troops had gone in. *The Washington Post* picked up the story.[6] So did *The Wall Street Journal.*[7] Many other outlets did, too.

Watching these events unfold on Israeli television (Apple TV is a remarkable technology) from my home in suburban Washington, DC, I noticed something very strange. I had tuned in expecting to see footage of the front. After all, the IDF had assembled ground forces at the Israel-Gaza border, including armored and infantry units.[8] But the Israeli anchors and reporters were not reporting a ground war. They were genuinely puzzled by the reports in major foreign media outlets. Their Israeli military sources could not confirm the story.

As it turns out, the Israelis may have pulled off a remarkable information operation. In response to the media reports of a ground invasion, Hamas scrambled its commando fighters — many of whom had been trained in Iran — to file into what the Israelis nicknamed the "Hamas Metro." The Metro was a labyrinth of tunnels that Hamas had spent years and hundreds of millions of dollars digging. The terrorist group hoped to surprise Israeli troops entering Gaza, with commandos popping up and quickly disappearing back into the Metro's many openings. Their goal was to kidnap or kill IDF soldiers.

Israeli intelligence was aware of this plan for years. So when Hamas responded to the false reports of a ground invasion, Israeli jets began to pound the Metro.[9] The Israelis claim that 160 aircraft dropped 450 missiles on 150 targets in northern Gaza during an intense operation.[10] The Metro sustained significant damage, and many commando fighters were killed, although the exact number is still debated. Israeli tanks, artillery, and infantry units near the Gaza border targeted Hamas rocket teams that emerged to strike Israel.[11] The IDF also destroyed rocket production facilities.[12]

The press scrambled to grasp what was happening. The Israelis did their best to explain what the Metro was and why they were focusing their efforts on it. The IDF's international spokesman, Lieutenant Colonel Jonathan Conricus, stated that the Metro ran under civilian neighborhoods throughout the Gaza Strip. The Israelis were reportedly taking great pains to strike only the roads directly over the tunnels, and not the older buildings sitting atop the recently constructed labyrinth.[13]

As the Israelis explained, the problem of minimizing collateral damage while destroying terrorist infrastructure intentionally built beneath a densely populated civilian area was no simple task. Hamas was wielding a cynical tactic known as "human shields," the use of civilians to shield weapons or fighters from lawful attack. It is a tactic that my colleague Orde Kittrie, a specialist in international law, has been documenting for years, including in his 2016 book on "lawfare."[14]

To be clear, using human shields is a war crime. It is a violation of the Fourth Geneva Convention and customary international law. Hamas is certainly not the only terrorist group to embrace this tactic. Al-Qaeda, the Taliban, the Islamic State, and Hezbollah have all used human shields in the past.[15] As a result, in 2018, the US Congress passed a law requiring the president to impose sanctions against groups such as Hamas that use human shields.[16] Unfortunately, the US government, under both Democrats and Republicans, has thus far failed to fulfill this statutory requirement.

By striking the empty streets above the Hamas Metro, however, the Israelis were able to significantly reduce civilian casualties. Lamentably, even though the IDF endeavored to minimize collateral damage, reports suggest that 44 Gazan civilians perished during the May 2021 conflict.[17]

In the aftermath of the Metro operation, the IDF reported that an estimated 300 to 400 Hamas operatives were killed underground.[18] The Israelis released video footage from the operation and announced that more than 60 miles of tunnels were destroyed.[19] Those 60 miles may have accounted for a mere 20 percent of the Metro network.[20]

Predictably, Hamas denied all of it. One official from Hamas' al-Qassam Brigades told *Al-Monitor*, on condition of anonymity, that he did not think the IDF was able to destroy Hamas' tunnels. In a sign that Gaza's municipal leadership was likely collaborating with Hamas, Gaza City Mayor Yahya al-Sarraj said that he "did not see any tunnels or facilities belonging to the Palestinian resistance during the rubble removal and road opening operations." He further claimed that Israel "used the tunnel issue as a pretext to destroy the infrastructure of Gaza City and deepen the suffering of its citizens."[21]

The IDF appeared to be prepared for such denials. Using aerial photographs, the Israelis documented the proximity of the tunnels to schools and other civilian buildings.[22] For example, the IDF identified a tunnel shaft in southern Gaza that was located adjacent to a kindergarten and a mosque. Another tunnel was located under a beachside hotel in northern Gaza.[23] Yet another military tunnel ran underneath a school.[24]

As the war dragged on, Hamas repeatedly alleged that Israel was deliberately targeting civilians. As a direct result, anti-Israel protests were spreading on the streets of capitals around the world. Few, if any, protestors at these anti-Israel rallies criticized Hamas for launching the war or for operating a commando tunnel system that deliberately put Gazan civilians in harm's way. If Gazans were exercised about this, they were certainly not able to hold protests under Hamas rule.

For Israel, however, the court of public opinion would have to wait. The IDF was still trying to halt the rocket fire, and its spokesman was trying to soothe some raw nerves among the press corps. The foreign reporters who had broadcast the news of Israeli troops entering the Gaza Strip were forced to retract their stories, and they were furious. As *The New York Times* subsequently reported, "Representatives of *The Times, The Washington Post, The Wall Street Journal, National Public Radio,* and *Agence France-Presse,* all of which had mistakenly reported a ground invasion early Friday, peppered [Conricus] with questions about whether they had been turned into accessories to the military, why it had taken hours for the invasion report to be reversed, and how they would be able to trust the military's statements going forward."[25]

Conricus took the blame. He insisted that he had misunderstood information coming from the field. The IDF Twitter feed and WhatsApp group issued a correction roughly two hours into the operation.[26] Conricus subsequently told reporters in an off-the-record briefing, which was later leaked, that he did not "attempt to try to fool anybody or to cause [reporters] to write anything that isn't true." Interestingly, Conricus also said that the IDF did, in fact, intend to draw out Hamas fighters "from their hiding places" to allow "their positions to be detected and destroyed — and to trick other Palestinian fighters to stream into the underground tunnel network, which Israeli generals were confident they could now destroy from the air."[27]

Did the Israelis deliberately mislead the press? Perhaps. But watching Israeli television live from my home in America, I found it very odd that professional Western reporters would have printed this story when the Israeli press would not. Perhaps it stemmed from a lack of local language skills. Or perhaps the Western press did not want to rely on Israeli reporters. That would be a mistake, however. Journalism is a serious business in Israel, with reporters doggedly chasing stories that just as often challenge government reports as they corroborate them.

In the end, the ground invasion story was not well-sourced. The incident was a reminder that while the Palestinian-Israeli conflict is one of the world's most polarizing conflicts, covered by thousands of journalists, the reporting still is often hit or miss — at best.

FOUR
AL-JALAA TOWER

An equally important moment of the 2021 Gaza war was the destruction of the Al-Jalaa tower. As the war stretched into its fifth day, Hamas rockets were still flying. Even after the Israelis had rendered the Hamas Metro out-of-order, they had not yet turned the tide of the war. It was at this point that the IDF took a dramatic step to counter a Hamas technological operation.

At 2:00 p.m. local time on May 15, tenants in the Al-Jalaa tower, a 12-story building in Gaza City, were notified that they were being given a short time to evacuate. The building contained approximately 30 apartments and 50 office suites. At the very top of the building were the offices of the Associated Press (AP) and Al Jazeera Gaza bureaus.

One of the owners of the building, Jawad Mahdi, received a call from a fluent Arabic speaker representing the Shin Bet with instructions to vacate the premises.[1] Mahdi reportedly then visited each floor to tell everyone to evacuate. The AP reportedly tried to convince the Israeli government to halt the pending military operation. However, a decision had already been made. Prior to the military strikes, there were two warning shots, fired 15 minutes apart.[2] At 3:00 p.m., the Shin Bet called back to ensure that the building had been fully evacuated. At 3:12 p.m., the military operation began.[3]

The tower's destruction was dramatic. Israeli television stations ran the footage on repeat. It did not look like an airstrike. If anything, it looked like a controlled detonation, with the building collapsing inward. Remarkably, the Israelis reported "no deaths whatsoever" due to the measures the military took, including warning civilians in advance.[4]

The destruction of the building would later be deemed legal by scholars of international law and military history.[5] At the time, however, the Hamas public relations machine swung into high gear. The Israelis were getting hammered with criticism from around the world, with allegations that the IDF had destroyed civilian infrastructure or even that it was deliberately targeting the press. Amnesty International tweeted, "We're calling on U.S. to intervene bilaterally & as UN Security Council member to end cycle of impunity & violations in Israel/[Occupied Palestinian Territories] by publicly denouncing war crimes & other serious violations including illegal settlement expansion, blockade of Gaza, dispossession of Palestinians."[6] Reporters Without Borders asked the International Criminal Court to investigate Israel's attack as a possible war crime. The group said it had reason to believe that the IDF's "intentional targeting of media organizations and intentional destruction of their equipment" could violate one of the court's statutes.[7]

The Israelis adamantly defended the operation. An IDF spokesman asserted that Hamas operatives were among the building's tenants. The terror group was reportedly using the building to conduct research and development (R&D), collect signals intelligence (SIGINT) and electronic signals intelligence (ELINT), and wage electronic warfare targeting both IDF operations and civilian systems in Israel. In fact, one of the primary goals of these Hamas operations was to disrupt or jam Israel's Iron Dome missile defense system, which was knocking Hamas rockets out of the sky and protecting Israeli civilians from widespread death and destruction.[8]

The United States, until this point, had been overwhelmingly supportive of Israel's military response to the Hamas rocket barrages. The Biden administration gave Israel full cover at home as well as at the United Nations.[9] But the Al-Jalaa operation appeared to give the White House pause. In a call with Prime Minister Benjamin Netanyahu, President Joe Biden "raised concerns about the safety and security of journalists and reinforced the need to ensure their protection."[10]

Israeli diplomats quickly volunteered to provide an intelligence briefing, complete with evidence showing that Hamas was operating in the building. According to one senior Israeli diplomatic source, Israeli intelligence officials shared the "smoking gun," with the understanding that the White House "found the explanation satisfactory."[11] Netanyahu tweeted after the call, thanking Biden for his "unreserved support for Israel's right to defend ourselves."[12] Two days later, Netanyahu appeared on *Face the Nation*, stating that Israel had struck the building because it housed "an intelligence office. . . that plots and organizes terrorist attacks on Israeli civilians. It is a perfectly legit target."[13]

This did not mean that the media were satisfied. The AP and Al Jazeera were still up in arms. AP Executive Editor Sally Buzbee said the wire service had offices in Al-Jalaa tower for 15 years and was never informed or had any other indication that Hamas might be in the building.[14]

The Biden administration expressed its solidarity with the media, even if the intelligence supported Israel's actions. US Secretary of State Antony Blinken conveyed his "unwavering support" in a phone call with AP President and CEO Gary Pruitt, expressing "relief" that the AP team in Gaza was safe. Blinken praised the "indispensability of [the media's] reporting in conflict zones."[15] White House Press Secretary Jen Psaki tweeted: "We have communicated directly to the Israelis that ensuring the safety and security of journalists and independent media is a paramount responsibility."[16]

The battle for public opinion took an odd turn on May 20 when *The New York Times* ran an op-ed by Laila al-Arian, who was identified simply as "an award-winning Palestinian-American journalist." Arian, who had worked for Al Jazeera for 13 years, stated that her family had owned an apartment in the building. She wrote her grandfather had bought it with his life savings and left it to his family. Not surprisingly, the op-ed excoriated Israel for the destruction of the building and the impact it had on her family.[17]

In chronicling her family's journey, Arian neglected to note one important fact: Her father is Sami al-Arian, who appeared in a Florida court in the 1990s for being a member of PIJ and providing financial support to the organization from the United States.[18] He ultimately pleaded guilty in 2006 to only one charge: conspiring to provide services to PIJ.[19] He was subsequently deported from the United States and moved to Turkey.[20]

The government of Turkey, incidentally, was among the harshest critics of Israel during the 2021 war. As longstanding Hamas supporters, this was no surprise.[21] Fahrettin Altun, the Turkish president's communications director, tweeted: "Israel continues to commit massacres and war crimes. By targeting the Associated Press and Al Jazeera offices in Gaza, the occupying Israel is also dealing a blow to the freedom of the press. I condemn these vile attacks of

Israel, which hit the press centers in order to hide their massacres."[22] There was, of course, some irony in Altun's comments: The Turkish government ranks as one of the world's top jailers of journalists.[23]

That *The New York Times* did not identify Laila al-Arian's full family history when it ran the opinion piece is odd. At minimum, the editors should probably have demanded that the allegations surrounding her father's ties to PIJ be included somewhere.

The following day, the IDF provided further clarification on the Al-Jalaa operation, noting that the building housed not only Hamas assets, but also assets belonging to PIJ. The Israelis also underlined the clear military nature of the Hamas R&D unit that had operated in the building. An IDF spokesman noted that the unit was:

> . . . responsible, among other things, for terror activity carried out against the State of Israel. The R&D unit consists of subject matter experts (SMEs) which constitute a unique asset to the Hamas terrorist organization. These SMEs operate the most valuable Hamas technological equipment against Israel. The unit used these capabilities against Israel in a number of incidents in attempts to sabotage and disrupt the actions of the IDF and of civilians in the area adjacent to the Gaza Strip.[24]

In early June, Gilad Erdan, Israel's ambassador to the United States and United Nations, explained a bit more. He stated that Israel had "no choice" but to strike the building, because "Hamas placed a secret unit [inside the tower] that developed technologies that were aimed to jam the capabilities of our Iron Dome."

Erdan explained, "If we hadn't knocked down this building, and [Hamas] jammed the Iron Dome capabilities, we would have no other choice but to initiate a ground operation. And in that operation, as you probably understand, many more civilians would pay with their own lives." [25] In a separate appearance, Erdan noted that "Israel does not think that [AP] workers were aware of the Hamas activities in the building, because it was a secret Hamas unit."[26]

But with the latter assertion, the Israeli diplomat may have been extra diplomatic. Former aide to President Barack Obama Tommy Vietor tweeted on May 15: "I'm sure Hamas offices were in that building & that they purposefully co-locate operations with civilians. But that is not a new problem."[27] In an exchange with other users on the social media platform, Vietor explained that he had "talked to someone who *used* to work out of that building periodically who said he believed there may have been Hamas offices there." Vietor later added, "I'm sure that Hamas operates in civilian areas for protection. A journalist friend who used to work out of that building told me Hamas worked out of it, too. I still don't think the IDF should have bombed the building."[28]

Matti Friedman, a journalist who worked at the AP's Jerusalem bureau from 2006 to 2011, had previously aired his concerns about the AP's policy of abiding by Hamas censorship.[29] In a 2014 essay for *The Atlantic*, Friedman alleged, "The AP staff in Gaza City would witness a rocket launch right beside their office, endangering reporters and other civilians nearby — and the AP wouldn't report it. . . Hamas fighters would burst into the AP's Gaza bureau and threaten the staff — and the AP wouldn't report it."[30]

Mark Lavie, a former colleague of Friedman at the AP Jerusalem bureau, confirmed the claims from Friedman's *Atlantic* article. Lavie added that the cover-up was "by far the worst journalistic fiasco I have been involved in, and we're talking 50 years of journalism here. No denials. . . can erase the truth–and this is the truth:

The AP suppressed a world-changing story for no acceptable reason.
. . It fit a pattern, described by Matti, of accepting the Palestinian
narrative as truth and branding the Israelis as oppressors."[31]

In early June, an AP spokesperson thanked Erdan for a recent
opportunity to discuss the episode. The spokesperson called it:

> . . . a positive and constructive conversation. Israeli
> authorities maintain that the building housing our
> bureau was destroyed because of a Hamas presence that
> posed an urgent threat. We have yet to receive evidence
> to support these claims. AP continues to call for the full
> release of any evidence the Israelis have so that the facts
> are public.[32]

Al Jazeera appeared decidedly less open to being convinced.
Mosefa Souag, the network's acting director-general, called the
strike "barbaric" and demanded that Israel be held accountable.[33]
But there was far more to this story than Souag let on.

Al Jazeera is owned by the government of Qatar. The tiny
Persian Gulf emirate created the station in 1996.[34] Early on, one
of Al Jazeera's more popular programs was *Religion and Life*, hosted
by Yusuf Qaradawi, a cleric widely known as the "spiritual guide"
of Hamas. Famously, Qaradawi endorsed Hamas' tactic of suicide
bombing as legitimate according to Islamic law.[35]

This is all relevant because Qatar is a longstanding patron of
Hamas. In 2006, shortly after the elections that earned Hamas a vic-
tory, Qatar offered $50 million to what was then a Hamas-dominated
PA government.[36] In 2008, PA officials claimed that Qatar provided
Hamas with "millions of dollars a month," nominally intended
for the people of Gaza.[37] In February 2012, Doha announced that
Hamas would receive $250 million for reconstruction projects in

Gaza, including 5,000 new homes and repairs to 55,000.[38] The following August, Qatar reportedly opened an office in the Gaza Strip to oversee its various construction endeavors in the coastal enclave.[39] More famously, in October 2012, Qatar's emir pledged $400 million to Hamas during a high-profile visit to Gaza. This was the first big tranche, but much more flowed to Hamas from Doha in subsequent years.[40]

In 2014, David Cohen, then-US Treasury undersecretary for terrorism and financial intelligence, confirmed that "Qatar, a long-time U.S. ally, has for many years openly financed Hamas."[41] Qatar is also the headquarters for several senior Hamas officials. According to Qatar scholar Allen Fromherz, "After Jordan closed the offices of Hamas in 1999, Qatar offered to allow Khaled Meshal and some of his deputies to relocate to Qatar as long as they did not engage in overt political activities." Fromherz noted that Meshal reportedly "regularly shuttle[d] between Doha and Damascus," where Hamas' external leadership maintained its main headquarters until 2012.[42]

As part of the 2011 deal for the release of kidnapped Israeli soldier Gilad Shalit, Israel released 15 Hamas prisoners and deported them to Qatar.[43] After Hamas' leadership left Damascus in 2012, a significant cadre of Hamas leaders relocated to Qatar.[44] In 2014, after Saleh al-Arouri was forced to leave Turkey, he also found a new home in Qatar. Arouri, the commander of Hamas' West Bank military unit responsible for the triple kidnapping and murder that helped start the 2014 Gaza war, joined a gaggle of other Hamas officials who made the country their home.[45]

During a research trip I took to Qatar in 2013, Western diplomats noted how they often saw senior Hamas figures dining out at popular Doha restaurants.[46] They were viewed locally as celebrities. Al Jazeera, the flagship television station owned by the Qatari government, also lauds the group's leaders as heroes. The channel is still among the most watched in the Arab world, thereby normalizing a terrorist organization on a grand scale.[47]

In 2017, Hamas held a press conference at the Sheraton Grand Doha hotel to announce the release of a new political document.[48] The document, promoted as a less extreme version of the group's founding charter, was a Qatari-led effort to rebrand the terrorist organization as more moderate. In short, Doha does not merely finance Hamas — it also serves as the group's political consultant.

After years of tolerating this activity and even trying to work with Doha to influence Qatari assistance, the Israelis have finally learned their lesson. In the wake of the 2021 Gaza war, outgoing Mossad Director Yossi Cohen renounced Qatar as a country with which Israel could partner to contain Hamas.[49] After the conflict ended, aggrieved Israeli families also filed suit against Qatari banks, alleging that they funded Hamas activity.[50]

But the story doesn't end there. It's important to note that the Taliban, al-Qaeda, and other terrorist groups — lately many Syrian jihadi factions, too — have all benefited from Qatari largesse over the years. This did not go unnoticed by the US government, particularly during the war in Iraq. John Hannah, a former colleague of mine who served as national security advisor to Vice President Dick Cheney, recalled clashes with Qatar in 2004, specifically over Al Jazeera's uncanny ability to be on the scene when terrorists struck.

Writing for *Foreign Policy* in 2017, Hannah noted, "U.S. analysts lost count of the number of times Al Jazeera cameras happened to be on location just in time to capture a spectacular attack on U.S. forces. The circumstantial evidence of Al Jazeera's collusion with the terrorists targeting American soldiers was compelling."[51] Back in 2004, General John Abizaid, then commander of U.S. forces in the Middle East, had similarly noted Al Jazeera's uncanny knack for being "at the scene of the crime whenever a hostage shows up or some other problem happens."[52]

In 2003, Patrick Kennedy, the chief of staff of the Coalition Provisional Authority in Iraq, penned a scathing letter to Al Jazeera. Hinting at mounting allegations that Al Jazeera maintained friendly relationships with anti-American insurgent groups in Iraq, Kennedy asked, "What procedures will be followed when [an Al Jazeera] staff member receives information regarding a pending attack, explosion, or other unspecified incident which may result in injury or death to any person, including civilians, civil authorities, or military personnel?"[53]

That is not all. In November 2001, the US military bombed Al Jazeera's Kabul office in Afghanistan. US Assistant Secretary of Defense Victoria Clarke stated, "the building we struck was a known Al Qaeda facility in central Kabul."[54]

How much Al Jazeera knew about Hamas' operations in the al-Jalaa building will likely never come to light. However, it is worth noting that when the war ended, the Qatari government immediately pledged $500 million for postwar construction in Hamas-controlled Gaza.[55] Doha was getting ready to help Hamas rebuild again — framing it all as humanitarian assistance, of course.

Weeks later, the deputy chief of Hamas in Gaza, Khalil al-Hayya, presented Al Jazeera's Gaza bureau chief, Wael al-Dahdouh, with an award for "outstanding coverage" of the recent conflict.[56]

FIVE
THE COLLAPSE OF PEACE, A NEW WAR

The international reporting out of Israel during times of conflict almost always portrays Israel as the aggressor. This ignores the fact that Israel's early battles against Hamas in the 1990s were largely battles for peace. The country, in partnership with the United States, was committed to a diplomatic process, however flawed it may have been, to achieve a two-state solution.

To be sure, there were Israeli politicians, such as Prime Minister Benjamin Netanyahu, who were determined to encumber or scuttle the Oslo process. But even Netanyahu signed the Wye River Accords, an important milestone of the peace process, in 1998.[1] And when push came to shove, Israeli voters removed Netanyahu from office in 1999, heralding the rise of Ehud Barak, the man who ultimately labored in vain to bring a peace deal across the finish line.

When the peace process collapsed with the launch of the Second Intifada in October 2000, the Israelis unknowingly entered into a new war. Theirs was no longer a battle for peace. Hamas had almost single-handedly destroyed that possibility. Rather, after the launch of the Second Intifada, Israel fought to contain the wave of terrorism that Hamas had unleashed on its people.

As it happened, Israel was not alone in this fight. America was battling al-Qaeda in the wake of the 9/11 attacks. After September 11, 2001, the White House designated Hamas a terrorist group under Executive Order 13224, a newly created tool designed to block the funds of terrorists.[2] The American listing was both legal and justifiable. After all, the group embraced the tactics of al-Qaeda, such as suicide bombings, and received funding and other assistance from Iran, a member of President George W. Bush's notorious "Axis of Evil."[3]

Hamas certainly did not try to hide its terrorist activities. It barely tried to obscure its funding sources, either. With the Second Intifada in full swing, Hamas Politburo chief Khaled Meshal attended a conference in Iran in April 2001 alongside representatives of Hezbollah and PIJ. Meshal called on the regime to provide political, financial, and military support.[4] Israeli intelligence at the time assessed that Hamas leaders were traveling to Tehran "every three to four weeks."[5]

Hamas and PIJ suicide bombings wreaked havoc throughout Israel during the Second Intifada, with bombers self-detonating in restaurants, malls, and buses. In 2002, Israel reached a breaking point after a Hamas suicide bombing at a hotel in the coastal town of Netanya on the first night of Passover. The attack, known as the "Passover massacre," killed 30 people and injured 140.[6]

In April 2002, the IDF launched Operation Defensive Shield. Across Palestinian towns and refugee camps, Israel targeted the assets of the terrorist groups that were killing its citizens. This did not halt Hamas' operations, however. On July 31, 2002, the group carried out an attack at a cafeteria at the Hebrew University of Jerusalem, killing seven — including five Americans.[7] Israel fought back by proactively targeting Hamas leaders on the ground in the West Bank and Gaza. As is always the case, the conflict yielded destruction and civilian casualties. Israel's critics accused the country of war crimes. Once again, Israel was forced to fend off attacks from its critics as it fought a war it did not seek.

With the intifada raging, the international community largely wrote off the peace process. Upon taking office in January 2001, the administration of President George W. Bush signaled it would not devote efforts to a lost cause. Bush refused to meet with Palestinian President Yasser Arafat,[8] who had enjoyed numerous meetings with Bush's predecessor.

Hamas, meanwhile, was gaining clout on the streets. The Second Intifada created ideal conditions for Islamism and rejectionism to surge in the West Bank and Gaza. The group, not surprisingly, spurned Arafat's offer to join a new Palestinian government in June 2002.[9]

As the Palestinian Authority crumbled, Arafat jumped at a proposal by the Quartet — the United States, United Nations, European Union, and Russia — known as the "roadmap" for peace. The roadmap promised a *de facto* Palestinian state, with final borders to be set by 2005.[10] However, the Quartet called for an initial period of calm. At America's urging, Egypt tried to broker a deal whereby Hamas would halt attacks on Israel in exchange for an end to Israeli targeted assassinations of Hamas figures. The talks failed. Hamas continued to strike inside Israel, including a November suicide bombing in Jerusalem that killed 11 and wounded 50.[11]

Hamas was not the only problematic actor during the Second Intifada. Shortly after the violent campaign began, Arafat's secular

Fatah faction created the al-Aqsa Martyrs Brigades, which co-opted Islamist symbols and slogans, in an obvious effort to compete with Hamas on the Palestinian street. Arafat could thus claim to be the reasonable leader interested in negotiations while also catering to Palestinians vehemently opposed to recognition or negotiations with Israel.

By 2002, the Brigades claimed responsibility for dozens of attacks in Israel. On March 21, 2002, for example, a Brigades suicide bomber detonated himself in the middle of a bustling thoroughfare in Jerusalem, killing three and injuring 86. Another Brigades suicide bomber killed 10 and injured 50 at a bar mitzvah celebration.[12] The Brigades also became the first Palestinian terror group to deploy a female suicide bomber, when a 28-year-old nurse detonated herself at a Jerusalem shopping area, killing one Israeli and injuring 150 others.[13]

The violence perpetrated by the Brigades ultimately eroded American and international trust in Arafat, Fatah, and the PA. Moreover, the Palestinian people, while perhaps supportive of the Brigades' attacks, still viewed Hamas as the original resistance faction. Arafat's stock continued to fall when the IDF encircled his presidential compound in Ramallah, known as the *Muqata*, and kept him under house arrest.

With Arafat cornered, Israel launched a campaign of targeted assassinations against Hamas leaders. Hamas founder and spiritual guide Ahmed Yassin was killed on March 22, 2004, when an Israeli helicopter launched a missile at him as he left a Gaza City mosque. At least seven other people died in the strike, and two of Yassin's sons were among the 15 wounded. Soon thereafter, some 200,000 Palestinians flooded the streets for a funeral procession.[14]

After Yassin, the IDF stalked his successor, Abdel Aziz al-Rantisi. Rantisi went into hiding, fearing his own assassination. Then, on April 17, he visited his family in Gaza City. Shortly after the visit, Israeli helicopters fired missiles at his vehicle, killing him.[15] Several months later, on August 21, 2003, an Israeli missile strike destroyed a car carrying Ismail Abu Shanab, Hamas' third-most senior leader.[16] One missed opportunity for the Israelis was Mahmoud al-Zahar, who survived a September 2003 Israeli strike against his home in Gaza.[17]

By 2003, *The New York Times* observed that "each Israeli killing only seems to enhance the popularity of Hamas on the street."[18] As one Hamas spokesman later stated, "after the assassinations of Sheikh Yassin. . . Abu Shanab, and Dr. Rantisi, we have gained strength from these painful losses, and our organization became more powerful. We are not a figurehead organization; we are a resistance movement with deep roots."[19]

The face of Hamas soon became Khaled Meshal. The head of the Hamas Politburo, Meshal moved to Damascus in 1999 after Jordan expelled the group.[20] Meshal increasingly looked to the regime in Tehran for both funding and training.[21]

With Hamas suicide bombings still killing and maiming civilians in Israeli restaurants, nightclubs, and malls, the IDF began to erect a security barrier separating Israel from the West Bank and Gaza Strip to prevent terrorist infiltration. As construction progressed, Hamas' ability to conduct attacks diminished. Violence against Israel plummeted. However, in this conflict, there are no permanent victories. A new Palestinian activist campaign drew attention to how the barrier impeded freedom of movement. Without regard for Hamas' campaign of violence that necessitated the barrier, international criticism of Israel exploded, with former US President Jimmy Carter leading the way.[22] Israeli officials attempted to explain that the fence was a measure of last resort to prevent further bloodshed caused by Palestinian terrorists.[23] Their arguments often fell upon deaf ears.

Critics also claimed that Israel erected the fence to facilitate a land grab in the West Bank. Indeed, the barrier included territory that had been on the Jordanian side of the Green Line, the armistice line of 1949. Still, this was not an entirely fair characterization. As analyst David Makovsky notes, Israel worked hard to abide by international law in setting the course of the fence. The barrier traced roughly along the 1949 line. Admittedly, the new line established by the fence included some Jewish settlements in the West Bank to protect them from Hamas violence, too.[24] This approach was validated by an Israeli Supreme Court opinion asserting that the IDF's legal mandate was to balance security requirements with concerns about the impact on West Bank Palestinians.[25]

Despite the international pressure, Israel continued to pour resources into the barrier, at significant financial cost. Between the barrier itself, the co-located military bases designed to monitor the perimeter, and systems needed for monitoring, the fence cost at least $1.5 billion.[26] But for Israel, it was worth every cent. The barrier has halted Hamas suicide terrorism.

But the battle continued. Hamas was still able to smuggle goods and weapons into Gaza through tunnels abutting Egypt's Sinai Peninsula. Egypt, then under the rule of longtime President Hosni Mubarak, was turning a blind eye to this activity.[27]

According to one senior Israeli official, the Israelis had found 70 or more tunnels originating in Egypt and leading to Gaza between 1993 and 2003, with the majority discovered during or after the Second Intifada.[28] Hamas and other terror groups dug the tunnels more than 60 feet below ground to evade Israeli detection. These tunnels required a significant investment, each costing up to $200,000 to burrow.[29]

Israel's Engineer Corps got to work destroying a great many of these tunnels. However, the IDF noted that the Palestinians were able to dig them as fast as they were found. Alarmingly, the weapons smuggled underground included armor-piercing munitions, automatic rifles, mines, and rocket-propelled grenades. Raw materials necessary to build homemade "Qassam" rockets, as well as high explosives for suicide bombings, also passed through the tunnels.

On October 9, 2003, the IDF launched Operation Root Canal in the Gazan town of Rafah, where many of the tunnels emptied out.[30] The September 2003 arrest and subsequent interrogation of a tunnel digger had revealed that Hamas had smuggled eight anti-aircraft missiles through these tunnels.[31] That alone justified action in the IDF's eyes. The Israelis continued to destroy tunnels. During raids on Hamas strongholds, the Israelis found that the group hid its smuggled arms and explosives under kindergarten playgrounds.[32]

In December 2003, even as Hamas smuggling increased in Gaza, Israeli Prime Minister Ariel Sharon announced a surprising plan for unilateral "disengagement" from the Gaza Strip. Downplaying the threat of an unchecked Hamas, the former IDF general believed Israel would engender international goodwill, particularly because the disengagement would involve dismantling settlements.[33]

In a December 2003 speech, Sharon erroneously predicted that the withdrawal would "relieve the pressure on the IDF and security forces in fulfilling the difficult tasks they are faced with. The Disengagement Plan is meant to grant maximum security and minimize friction between Israelis and Palestinians."[34]

Two years later, in August and September of 2005, as the intifada wound down, Israeli troops evacuated the Gaza Strip. It was immediately clear that the withdrawal was a mistake. As journalist Zaki Chehab notes, Hamas and other terrorist groups could operate with greater ease in the Gaza Strip. They could manufacture explosives and other weapons without fearing IDF raids, and tunneling became easier without the IDF monitoring the border. As then-future Prime Minister Benjamin Netanyahu noted, the withdrawal was a victory for Hamas since the group "could claim that terror works."[35]

After Israel's departure, Hamas began to refine a key terror tactic, launching more rockets and mortars into Israeli territory. One Hamas commander acknowledged Iran's role: "To achieve our goal, we are allowed to ask for help to obtain power from wherever we can, from whoever provides it. . . The only one that provides [the rockets] is Tehran."[36] Hamas and a handful of other Palestinian terror groups in Gaza launched a campaign of firing hundreds of unguided rockets at the towns abutting the Gaza Strip. The rockets killed only a few people but wounded many others and caused millions of dollars in damage. More importantly, the group was sowing terror among the Israeli population. Israelis living near Gaza never knew when the next salvo would come or where the rockets would land. A new era of terrorism had begun.

SIX

FIREBALLS IN THE SKY

Israel has absorbed thousands of rocket and mortar attacks over the years. In the early days, the rockets simply made impact while Israeli civilians scrambled desperately to their shelters as sirens shrieked. Apologists for Hamas insisted that these rockets were glorified "fireworks."[1] Such rhetoric only increased with the advent of Iron Dome. The missile defense system made these rockets look utterly benign.

Such thinking was always dangerous. On the night of May 11, 2021, Hamas showed why. Perhaps without even trying, the group managed to strike an oil storage tank adjacent to Israel's Eilat-Ashkelon pipeline.[2]

Immediately after the strike, Israeli television aired jarring footage of the resulting fireballs reaching high into the air. An Israeli energy official initially confirmed the report.[3] However, subsequent reporting was scarce, and the video ceased to air on Israeli television. It appeared that the Israeli government had issued a gag order. Israel does not like to reveal its vulnerabilities, especially during times of conflict. As one Israeli contact of mine told me in a not-for-attribution conversation, "We don't discuss such things."

Still, some facts about the attack could be discerned. The pipeline was owned by the Europe Asia Pipeline Company.[4] The company stated that the rocket attack did not affect its main terminal in Ashkelon. Rather, Hamas had hit an isolated oil storage tank.[5] The size of the tank was unknown.

Whether Hamas deliberately targeted the oil pipeline was the subject of some debate. It was initially unclear whether the group used a drone or guided munition or if it was simply dumb luck that an unguided rocket or mortar snuck through Israel's Iron Dome air defense system and hit the target. During a visit I took to the Gaza border one month after the war, Israeli officials stated with high certainty that it was something of a lucky strike. The IDF believes that it was a mortar fired from northern Gaza. Mortars can travel up to eight kilometers. In this case, the target was about six kilometers away.[6]

Hamas certainly indicated in advance that such a strike was possible. The terror group had previously tried to fire large salvos of rockets at sensitive sites in Israel, hoping to deliver a strategic blow to its enemy. During the war, Hamas released a statement saying it was "directing a rocket strike involving 15 rockets [at] Dimona," home to Israel's secretive nuclear facility.[7] That attack failed. The facility in Dimona is 75 miles from Gaza, giving Iron Dome more time to neutralize incoming projectiles. The secretive facility is also widely believed to have greater defenses given the sensitivity surrounding the site.

Ashkelon, by contrast, is a town just to the north of the Gaza Strip. To the chagrin of its residents, the city is a much more reachable target. Before the attack, Hamas vowed to "turn the town to hell."[8] The terror group fell just shy of that goal. As I heard from the

IDF, the mortar fell a mere 700 meters from the vital pipeline itself, whose destruction could have done far more significant damage.[9]

The strategic value of hitting an Israeli energy asset is not difficult to grasp. The Gaza war — specifically attempts by Hamas to target the Tamar gas platform using underwater drones — prompted Chevron to shut down the facility. The fact that this could happen was, in and of itself, a blow to Israel's progress in recent years toward energy security and monetizing its gas finds.[10]

As my colleague Brenda Shaffer notes, the Eilat-Ashkelon pipeline "at times is used to transport Caspian and Russian oil to Asia, as well as Gulf-produced oil to Europe. However, since these oil trade flows are not frequent, the pipeline is not used regularly. Today, most of the Gulf oil is exported to Asia and Russian and Caspian oil to Europe. Thus, this route is not in great need. However, it could have geopolitical significance if the Persian Gulf was blocked and the Red Sea route was used to bring oil to market. Thus, the UAE [is] interest[ed] in having access to this export route."[11]

In fact, the United Arab Emirates (UAE) had recently signed a memorandum of understanding with Israel to utilize the pipeline, inked as part of their 2020 normalization efforts.[12] At the time, Hamas spokesman Fawzi Barhoum called the UAE-Israel normalization agreement "dangerous" and a "stab in the back to the Palestinian cause."[13] In reality, there was a very low likelihood that the tank explosion was a deliberate message to the Emiratis. As IDF officers from Israel's Southern Command told me, the successful strike was quite lucky.

For Iran, the target had real significance. The pipeline was built in 1968 as a joint project between Israel and the previous regime in Iran, with which Israel enjoyed close relations. When Iran cut all ties with Israel following the 1979 Islamic Revolution, Iranian oil transportation through the pipeline ceased.[14] The pipeline's legal status has been in arbitration for several decades. In 2016, the Swiss High Court ruled that Israel must pay Iran approximately $1.1 billion for its share of the pipeline.[15]

Iranian propaganda in recent years has focused on Hamas' targeting of Israeli energy sites and other vital Israeli interests, such as Dimona.[16] Similarly, Hezbollah has threatened to hit the Israeli chemical plant in Haifa.[17] Such threats are, in effect, open declarations of an intent to carry out mass casualty attacks, or even chemical or nuclear attacks. Remarkably, they garner little attention.

SEVEN
A WAR IGNORED

While Hamas' openly genocidal threats are often ignored, there is another dynamic that gets even less airtime: the internecine Palestinian conflict. I have spent years studying this conflict. I even wrote a book about it.[1] There is little that surprises me anymore in this business. However, I am genuinely surprised at how little coverage this issue receives, particularly considering the flood of coverage of the broader Palestinian-Israeli conflict.

In November 2004, when Arafat died from a mysterious illness, Mahmoud Abbas, his heir-designate, was officially named as the new head of the PLO. Abbas lacked his predecessor's charisma. But his problems did not end there. He also had to grapple with the economic devastation caused by the Second Intifada. Palestinians further recognized that Fatah engaged in massive corruption schemes during the peace process. In short, Abbas had a legitimacy problem.

Amidst the Bush administration's democracy agenda, the White House encouraged Palestinian elections. The goal was to reinforce democracy to combat terrorism on an ideological level

— a policy Bush pursued in Iraq and Afghanistan, among others. The Bush White House believed that Abbas could strengthen his position at the ballot box.

The strategy was risky. Fatah faction members were squabbling amid flagging public support. Although polls showed Fatah enjoyed a small lead,[2] Hamas had gained popularity over the years, in part by deliberately boycotting the political structures created by the Oslo process. Instead, the group gained adherents in Gaza as well as the West Bank through its welfare system of mosques, charitable associations, sports clubs, and other services. Hamas also influenced the Palestinian people through its media network. In addition to its print and internet publications, Hamas broadcast its message via a television channel called Al-Aqsa TV.[3]

Hamas shocked the world on January 25, 2006, when the Islamist party won a majority of seats in the Palestinian parliament. According to one source, more than one million Palestinians voted. Hamas claimed 76 of the 132 parliamentary seats (74 under the Hamas banner, plus two Hamas-aligned independents), granting Hamas the right to form a government.[4]

Hamas soon announced a new coalition to be led by Ismael Haniyeh, a protégé of the late Hamas founder, Ahmed Yassin. The Palestinian territories soon fell into disarray. Fatah, which took only 45 seats in the election, was unprepared and unwilling to relinquish power. In a desperate bid to prevent a Hamas takeover, Israel and the United States offered their support.

For Israelis, the 2006 Hamas win severely dampened hopes for successful negotiations, let alone peace. Israel's unilateral withdrawal from Gaza in 2005 had backfired. Hamas could claim, with some credibility, that it drove Israel out of Gaza. The group could also now say it was the legitimate voice of the Palestinians by way of a free and fair election. Hamas leaders stated unequivocally that the terror group would neither disarm nor pursue peace talks.[5]

Hamas' electoral victory also pulled the rug out from under America's regional democratization efforts. The White House adopted a policy of "no recognition, no dialogue, and no financial aid" toward the Hamas-controlled Palestinian government until specific conditions were met. The Bush administration demanded that Hamas recognize Israel, renounce violence, and accept all previous Palestinian agreements with Israel.[6] None of that would happen any time soon.

In the Palestinian political arena, the elections dealt a debilitating blow to Fatah's historical primacy. As a result, Hamas-Fatah tensions ran high. Hamas members hung the party's green banner above the entrance to parliament in place of the traditional red, white, green, and black national flag. Fatah members tore down the banner, sparking a fight that was broken up by police.[7] Following the elections, there were other reports of "attacks on public institutions; armed personal and clan disputes; attacks on international organizations; abductions of [foreign nationals], including journalists; armed conflicts between security services and armed groups; and attacks on officials."[8]

Amid the political chaos, the Palestinian terror factions did not forget to attack Israel. As previously noted, on June 25, 2006, Hamas conducted a raid near the Kerem Shalom crossing at the Israel-Gaza border. Hamas fighters, along with militants from other Iran-backed terror groups, utilized an underground tunnel to ambush an Israeli tank. They killed two Israeli soldiers and captured Corporal Gilad Shalit, dragging him to the Gaza Strip, where he would remain in Hamas custody until 2011. In response to the commando raid, the IDF launched Operation Summer Rains against Hamas targets, adding to the chaos in Gaza.[9]

Remarkably, the Israeli outrage over the Hamas kidnapping was almost a side plot at the time. The events at Keren Shalom were quickly overshadowed by war on Israel's northern border, which began on July 12, 2006, when Hezbollah fighters attacked two IDF armored jeeps patrolling the Israel-Lebanon border. Hezbollah killed three soldiers and kidnapped two: Eldad Regev and Ehud Goldwasser. The result was a 33-day war marked by thousands of Hezbollah rockets fired into Israel's north. Ultimately, the United Nations brokered a ceasefire that went into effect on August 14, 2006.[10]

When the war ended, the focus returned to the Palestinian political deadlock. Seeking to regain control, Abbas called for an early election to end the crisis. Fatah activists celebrated Abbas' political maneuver, while Hamas accused him of launching a coup against its democratically elected government.[11] The political crisis worsened. In January and February 2007, Hamas abducted Fatah and PA figures. The victims were often beaten and, in some cases, had "their limbs. . . fired at to cause permanent physical disabilities." According to the Palestinian Centre for Human Rights, Hamas fighters stormed homes and executed Fatah figures point-blank, marking a dangerous turning point in the internecine Palestinian conflict.[12]

In a bid to halt the fighting, King Abdullah of Saudi Arabia invited leaders from both Palestinian political factions to Mecca for talks. Both Hamas and Fatah sent senior delegates, demonstrating a seriousness of purpose and perhaps concern for the future of the Palestinian national project. On February 8, 2007, Riyadh announced the Mecca Agreement, designed to end the internal conflict and re-establish political order.[13] The two sides agreed to form a national unity government. Yet violence soon erupted again — thanks in part to Iranian efforts to undermine a deal brokered by Tehran's Sunni regional rival.[14] In March 2007 alone, there were 46 reported kidnappings of civilians in the Gaza Strip and more than 25 killings. Yasser Abed Rabbo, a senior PLO member, described the situation as "anarchy."[15]

Factional violence between Fatah and Hamas continued through the spring — albeit unbeknownst to most of the world, thanks to poor media coverage. That period was marked by kidnappings, machine gun clashes, homemade-bomb attacks, and other acts of violence. Sensing that the situation could get even worse and perhaps threaten regional security, the Egyptian government stepped in again to broker calm. However, this ceasefire lasted for only a few weeks.[16]

Finally, on June 7, 2007, Hamas launched a military offensive to conquer the Gaza Strip. Among the group's key military assets was an underground tunnel that snaked its way into a Fatah military structure.[17] In just six days, Hamas forces controlled the streets and PA buildings, including Abbas' presidential compound and a massive security compound known as *al-Suraya*. By June 14, all of Gaza was under Hamas' control. Abbas appointed outgoing Finance Minister Salam Fayyad, an economic reformer respected by the international community and many Arab leaders, to lead an emergency government in the West Bank. In so doing, Abbas all but conceded that he had lost the Gaza Strip.

The fighting between Hamas and Fatah on the streets of Gaza was certainly not a surprise given their long history of animosity. What was surprising, though, was the utter collapse of the PA security forces. These fighters were trained and armed by the United States and other Western nations. During the battle, these fighters either fled or even switched sides. It was an embarrassing and lop-sided defeat.[18] The PA had lost Gaza, and it was barely clinging to power in the West Bank.

Hamas was a brutal enemy. According to one report, the civil war was characterized by "extra-judicial and willful killing," including incidents in which Hamas fighters pushed Fatah members off tall buildings. Hamas fighters killed PA supporters who were already injured[19] or shot Fatah fighters in their limbs at close range to ensure permanent wounds.[20] In total, the June 2007 civil war claimed the lives of 161 Palestinians, including seven children and 11 women. At least 700 Palestinians were wounded.[21]

Iran was widely suspected of being behind the orchestrated assault in Gaza. Iranian assistance had likely helped Hamas build tunnels and train fighters. Authors Beverly Milton-Edwards and Stephen Farrell were able to establish that Iranian support increased "exponentially" after the 2006 elections.[22] Senior Hamas leader Mahmoud al-Zahar later admitted that Iran had given him $22 million in cash in 2006.[23] Months before the Gaza takeover, Yuval Diskin, the head of Israel's Shin Bet, noted, "We know that Hamas has started to dispatch people to Iran, tens with the promise of hundreds, for months and maybe years of training."[24]

Hamas never denied Iran's support during this time. Journalist Zaki Chehab stated in his 2007 book *Inside Hamas*, "The Iranian connection is real and long-standing. It is one whose deep roots I witnessed at first hand."[25] Hamas leaders also later admitted that the group's fighters received training in Iran.[26]

During this time, the US government strove to prevent the flow of cash from Iran to Hamas. In July 2007, the US Treasury Department issued sanctions against Iran's Martyr's Foundation for funneling money from Iran to Hamas, among other groups.[27] Later that year, Treasury targeted Iran's Quds Force and Bank Saderat for funding Hamas, along with Hezbollah and PIJ.[28] Through these designations, Treasury's message was clear: Iran was providing Hamas with significant financial support.

With Gaza under Hamas control, concerns swirled that the coastal enclave would soon become an Islamic emirate.[29] Veteran British journalist Marie Colvin reported that "only believers feel safe" in Gaza. Un-Islamic dress sometimes resulted in beatings, and women were increasingly harassed if they did not dress appropriately.[30] Hamas banned free expression and generally exploited the population for its own members' benefit.[31]

The first sign of trouble came when Hamas announced on television the "end of secularism and heresy in the Gaza Strip." On June 14, 2007 masked gunmen raided Christian religious sites. Hamas gunmen stormed a Christian school and a church, destroying nearly everything in sight.[32] Later that month, Hamas kidnapped a Christian woman and forced her to convert to Islam.[33] Other attacks against Christians continued in the months that followed.[34] One Christian publication counted more than 50 attacks. Targets included barbershops, music stores, and even a UN school where boys and girls played together.[35]

Christians were not the only targets. Amnesty International documented that some 1,000 people across 23 different locations, mostly aligned with Fatah and the PA, were detained during the first months of Hamas rule.[36] The Palestinian Centre for Human Rights began documenting Hamas torture, citing Fatah members who "sustained fractures to the feet" as a result of beatings with sticks. In other instances, Fatah men were "handcuffed and blindfolded" and had cloth stuffed in their mouths to muffle their screams.[37]

There were also widespread reports of abductions. In July, Hamas arrested the director of Gaza's electricity company. He was not released until the end of the year.[38] In August, Hamas arrested a bank manager but gave no reasons for doing so.[39] In some cases, Fatah leaders were abducted just to be intimidated.[40] Law and order was clearly breaking down. A month after the Gaza civil war, Gaza's attorney general reported that his office had been inactive. *Sharia* courts run by Hamas-appointed judges became the primary arbiters of disputes in Gaza. As Amnesty International noted, the judges lacked "adequate independence, impartiality, training, oversight, and public accountability."[41]

Journalism suffered, too. Reporters and cameramen were barred from doing their jobs.[42] Hamas began to issue government press cards to journalists and explicitly banned reporting that could "cause harm to national unity."[43] The Palestinian Journalists Syndicate complained that the move was designed to intimidate and stifle the press.[44] *The New York Times* reported that journalists were beaten and intimidated.[45] Meanwhile, Hamas halted the production of three Fatah-aligned newspapers, marking the first time West Bank newspapers were banned in Gaza.[46] Hamas also closed pro-Fatah television and radio stations. Soon, Hamas controlled all electronic media in Gaza, except one radio station linked to Iran-backed PIJ.[47]

The London-based newspaper *Asharq Al-Awsat* reported that Gazans felt "miserable and suffocated" under Hamas rule. The United States, European Union,[48] and Canada[49] suspended their assistance to the enclave. Ultimately, Washington and Brussels developed mechanisms to deliver aid to Gazans with the goal of circumventing Hamas-controlled entities.[50]

In October 2007, Israel severed financial ties between Israeli banks and the Gaza Strip and even cut fuel deliveries. Israel threatened punitive disruptions of electricity — which Israel provided to Gaza pursuant to the Oslo Accords — in response to Qassam rocket salvos.[51] By December 2007, goods Israel had barred from entering Gaza included batteries, tobacco, coffee, gasoline, diesel, and chocolate.[52] Gazan produce traditionally sold to Israel rotted at the border.[53]

Gazans were generally miserable under the new regime. There was no way of legally protesting; demonstrations were outlawed. Still, that did not stop Gazans from trying. At one anti-Hamas rally in November 2007, a group of female Fatah protestors gathered in front of a Gaza police station controlled by Hamas, chanting, "Shi'a, Shi'a, Shi'a!" — a sign that Gazans did not forget from where Hamas received its training and funding: Iran.[54]

EIGHT
A CANCELED VOTE

The divisions between Hamas and Fatah, and between the West Bank and Gaza, endure to this day. For nearly 15 years, the bitter split has represented the greatest diplomatic impediment to the prospect of a two-state solution. Of course, this has not stopped American, European, and UN diplomats from mounting successive efforts to achieve peace. But none of the world's top diplomats have been able to answer one simple question: How can one negotiate two states for two people when the Palestinians are physically divided and disagree vehemently over their own leadership?

Fractured intra-Palestinian politics were a major contributing factor to the Gaza war of 2021. One would not know that from the reporting at the time. As is almost always the case, the conflict was cast as one in which Israel and the Palestinians were locked in a bitter cycle of violence. But that narrative assumed that the Palestinians were united. Remarkably, the old adage that "all politics are local" somehow did not seep into the analysis.

West Bank Palestinians lead a quiet existence relative to the hot wars their brethren in Gaza too often endure. Admittedly, many Palestinians chafe under the control of Israeli forces in certain areas of the West Bank. Many also chafe under the autocratic leadership of PA President Mahmoud Abbas. The octogenarian leader, who first took power in 2005 after the death of Yasser Arafat, has managed to extend his grip on power for a full 16 years and counting.

Some Palestinians might say Abbas is better than Arafat, who presided over the unraveling of a peace process that could very well have yielded the Palestinians a state. However, Abbas has arguably overseen an equally insidious era of Palestinian politics. During his tenure, corruption has been rampant. Billions of dollars in international funds that should have benefited his people have instead lined the pockets of the elite — all the while leaving the masses seething and blaming Israel for their woes.[1] Successive polls show that the Palestinian people thoroughly detest Abbas, and corruption is the primary reason.[2]

With little more than a shrug from Western governments, Abbas has quietly forged a system that has made it nearly impossible to unseat him. Due to the steadily growing paranoia of the aging Palestinian leader, there is no plan for an orderly succession. Palestinian basic law stipulates that in the absence of a Palestinian president, the speaker of parliament should take over in preparation for elections. After the 2006 elections, the speaker of parliament was a member of Hamas, Aziz Dweik.[3] For years, Washington feared Dweik would preside over the PA for several weeks until elections were held, prompting a cut in US and other international aid.

Abbas has since dissolved the parliament.[4] But the succession question still lingers. It is a question that he would rather not answer.

Some believe Mohammed Shtayyeh, the PA prime minister, could succeed Abbas.[5] However, it is unclear how much support he enjoys among the Palestinian elite, let alone the broader population. Others say Mahmoud al-Aloul, Fatah's deputy leader, could fill the role.[6] However, he also lacks a credible following.

Admittedly, succession could be determined the way it was after Arafat's passing in 2004, through a Palestinian leadership conclave. The PLO chieftains back then got together in Ramallah and selected Abbas. The opaque selection process was reminiscent of how the Vatican selects the pope — without the white smoke. But this approach leaves open the possibility that another corrupt leader will ascend to power, thereby perpetuating the Palestinian people's misery. Moreover, it would exclude the Palestinian people from selecting their own leader.

For many years, Abbas appeared to be bothered very little by the talk of succession. He understood that most Western nations supported him because they supported stability in the West Bank. Also, Abbas begrudgingly engaged in security cooperation with Israel to neutralize Hamas, thereby cementing his importance to the Israelis and the United States.

But this dynamic changed in December 2017 when the Trump administration recognized Jerusalem as Israel's capital. Abbas' currency on the Palestinian street began to drop as a result. Adding insult to injury, the Arab world did not join forces with the aging Palestinian leader to contest the move. As President Donald Trump (or perhaps his son-in-law, Jared Kushner) understood, the Arab states were drifting out of the Palestinian orbit. They were increasingly drawn to Israel's impressive military and intelligence capabilities. It was hard not be impressed given that the Israelis were targeting Iranian assets all over the Middle East — even inside Iran — with impunity. (See chapter nine.) In early 2020, the Trump administration unveiled its so-called Deal of the Century (also known as Peace to Prosperity) — a document that frontloaded benefits for Israel and called for the Palestinians to get their political house in order. Months later, Netanyahu announced the prospect of annexing roughly one-third of the West Bank. To thwart annexation, Abu Dhabi offered normalization — a move that the UAE had already been mulling.[7]

On September 15, 2020, two Arab states officially crossed the Rubicon. The United Arab Emirates and Bahrain signed the Abraham Accords with Israel.[8] The normalization agreements were undeniably a shock to the Palestinians, who began to realize that the Palestinian cause, celebrated by Arab states for more than seven decades, was beginning to lose its luster. It was not as if the Emiratis or Bahrainis rejected Palestinian nationalism. In normalizing with Israel, the two governments conveyed the somewhat harsh reality that the Palestinian issue was no longer a top national priority.

Other Arab countries seemed to convey that, too. Morocco soon signed a normalization agreement with Israel,[9] followed by Sudan.[10] There was speculation that others might join this trend, including Oman and Saudi Arabia. Trump, however, was voted out of office in November, prompting the rest of the Arab world to closely monitor the Biden administration for signs of whether the new American leadership would encourage additional normalization agreements.

Abbas and his inner circle were jolted by this wave of normalization. So was Hamas. The Abraham Accords were a wake-up call. The Palestinians wanted to put their national aspirations back on the international policy agenda after several years of what felt like exile under Trump. Hamas and Fatah subsequently met in Istanbul for reconciliation talks that few, if any, believed would yield a political breakthrough.[11] After all, the two sides had met and failed to agree many times before. The Egyptians, Saudis, Turks, Russians, and others had all tried brokering agreements, and they all failed.

Remarkably, on September 24, 2020, the two sides emerged aligned. "We have agreed to first hold legislative elections, then presidential elections of the PA, and finally the central council of the Palestine Liberation Organization," said senior Fatah official Jibril Rajoub, whose brother Nayef is a senior Hamas official.[12] The plan was for elections to take place in both the West Bank and the Gaza Strip.

The likelihood the two sides would follow through on this was still decidedly low. However, according to an Egyptian official with whom I spoke, Abbas received encouragement from French officials during a medical visit to Germany.[13] He was told that particularly after President Joe Biden's electoral victory, holding elections would be a way to rebuild confidence in both Washington and Brussels. Abbas apparently took that advice to heart. On January 15, 2021, days before Biden's inauguration, Abbas announced that PA parliamentary elections would take place on May 22 and presidential elections would follow on July 31.[14]

Abbas' announcement was nothing short of remarkable. The aging politician had already extended his four-year term to 16. He faced no overt pressure to take this step. Yet he did so anyway — and to the delight of Hamas. The group called for fair elections that would allow Palestinians to "express their will without restrictions or pressures" — a less-than-subtle message to the United States, Israel, and other governments that opposed their electoral victory in 2006.[15]

As election plans took shape, Abbas issued a direct challenge to Israel. He insisted that elections could not happen without the Arab residents of East Jerusalem, which Israel considers to be part of its capital. "We are very interested in having elections but not at any price," Abbas warned.[16] The PA followed up with a formal request to Israel for the Palestinian right to vote in Jerusalem.[17]

Despite the fact that Israel had allowed Palestinians to vote in eastern Jerusalem in 1996 and 2006 and was amenable to work-arounds, such as online ballots, the issue appeared to set the stage for a showdown. While the Israelis indicated that "no decision ha[d] been taken," the PA engaged in an aggressive messaging campaign during which Mutasem Tayem, director-general of the PA's Jerusalem Unit, said Arab residents with Israeli-issued identification cards must be able to vote "despite all Israeli measures aiming to prevent them from participating."[18]

One Israeli official told me that the Netanyahu government refused to be drawn into the Palestinian election debate.[19] For one, both sides had found compromises in the past. Moreover, officials in Israel's Ministry of Foreign Affairs viewed Abbas as goading Israel to bar Palestinian voters from casting ballots in eastern Jerusalem. The Israelis saw this as a convenient excuse for Abbas to eventually cancel elections he did not really want to hold. The Israelis, who were preparing for their own elections in March, did not like the optics. Finally, Prime Minister Benjamin Netanyahu, a politician known for being less than enthusiastic about the peace process with the current Palestinian leadership, did not want the Palestinians to become an election issue for Israeli voters, not least because he was campaigning for support among Israel's Arab parties. To Netanyahu's delight, the peace process had been a minor issue in all three of Israel's inconclusive elections heading into 2021.

Israel thus opted for a policy of silence. Israelis would table their own concerns about Hamas' participation in Palestinian electoral politics until after Israel's own March 23 elections. As one senior Israeli official, speaking on the condition of anonymity, said to me, "The Palestinians would have to continue waiting for a savior to blame." The official clearly believed that the Palestinian leadership did not actually want the vote to take place, even as it made plans for the elections.[20]

If the Palestinian leadership was ambivalent, it was for good reason. September 2020 opinion polls among Palestinians indicated that Hamas leader Ismael Haniyeh would beat Abbas 52 percent to 39 percent in a head-to-head contest. If convicted terrorist Marwan Barghouti ran, he was slated to win 55 percent of the vote. In parliamentary elections, Fatah would receive 38 percent of the vote, and Hamas 34 percent — a very tight race.[21]

Subsequent opinion polls in December did not improve for Fatah. The parliamentary split between Fatah and Hamas was identical. Abbas was losing ground to Barghouti and was still projected to lose to Haniyeh. Even worse for Abbas, 66 percent of respondents were demanding the ailing octogenarian's resignation.[22]

As talk of Palestinian elections gained steam, the international community maintained an uneasy silence. The Biden administration's silence was particularly notable. Rather than addressing the looming challenge of a terrorist group participating in the Palestinian election — a longstanding bipartisan red line in Washington — the Biden administration prioritized allocating additional funds to the PA. The Trump administration had voided a great deal of US funding for the PA. Seeking to take America's Middle East policy in a new direction, the Biden administration announced plans to provide $15 million in COVID-19 support,[23] $10 million for "peace-building" programs, and $75 million in other assistance.[24] A leaked administration memo expressed a desire to prioritize renewed ties with the PA, while articulating mere "concern" that Hamas could beat Fatah in the forthcoming elections.[25]

Deeper concern was building, though. Reports out of Israel revealed that the Hamas ticket included inmates in Israeli jails and a terrorist commander.[26] *Asharq Al-Awsat* reported that the Biden administration did quietly ask Abbas for "clarifications on the partnership with Hamas in the upcoming elections."[27] One Palestinian outlet claimed that the United States asked Abbas to postpone or cancel the elections, which Abbas allegedly rejected.[28]

Broadly speaking, the White House's primary goal was to "renew the legitimacy in the Palestinian Authority."[29] In my private conversations with Israeli and Palestinian officials, they attested to this. Meanwhile, US officials specifically noted in not-for-attribution briefings that the State Department would not interfere, saying that Washington had little right to make demands of others' electoral processes, particularly after the disastrous events of January 6, 2021, when protestors stormed the halls of Congress in response to Trump's electoral loss.

But this position was decidedly awkward considering that Biden, while serving as a US senator, had spearheaded the Palestinian Anti-Terrorism Act (PATA) of 2006. That law explicitly prohibits US assistance if the PA is "effectively controlled by Hamas."[30]

Jordan and Egypt, traditional Palestinian allies that oppose the Muslim Brotherhood (of which Hamas is a splinter faction), were also relatively quiet. Qatar-based Al Jazeera reported that the two governments expressed "uncertainty about the readiness of the Fatah movement for the elections."[31] Officially, however, neither country appeared eager to stand in the way of the forthcoming vote.

One country that appeared to welcome Palestinian elections was the United Arab Emirates. Mohammed Dahlan, the former Gaza Strip security chief and a rival of Abbas, had been living in exile in the Emirates since 2011 and was champing at the bit to re-enter Palestinian politics. He had no plans to run in the legislative elections but was clearly eyeing the presidency, even though his legal status in the Palestinian territories potentially encumbered his candidacy.[32]

As *The Times of Israel* noted, "[w]ith Abu Dhabi's backing, Dahlan's movement has quietly funded aid projects in the Gaza Strip and in East Jerusalem over the past several years."[33] In fact, Dahlan delivered 60,000 COVID-19 vaccine shots to Gaza, donated by the Emiratis, amid rumors he would run.[34] Dahlan's polling numbers were not particularly impressive, but Palestinians believed he could play a spoiler role, particularly if his candidacy eroded support for Abbas.

Posing an even greater threat to Abbas was Marwan Barghouti,[35] the polarizing Palestinian figure who was sentenced to multiple life terms in Israel for acts of terrorism committed under his command during the Second Intifada. Some Palestinians see him as their Nelson Mandela, the famous South African figure who emerged from a terrorism-related prison sentence to lead his country. Mandela, of course, never directly engaged in violence the way Barghouti did. Nevertheless, Barghouti had a consistently strong showing in the opinion polls.[36]

Another formidable candidate was former Fatah Central Committee member Nasser al-Qudwa, who on Twitter declared his intention to form "an electoral slate within the framework of a broad democratic forum that includes various segments of society, not the Fatah movement alone."[37] In retribution for Qudwa's audacity, Abbas expelled him from the Fatah party.[38] Undeterred, Qudwa and his supporters founded a new political party — the Palestinian National Democratic Forum — and even invited Barghouti to join it.

Also in the mix was former Palestinian Prime Minister Salam Fayyad, a soft-spoken reformer who ran under the banner of the "Third Way" in 2006.[39] Fayyad, who currently teaches at Princeton University, was once the best hope the Palestinians had for a functioning, democratic state. However, Abbas ran him out of Ramallah after the two clashed over core issues, including corruption. Fayyad declared that his new electoral list would be composed of "independent personalities" who sought to govern with "transparency and honor."[40]

By March 2021, there was no dearth of candidates or candidate lists. Nor was there a problem with projected voter turnout. An estimated 93 percent of eligible voters had registered to cast their votes.[41] Longtime observers of Palestinian politics, who had little to write about for many years, due primarily to Abbas' suffocation of the political system, cautiously began to assess possible outcomes.[42] The consensus was that the Palestinians had advanced too far in the electoral process to turn around.

The Israelis were not so sure about that. After their own March 23 elections, Israeli officials finally began to voice their concerns. Shin Bet chief Nadav Argaman visited Majed Faraj, the head of the PA security services, in an effort to postpone the election.[43] Argaman also met with Abbas and delivered the same message, only to be rebuffed by the Palestinian president, who told him, "You built Hamas." This was a reference to the network of mosques and social services first built by Ahmed Yassin — supported by Israel before Yassin founded Hamas.[44] The IDF's outgoing liaison to the Palestinians also issued a rare public warning, saying Israel should be prepared to halt all security coordination with the Palestinians if Hamas won the election.[45]

One senior Israeli official told me that the Palestinians still had an opportunity to "climb down from the tree."[46] They could postpone the election by citing legitimate concerns about COVID-19. Polling stations without proper public health procedures could further strain West Bank hospitals, which were well over capacity in March, according to the World Health Organization.[47] Gaza's infection rate had been surprisingly manageable even though overall Palestinian vaccination numbers remained low.[48] Whether Abbas wanted to use the coronavirus as an excuse to cancel elections was another story.

Abbas was undoubtedly aware of his dismal survey numbers. With his Fatah party generally in disarray and roundly hated by the Palestinian people,[49] the PA elections looked like they were heading for a repeat of 2006. Even if Hamas did not score a huge victory, the terrorist group would undoubtedly play a significant role in the new government. A recent change in the Palestinian election law stipulating proportional representation in parliament guaranteed that Hamas would win seats. (Fatah leaders thought the law might help win them a few more seats.)[50] This presented a major risk to the PA. The aforementioned PATA law that Biden had championed prohibited US aid to the PA if there was any Hamas participation whatsoever.

Back in Washington, PATA was not the only legislation to consider. Congress had also passed the Anti-Terrorism Clarification Act of 2019 to ensure that American victims of attacks by the PLO or other Palestinian organizations could sue the PA for damages.[51] One can only imagine the liabilities of a PA represented by Hamas lawmakers.

The Europeans, by contrast, seemingly had no problem pushing the Palestinians to continue down the path toward elections. According to the Associated Press, Palestinian election officials in January 2021 invited the European Union to send monitors.[52] The European Union did not send its own people, however. It instead sent representatives from the company DT Global Europe, under the umbrella of an Election Exploratory Mission. A company spokesperson was unable to share additional details, citing "a strict privacy setting." When asked about the participation of Hamas, the spokesperson noted only that the company was compiling its analysis of the political environment, and that it was the "EU officials who will receive this analysis and act on the information as they consider best."[53]

As Israel and other regional states warned that Hamas was likely to emerge as the big winner in the Palestinian elections, the Biden administration began to waver. American officials reportedly began to signal that the United States would not complain if the PA canceled the elections.[54] This came as Israel delivered its bluntest warnings yet that a Hamas victory would torpedo the delicate relationship between Jerusalem and Ramallah, particularly in security coordination — an arrangement that had undeniably helped prevent Hamas from overtaking the West Bank since the group conquered Gaza in 2007.[55]

On April 30, Abbas canceled the elections. As expected, he blamed Israel for failing to clarify if elections would be able to proceed in Jerusalem. He stated that the elections would be postponed, not canceled, "until the participation of our people in Jerusalem is guaranteed."[56]

The Palestinians, not to mention the rest of the Middle East, understood that this was the only way for Abbas to save face. Still, Palestinian voters were understandably frustrated. The most aggrieved party was Hamas. The group's leadership (correctly) viewed the elections as an opportunity to rewrite history after Abbas negated the results of the 2006 elections at the urging of Israel and the United States. History, it appeared, was repeating itself — at least on some level.

Hamas' commitment to violence and its underlying extremist ideology were obvious hurdles to the group's participation in the first place. Remarkably, neither the PA leadership nor its champions in Washington or Brussels addressed the problem preemptively when the idea of new elections was introduced. The entire episode created needless friction between the PA and Hamas, the latter of which until then had been sidelined in the Palestinian political process. For the terror group, the prospect of elections briefly inspired new hope of participating in the Palestinian political system. Smarting from this political setback, Hamas was eager to demonstrate its leadership to the Palestinian people. It would do so by starting a war with Israel.

NINE
THE WAR BETWEEN WARS

In the lead-up to the May 2021 conflict, the Islamic Republic in Iran was also looking for a fight. Admittedly, the regime in Iran is always looking to target Israel. That explains why Tehran has financed, armed, and trained Hamas and other terrorist organizations, including Hezbollah in Lebanon and Palestinian Islamic Jihad in Gaza.

Historically, Israel has endeavored to simply beat back Iran's proxies through brief but painful wars when provoked. Hezbollah, Hamas, and PIJ have all taken their lumps in the region's many flare-ups over the years. Israel always walked away bloodied but intact. However, Tehran never paid a price. The regime obviously preferred it that way. The people who were fighting and dying were Palestinian and Lebanese, not Iranian.

But over the last decade, that dynamic has started to change. Beginning in 2012, Israel saw that Iran was actively working to exploit the chaos of the civil war in neighboring Syria. The Islamic Republic was sending Shiite militias, advanced weaponry, and other military hardware closer and closer to the Israel-Syria border.

Tehran was looking to create a new front on Israel's northern border. Simply put, the regime hoped to create one or more Syrian versions of Hamas. All the while, Tehran was sending advanced weapons to Hezbollah via Syria to strengthen the Lebanese terror group's capabilities for the next round of fighting.

Israel began to target these military assets in Syria, often quietly and in the dead of night. Yet the shipments from Iran continued. Iran was clearly willing to absorb these tactical strikes so long as it could continue its smuggling efforts. The regime, in other words, would continue to move whatever weapons it could to its proxies, even if only a small percentage squeezed through. This opened a new front in what the Israelis call "the war between wars," or WBW.[1]

The WBW first began as a covert Israeli campaign inside Iran to undermine Tehran's nuclear program, which Israel considers its top security threat. But as Iranian weaponry flooded into war-torn Syria, the government of Prime Minister Netanyahu had little choice but to operate there, too. The IDF began to hammer Iran's military assets in Syria systematically — assets intended to aim at Israel one day. The IDF targeted Iran's Islamic Revolutionary Guard Corps (IRGC), Iran's proxy Shiite militias, and even the Bashar al-Assad regime in Syria on a consistent basis. This shadow war cannot be ignored as a contributing factor in, if not one of the causes of, the 2021 Gaza war.

When the civil war in Syria first erupted, one senior Netanyahu advisor privately joked with me in 2012 that the conflict was like the movie *Alien vs. Predator* for Israel. The Iranian axis was battling Sunni extremists — both Israeli foes. When I returned to Israel in 2013, however, the official was in a decidedly less jocular mood. The reason was apparent: The Israelis were discovering new and troubling threats in Syria. In February 2013, Israel struck a biological research center as well as anti-aircraft systems destined for Hezbollah in Lebanon.[2] The following May, *The New York Times* reported that Israeli warplanes struck an additional shipment of advanced weapons bound for Hezbollah.[3] Attacks continued through the year.

In January 2014, the targets included missile launchers,[4] advanced weapons destined for Hezbollah,[5] and even Syrian military sites.[6] In June, the Israelis carried out strikes against nine military targets associated with Iran in Syria, in retribution for an attack that killed an Israeli teenager.[7] The Israeli Air Force struck targets near the Damascus International Airport in December — likely more weapons intended for Hezbollah.[8]

In January 2015, the IDF killed six Hezbollah members and six Iranian soldiers, including commanders.[9] Reported among the dead was Jihad Mughniyeh,[10] the son of Imad Mughniyeh, a Hezbollah commander whom Israel had killed in Syria in 2008.[11] In April, the IDF reportedly took out additional Hezbollah and Assad regime weapons depots.[12] This was followed by an Israeli airstrike against militants placing explosives along Israel's border.[13]

In February 2016, Israel reportedly again struck Syrian army outposts.[14] The Israelis took out a weapons convoy headed for Hezbollah the following May.[15] On May 13, Lebanese media reported that Hezbollah's top commander in Syria, Mustafa Baddredine, was killed in an apparent Israeli strike.[16] Remarkably, the Israelis were simultaneously targeting Islamic State assets in Syria, too.[17]

In 2017, the WBW continued apace. Israel was blamed for carrying out attacks on an airbase in the Damascus area,[18] a Hezbollah convoy carrying weapons to Lebanon,[19] and the leader of an Iran-backed militia.[20] In April, Israel reportedly struck Hezbollah-bound assets at the Damascus airport.[21]

In June 2017, tensions flared when ten projectiles were fired into Israel, prompting the Israelis to strike military positions across Syria.[22] The following month, Israel targeted a suspected Syrian chemical weapons facility.[23] The Israelis continued to strike military targets across Syria through the end of the year.[24]

In February 2018, the shadow war emerged further from the shadows. The drama began when the Islamic Republic dispatched a drone from Syria that penetrated Israeli airspace. Israel destroyed the drone with an Apache helicopter, then sent eight F-16s to strike the Syrian airbase known as T4, from which the drone was dispatched. While the Israelis successfully destroyed a number of Iranian targets at T4, one F-16 jet was struck by a Syrian surface-to-air missile (reportedly because of pilot error). The pilot and his navigator managed to make it safely back to Israel.[25]

The IDF had long warned that the T4 base was crawling with fighters from Iran's Quds Force, the IRGC's expeditionary arm. Netanyahu had paid multiple visits to Moscow hoping to convince President Vladimir Putin to curb the threatening activities of Iran and its proxies. The Russians had established a formidable presence in Syria since 2015, when Putin dispatched his forces to the country to save the Assad regime from collapse.

Whether Russia had advance knowledge of the Iranian drone operation is unclear. Nor was it clear whether Russia was involved in unleashing the Syrian surface-to-air missile that downed the Israeli F-16. But after many Israeli airstrikes in Syria in recent years, this was the first time Syrian anti-aircraft weapons had managed to hit a target.

The T4 incident was not the first drone incursion into the Golan Heights. In 2017, the IDF intercepted several Iranian-built, Hezbollah-operated drones that penetrated Israeli airspace from

Syria.[26] But there was something about this particular drone from T4 that struck a nerve among the IDF brass. After the initial skirmish, the Israeli military launched additional airstrikes against Iranian and Syrian targets, including air defenses. This second wave was the largest aerial attack against Syria since the 1982 Lebanon War, when the Israeli Air Force destroyed Syrian surface-to-air missile batteries and warplanes.[27]

Two months after the T4 incident, Israel struck an Iranian airbase in Syria, killing seven members of the Iranian military.[28] In May 2018, eight Iranians and seven other Iran-backed fighters were killed by a reported Israeli strike at an IRGC installation.[29] Later that month, the Israelis struck more than 50 Iranian targets throughout Syria as part of Operation House of Cards, designed to neutralize Iranian assets across the country.[30] But that was hardly the end of the WBW. In June, Israel was believed to have carried out a strike much farther from home, in Iraq, against an Iran-backed militia. That strike killed 20 and destroyed other military assets.[31]

Iran was either unwilling or unable to respond to these strikes. Either way, by 2019, Israel was openly eschewing its policy of plausible deniability. Perhaps Netanyahu wanted to wield the WBW for political gain as Israel descended into political deadlock and was repeatedly unable to form a government. Or perhaps the Israeli security apparatus believed that making Iran's defeats public would be more demoralizing for Tehran. Whatever the reasons, Netanyahu openly claimed credit for a strike against Syrian targets in February 2019.[32] In March, Israel's acting foreign minister, Israel Katz, appeared to confirm strikes against Iranian assets in Aleppo.[33] In April, Netanyahu hinted again that Israel was behind a strike against an Iranian weapons factory.[34] In May, the IDF claimed credit for targeting a Syrian anti-aircraft battery.[35]

The tempo did not slow, either. The IDF targeted an Iranian drone at a base in Syria in June 2019.[36] The following month, the Israelis struck a military research center and a base housing Hezbollah fighters.[37] In August, the IDF targeted Iranian forces reportedly planning to launch "killer drones" at Israel. [38]

In May 2020, the Syrian Observatory for Human Rights reported that Syria had sustained nearly 40 airstrikes that year, resulting in the death of 225 Iranian and Assad regime soldiers.[39] Israeli reports suggested that Iran was looking to draw down in Syria after sustaining multiple Israeli strikes.[40] The evidence never quite supported this assertion, but it was certainly likely that the regime in Tehran, as well as the Hezbollah leadership in Lebanon, was growing frustrated.

In June 2020, the Israelis reportedly struck Syrian onion and cattle plants that Iran had converted into weapons warehouses.[41] Another strike took out a weapons convoy headed for Hezbollah in Lebanon.[42] In September, the IDF once again targeted the T4 airbase, knocking out the runway to prevent Iranian weapons transfers to Hezbollah and other terrorist proxies.[43] In December, a suspected Israeli airstrike took out Muslim Shahdan, a top IRGC commander.[44]

In December 2020, IDF Chief of Staff Aviv Kochavi announced that Israel had struck more than 500 targets in Syria during 2020 alone, targeting Iranian and Iran-backed smugglers, fighters, and weapons systems.[45] Kochavi was being understated. One year prior, outgoing IDF Chief of Staff Gadi Eizenkot revealed that Israel had destroyed thousands of military targets in Syria.[46] But as one senior Israeli official quipped at the time, when I pressed him for exact numbers, "Who's counting?"

For much of the WBW, Israel operated with the implicit blessing of the Trump administration, which was unequivocally supportive of Israel's right to diminish the Iranian military build-up on its borders. After Trump's departure, it was unclear whether President Joe Biden would give Israel the green light to continue. After all, Biden had already signaled his intent to re-enter the 2015 Iran nuclear deal, which Trump exited in 2018. Biden certainly did not appear to be openly pro-regime. Still, it remained to be seen whether Israel could continue to operate with impunity.

That question appeared to be answered on January 28, 2021, when Israel struck Iranian and Hezbollah forces in Syria for the first time in the Biden era.[47] In April, Reuters reported that Jerusalem had "dramatically expanded air strikes on suspected Iranian missile and weapons production centers in Syria" as part of Israel's operations to halt Iranian weapons proliferation to Tehran's proxies on Israel's borders.[48] If Washington was unhappy about this, it was not aired publicly.[49]

It is important to note here that Syria was not the only WBW battleground. In recent years, Israel and Iran have slugged it out on the high seas. In March, Israel reportedly struck an Iranian oil vessel bound for Syria.[50] *The Wall Street Journal* subsequently revealed (perhaps as the result of leaks from the Biden White House) that Israel had targeted maybe a dozen other Iranian vessels since 2019.[51] In April, Israel damaged an Iranian spy ship on the Red Sea[52] and reportedly hit an Iranian fuel tanker with a drone strike.[53] The following month, a mysterious explosion occurred on an Iranian oil tanker off the coast of Syria. Israel was once again suspected.[54]

The Israelis got it as good as they gave. In March 2021, Iran was suspected in an attack on an Israeli freighter near the Persian

Gulf.[55] Later that month, an Israeli-owned ship was hit by a missile off the coast of Oman.[56] The following month, another Israeli-owned ship was attacked off the coast of the United Arab Emirates.[57] Months after the Gaza war's conclusion, the Israeli ship *Mercer Street* was struck by an Iranian drone, drawing condemnation from the United States and the G7.[58]

The WBW has expanded significantly over the years. It was originally designed to weaken Iranian nuclear capabilities, which have advanced alarmingly. In November 2020, Iran's top nuclear scientist, Mohsen Fakhrizadeh, was killed in his car by a remote-controlled weapon.[59] The culprit was presumed to be the Mossad, which had been widely blamed for six other attacks against Iranian nuclear scientists since 2007.[60] There have also been targets of opportunity. For example, the Israelis were involved in the 2020 assassination of Abu Mohammed al-Masri, al-Qaeda's second-in-command, who was living under regime protection in Tehran.[61] The revelation of this arrangement raised new questions about the regime's long-standing relationship with the terrorist group that attacked America in September 2001.[62]

Israel was also battling Iran in cyberspace. Israel first announced itself on this battlefield in 2010 with the deployment of the "Stuxnet" worm, a joint US-Israeli cyber weapon that set back Iran's nuclear program for perhaps two years.[63] In 2018, Tehran also accused Israel of launching a cyberattack against Iranian critical infrastructure.[64] In 2020, Israel was suspected of being behind cyberattacks against two Iranian government agencies,[65] as well the Iranian port of Shahid Rajaee.[66]

These operations did not occur in a vacuum. The Iranians were also targeting Israel. In March 2021, Iranian hackers reportedly targeted Israeli medical researchers,[67] government agencies, academia, and tourism agencies.[68] In December of the previous year, Iranian hackers stole data from at least 40 different Israeli companies.[69] In a separate instance, Iranian hackers gained access to Israel's water system.[70] In fact, 2020 saw Iranian cyberattacks against Israeli companies across a wide range of sectors.[71] According to news reports in 2019, Iranian hackers almost infiltrated Israel's missile early warning system.[72] And in 2018, it was reported that Iran successfully penetrated the cellphone of Benny Gantz, the IDF's former chief of staff.[73]

But perhaps the most important event in the WBW was the 2018 operation in which Israel's Mossad spirited away reams of documents from a secret nuclear archive on the outskirts of Tehran.[74] Nuclear experts were sent scrambling to interpret loads of new information about Iran's nuclear program after the documents were revealed.[75] Several of those documents helped the UN nuclear watchdog, the International Atomic Energy Agency, identify nuclear sites previously obscured by the regime.[76] The documents also helped to raise awareness about the regime's prior advances in weaponization of its nuclear program.

For the regime in Tehran, the WBW has been deeply frustrating. The regime's desire for retribution has only grown. In April, just weeks before the war erupted, an Iranian general stated, "The Zionists [Israel] imagine that they can continuously target the Syrian territories and conduct mischief in different places and in the sea and receive no response. . . [T]he Resistance Front will give a principal response."[77] Similarly, IRGC commander Hossein Salami declared, "the evil deeds committed by the Zionists [Israel] in the region will turn against themselves and expose them to real dangers in the future."[78] Shortly thereafter, Salami declared that Israel's "biggest weakness is that any tactical action could bring about a strategic defeat. . . just a single operation can ruin this regime."[79]

Iran appeared to be threatening to deploy its own forces or its proxies to battle Israel. Of course, the Islamic Republic never wages war directly, at least not since the Iran-Iraq War of 1980–1988. Proxies are always a safer bet. Hamas has long been one of the non-state actors to benefit from Iranian military support. To Tehran's delight, the group's leaders were openly expressing their willingness to fight Israel again. The winds of war were blowing.

TEN
THE 2021 GAZA WAR

On May 10, Hamas launched seven rockets toward Jerusalem. One fell in the outskirts of the city, causing damage to a home and sparking a brushfire.[1] The very act of firing upon Jerusalem, Israel's capital, was sure to prompt a harsh response from Israel. Then, in what can only be described as a long string of war crimes,[2] Hamas continued to fire rockets indiscriminately at population centers. With remarkable precision, Israel's Iron Dome missile defense system started knocking them down. The IDF soon began to respond with air strikes. What the Israelis called Operation Guardian of the Walls was underway.

Amos Harel, a veteran Israeli military analyst, observed that during the previous Israel-Hamas war in 2014, the terror group fired a total of 4,600 projectiles over 50 days, an average of less than 100 per day. This time around, Hamas fired nearly 400 projectiles a day — four times more.[3] In fact, during one salvo, Hamas claimed to have launched a remarkable 137 rockets in roughly five minutes.[4]

During the war, the Israeli military ceded that it was dealing with the "highest daily rate of rocket fire that Israel has faced in the history of the country."[5] Hamas must have been pleased. Prior to the war, the group's spokesman explained that Hamas' goal was to "overcom[e] the so-called Iron Dome by adopting the tactic of firing dozens of missiles in one single burst."[6]

To a certain extent, it was a numbers game. During an IDF briefing at the beginning of the war, I was told that Hamas had entered the conflict with an estimated 30,000 projectiles in its arsenal.[7] But senior Israeli officials subsequently cited smaller numbers.[8] My best guess is that Hamas had 12,000 to 15,000 rockets at the ready. During the hostilities, Hamas launched approximately 4,350 of them.[9] Following the war, a senior Israeli official estimated that Hamas had 8,000 remaining.[10]

Hamas had Iran to thank for much of its arsenal. Over the years, the regime had smuggled thousands of rockets into the Gaza Strip. When smuggling entire rockets became more difficult, the regime smuggled rocket parts. When that became more of a challenge, the regime taught Hamas' rocket makers how to assemble the ordnances on their own, sometimes using only locally sourced parts. (The regime has done the same with Hezbollah in Lebanon.) In one Al Jazeera report from 2020, Hamas members recounted how they had built rockets using shells extracted from a vessel that had sunk off the Gaza coast during World War I.[11]

Numbers were only part of the challenge for Israel. Hamas' rockets were also increasingly sophisticated. Worryingly for Israel, they were more accurate than they had been in past conflicts. Several days into the conflict, analyst Michael J. Armstrong observed, "Accuracy has improved. . . About 50 per cent of the rockets arriving over Israel have threatened populated areas. That's up from 22 per cent in 2012 and 18 per cent in 2014. Fewer rockets land in empty fields after missing their targets."[12]

By the end of the conflict, roughly 3,400 rockets (around 78 percent of the 4,350 total) were fired into Israeli territory. Another 680 rockets (15.5 percent) exploded or landed in the Gaza Strip, and 280 (6.5 percent) fell into the Mediterranean Sea.[13] One assessment suggested that 91 Palestinians were killed by errant rockets that fell in Gaza, amounting to a significant percentage of the Palestinian death toll.[14] This received little coverage at the time.

Regardless of the exact numbers, the accuracy of Hamas' rockets forced Israel's Iron Dome to work overtime. Armstrong noted, "almost half of [the] rockets fired from Gaza . . . prompted an Israeli interception attempt, significantly higher than in previous conflicts in 2019 and 2014."[15] Iron Dome could not stop everything. Thirteen Israelis were killed during the conflict.[16] The rockets also occasionally caused significant property damage in towns across Israel.

For the IDF, the range of the Hamas rocket arsenal was also a concerning factor. Most of the Hamas rockets were short-range threats. The locally produced Ayyash rocket, however, boasted a range of more than 240 kilometers, capable of striking deep into Israel.[17] Hamas further claimed to have thousands of rockets with a similar range, thanks to Iran.[18] For example, Hamas managed to import Fajr-3 and Fajr-5 rockets from Iran and M-302 rockets from Syria. These projectiles have a range of 480, 750, and 180 kilometers, respectively.[19]

PIJ, a smaller Iran-backed proxy group with a smaller rocket arsenal, boasted similar capabilities during the war. The group proudly unveiled the new Badr-3 rocket, produced with Iranian support.[20] It also fired off many shorter-range rockets.

Amos Harel observed that Hamas' improved rocket capabilities represented a significant achievement for the group — not to mention for its Iranian patron. Hamas had demonstrated that it could assemble a formidable rocket arsenal despite Israel's close monitoring of the Gaza Strip.[21] During the war, the IDF specifically targeted 10 to 12 Hamas engineers involved in the rocket project, knocking out a significant percentage of the group's brain trust. However, Hamas' rocket-making know-how is likely institutional at this point.[22]

Another military achievement for Hamas was its introduction of unmanned aerial vehicles (UAVs) that pierced the skies over Israel. Israeli military officers told me that the group had been sending drones to probe Israeli airspace for months prior to the conflict.[23] Hamas stated that its drones were built locally, but weapons specialists noted similarities with Iranian drones.[24] Ephraim Sneh, a retired Israeli brigadier general and former deputy defense minister, noted, "The design [of Hamas weapons] is Iranian but the production is local." Or as Scott Crino, the CEO of US consulting firm Red Six Solutions, said, "Iran's hands are all over this."[25]

Upon closer examination, the "Shehab" Kamikaze drones Hamas launched at Israel during the May 2021 war resembled the Iranian Ababil-T and Qasef-series UAVs deployed in Yemen by the Iran-backed Houthis. However, the Shebab is smaller,[26] with a wingspan of only eight feet. Alarmingly, the drone's GPS system could be purchased commercially at the time for only $50 — a sign of the dangerous era of drone warfare that looms, and not just in the Middle East.[27] In fact, US officials had voiced concern about the proliferation of drones months before the war erupted.[28]

During the 2021 conflict, the IDF downed at least three drones.[29] The Israeli military also claimed it conducted a strike on the apartment of Samer Abu-Daka, the head of Hamas' UAV unit.[30] The IDF further claimed to have "struck a squad of terrorists operating explosive UAV launchers belonging to the Hamas terrorist organization in the Gaza Strip. The squad was struck while they were preparing to launch the UAV into Israeli territory."[31]

While the IDF conveyed the sense that it was all under control, it was not as easy as it looked. It's a complicated thing to monitor the skies for drones while thousands of rockets — not to mention the Iron Dome interceptors that were deployed to destroy them — soar across Israeli airspace.

The May 2021 Gaza war also witnessed another Hamas innovation: unmanned underwater vehicles (UUVs).[32] The Israeli Navy intercepted one of them, reportedly deployed to attack the Tamar offshore natural gas rig — a valuable financial asset for Israel. The UUV in question reportedly was a commercial vehicle converted for military use. The IDF stated that the UUV carried a whopping 30 to 50 kilograms (66 to 110 pounds) of explosives.[33] On May 18, the IDF shared footage of a Hamas team operating the UUV by remote control from a car. The Israeli Air Force destroyed both the UUV and the car.[34]

The Israelis had actually been preparing for this tactic for several years. In 2016, the Mossad was believed to be behind the assassination of Mohammed Zawahri, a Hamas engineer developing UUVs and UAVs in Tunisia.[35] An IDF officer told me after the May 2021 war that the IDF also hit one UUV three days before the conflict and another one in 2020. The Israelis knew there would be more.[36] The IDF destroyed numerous UUVs in their docks during the 2021 war.[37]

As if the threats from the air and the sea were not enough, the Israelis were also forced to deal with terror threats from underground.

Tunnels are a longtime tactic of Hamas, one well known to Israelis. The IDF destroyed a tunnel near the Gaza border roughly four months before the conflict erupted.[38] But once the war began, it quickly became clear that Hamas had prepared an advanced system of underground tunnels that the IDF targeted from above.

The Israeli technological responses to this growing array of threats are worth noting. Israel's high-tech defensive solutions to a wide range of systems allow a glimpse into the future of warfare.

First, there is missile defense. The Israelis have an advanced and multilayered missile defense system developed jointly by the Israeli Missile Defense Organization and US Missile Defense Agency. In addition to Iron Dome, the other layers are David's Sling (for mid-range threats) and Arrow (for long-range).[39] In 2020, Israel conducted an integrated test of these systems, simulating a variety of advanced threats. For Israel, this was the first time all three of its missile defense layers worked together simultaneously.[40]

Out of these three systems, Iron Dome undeniably has seen the most action. Israel decided in 2007 to develop the system to address a mounting rocket threat from Hamas and Hezbollah. Four years later, Iron Dome successfully intercepted its first short-range rocket,[41] and has since intercepted thousands more. The system has only improved over time, exceeding all expectations.

For Israel, this innovation could not come soon enough. For the last two decades, Israel has faced an astounding number of incoming enemy rockets. Hamas has consistently fired projectiles toward Israel since the early 2000s. In 2006, during the Second Lebanon War, Hezbollah fired approximately 4,000 rockets into Israel, devastating the country's north.[42] In 2014, Hamas also fired thousands of projectiles into Israel's south and center, even briefly shutting down Israel's international airport.[43]

Iron Dome's success rate of roughly 90 percent gives Israeli policymakers the breathing room to respond calmly and judiciously while Hamas and other terrorist groups try in vain to kill Israeli civilians.[44] Were it not for Iron Dome, many of the recent conflicts in Gaza might have escalated more quickly and devolved into far more destructive wars.

To augment its missile defense capabilities, Israel has made strides in the realm of lasers in recent years.[45] The goal is to develop a cheaper means of destroying the short-range weapons fired by Hamas (Iron Dome's "Tamir" interceptors are reported to have a steep price tag of $100,000 per munition).[46] Israel's work on lasers has advanced, including a test in June 2021 that successfully intercepted drones.[47] While lasers are not yet ready for prime time, the development of this and other systems will undoubtedly continue as Iran and its proxies work tirelessly to bring increasingly deadly weapons to the battlefield.

Surprisingly, these remarkable defensive systems are the source of some controversy in Israel. As I wrote in 2019 with my colleague Jacob Nagel, the former acting national security advisor to Prime Minister Benjamin Netanyahu, Iron Dome's efficacy in shooting down projectiles may paradoxically encourage Israel's enemies to increase their rocket launches. By granting Israeli officials the time and space to consider a proportional or surgical strike, Iron Dome can also have the unintended consequence of prolonging a conflict. In other words, the system raises the threshold for Israeli political and military leaders to launch a decisive response, even as the volume of rocket provocations increases.[48]

Iron Dome gets most of the attention these days, but in tackling the tunnel threat, Israel has been no less impressive. A mere two months before the 2021 Gaza war, Israel reported significant progress on an underground fence around the Hamas-controlled Gaza Strip.[49] Once the fence is fully assembled, it may well be the most sophisticated barrier in the world.

The Israelis first understood the tunnel threat after the 2006 kidnapping of Gilad Shalit and the opening stanza of the 2007 internecine war in Gaza. Both of those Hamas operations achieved success thanks to commando tunnels. However, the need for an anti-tunnel barrier became more apparent during the 2014 Gaza conflict, after Israel uncovered several Hamas commando tunnels that emptied out into Israeli territory.[50] Still, it was not until 2016, as more tunnels were discovered, that Israel set out to build this complex, multilayered barrier.

As Nagel and I wrote in *Real Clear Defense,* the new border fence has three levels: a deep underground barrier; an above-ground barrier; and an above-ground, high-tech layer that includes detection devices such as UAVs, unmanned ground vehicles, and more. The fence is also equipped with visual, electronic, and intelligence equipment, all of it powered by artificial intelligence (AI). To augment all of this, the Israelis built command-and-control bases along the barrier.[51]

The physical upper layer of the Gaza fence resembles the barrier Israel erected along the Israeli-Egyptian border. It stretches across Israel's entire 40-mile border with Gaza. Some of the elements of the barrier have not been disclosed publicly.

The underground layer includes a high-tech cement wall extending "tens of meters" beneath the ground. (The exact depth is not public.) It is equipped with a multidimensional sensor net to detect any activity near, at, or underneath the barrier. The barrier even stretches into the Mediterranean Sea to stymie Hamas naval commandos from penetrating Israel. Hamas frogmen in 2014 carried out a terrorist attack against an Israeli military base at Zikim beach.[52] It was a painful lesson that Israel did not want to learn again.[53]

Israel also set out to aggressively detect and destroy existing tunnels, even more than in the past. In total, more than 20 were found and neutralized after the 2014 conflict. Initially, the IDF worried that Hamas might accelerate efforts to attack Israel via tunnels before they could all be destroyed. Curiously, this "use it or lose it" calculus did not push Hamas to do so. After more than five years of tunnel detection and destruction, Israeli officials with whom I spoke in June 2021 say they are confident the Hamas tunnel threat is almost entirely neutralized.[54]

However, as with Iron Dome, there is controversy in Israel about the military message that barriers send. Some in the IDF believe the construction of expensive high-tech fences conveys weakness or a defensive posture. They argue that effective fences might prevent Israeli political leaders from taking decisive action during conflict, particularly if those leaders feel the barrier might shield the country from a wider conflagration.

On the other hand, barrier proponents argue that these measures prevent terrorism and loss of life. The West Bank fence brought the number of suicide bombings to near zero.[55] The Egypt-Gaza border fence brought smuggling down to negligible levels, too.[56] As with Iron Dome, it is hard to deny that this technology is effective.

The debates will continue in Israel. However, as Nagel told me in the aftermath of the 2021 Gaza war, the underground system did its job, protecting Israel from Hamas infiltrations and containing the conflict as much as possible.

The 2021 war also marked the first time Israel used AI to power its weapons systems during a conflict. One IDF officer told me that roughly 15 percent of the IDF's operations utilized this cutting-edge technology, including to help locate Russian-made Kornet anti-tank missiles in the Gaza Strip and to pinpoint Hamas targets operating underground. As the officer joked, the Israelis "often have the privilege" of being able to test out new techniques given how frequently conflict erupts.[57]

Israel's military-technological prowess is a major reason why Congress, on a bipartisan basis, has pushed US administrations to stand up a US-Israel Operations-Technology Working Group to catalyze a systematic cooperation with Israel. This working group — first conceived of by my FDD colleague Bradley Bowman — would help both the United States and Israel field cutting-edge military capabilities more quickly and stay ahead of adversaries sprinting to do the same.[58]

The Gaza war of 2021 truly provided a glimpse of future warfare. As *The Jerusalem Post* reported, Israeli "[s]oldiers in Unit 8200, an intelligence corps elite unit, pioneered algorithms and code that led to several new programs called 'Alchemist,' 'Gospel,' and 'Depth of Wisdom,' which were developed and used during the fighting." The Israelis reportedly utilized AI-powered drone swarms "to seek and attack hidden targets."[59] IDF officers said they believe that the efficiency of such AI-powered tools shortened the length of the conflict while also helping the IDF hit its intended targets without incurring collateral damage.[60]

But even the best technology and intelligence are no guarantee against the unforeseen events of war. Israel would soon learn this the hard way.

ELEVEN
UNREST IN THE STREETS

During the first days of the May 2021 conflict, I spoke with Israeli officials both past and present. If I am doing my job correctly, I pick up on common themes across multiple conversations. This time around, I quickly sensed a theme. My interlocutors all took the ongoing Hamas attacks in stride, fierce as they were. The IDF was not surprised by any of Hamas' strategies or tactics. What did surprise and even alarm the Israelis was the unrest in Israeli communities with significant Arab populations. There appeared to be no contingency plan for this.

In the towns and cities of Akko, Ramle, Jaffa, Haifa, Be'er Sheva, Jerusalem, and beyond, Arabs took to the streets, burned cars, and destroyed property. In some cases, Jewish crowds organized violent responses or launched their own riots in retribution.[1] As I watched Israeli television one evening, as one analyst on the Kan network blurted out incredulously, this was not something seen even during the outbreak of the Second Intifada in October 2000.

It began on May 10, when Arab youths tore through Lod, a town in central Israel near the international airport. The rioters burned cars, synagogues, and other buildings, threw stones, and even fired weapons.[2] By May 12, with the violence still out of control, Israel declared a state of emergency in Lod. Protesters threw rocks at police who responded with stun grenades. Twelve people were reportedly injured.[3]

On May 13, rioters damaged the theater in Acre, a "mixed" city of Arabs and Jews. The theater was known for putting on plays in Hebrew and Arabic. Its owner viewed the venue as a space for coexistence.[4] The day before, an Arab mob destroyed the Arabesque hotel on May 12, another symbol of coexistence in Acre.[5]

The violence seemed to be spiraling out of control everywhere. Bedouins in the south ambushed Jewish cars with stones. A Jewish man in Lod died after being struck by a heavy rock.[6] In Jerusalem, a car ramming attack targeted Israeli security personnel.[7] Some Jewish Israelis began randomly attacking Arabs. In the town of Bat Yam, teenagers yanked an Arab out of his car and beat him.[8]

Thus, amidst the ongoing rocket war, the Israeli government was also struggling to contain an internecine conflict. Apart from the damage caused by rockets, not to mention the confusion prompted by sirens calling citizens to run to their bomb shelters, an escalation on the streets was something the country could ill afford.

The Israeli police stepped up their presence in many of the towns impacted by the violence. This was noted repeatedly in the Israeli television coverage of the war. I observed that a number of television correspondents from channels 11 and 13 were reporting from across the home front, while seemingly fewer reporters were reporting from the towns that sustained Hamas rocket fire.

Out of the chaos, a voice of reason emerged: Police Commissioner Kobi Shabtai. Shabtai's message was (much like him) short and gruff, but it was also consistent and reassuring. "From my perspective, anyone who was involved in the riots in the mixed cities is a terrorist. [There were] terrorists on both sides," he said.[9] In this way, a consistent policy had been established. Israel would tolerate no violence from any civilian, under any circumstance — regardless of their religion or ethnic background. It was a confirmation of the rule of law.

With rocket salvos still being unleashed day and night, Israel deployed large numbers of border police to quell the riots.[10] Defense Minister Benny Gantz ordered an emergency call-up of ten Border Police companies.[11] It took four days to suppress the riots.[12] In the end, Israeli police arrested more than 1,550 suspects — Muslims, Christians, and Jews.[13] Weeks after the conflict was over, Israeli security services also arrested the imam of Lod's Great Mosque for inciting some of the violence.[14] One week later, ten residents of Ramle and Lod were arrested for throwing firebombs at a Jewish home during the war.[15] It was clear that investigations were ongoing.

During and after the conflict, a number of commentators, both in Israel and abroad, concluded that these riots stemmed from a lack of economic and political integration on the part of many Arabs living in mixed cities.[16] That certainly may have had something to do with it. Arabs have for years been under-represented in Israel — not because they are denied rights but because many Arabs boycott Israeli elections and Arab parties have consistently showed little or no interest in joining Israel's governing coalitions. Their ability to demand better resources and services has thus been curtailed by their own limited engagement.

Interestingly, this dynamic appeared to be on the cusp of change with the emergence of Mansour Abbas, an Islamist politician and the leader of the Ra'am party, who was actively engaging in coalition talks with other Israeli parties both before and after the Gaza war. In fact, immediately after the war, as he made plans to join a coalition led by Israeli politicians Yair Lapid and Naftali Bennett, Abbas negotiated the doubling of the budget allocated for the Arab sector over a five-year period.[17]

Notwithstanding the clear understanding that Israel needed to do more for its Arab communities, there was still an open question of whether the Arab rioters had coordinated with Hamas. American Jewish Committee Spokesman Avi Mayer claimed that "Hamas . . . instigated this violence weeks ago and just this past weekend called on Palestinians in Jerusalem to acquire knives and behead Jews in the street."[18] He noted that senior Hamas official Fathi Hammad had urged Palestinians in Jerusalem to "buy a knife, sharpen it, put it [to Jews' throats], and just cut off [their heads]. It costs just five shekels. With those five shekels, you will humiliate the Jewish state."[19]

Similarly, an advisor to Prime Minister Netanyahu asserted that "Hamas and the PA went into overdrive inciting hostility against Israel over the matter."[20] There can be no doubt that this incitement was already underway even before Hamas began firing rockets. In fact, more than a month before the conflict erupted, a popular trend was discernible on the Chinese-owned social media platform TikTok: Videos of Arab teenagers assaulting orthodox Jews were gaining popularity.[21]

Turkish President Recep Tayyip Erdogan's rhetoric was also on overdrive. The Islamist strongman stated that he was "furious at the cruelty of the terrorist state of Israel against Palestinians."[22]

He called Israelis "murderers" who "drag women on the ground to their death."[23] He told Russian President Vladimir Putin that the international community needed to "give Israel a strong and deterrent lesson."[24]

Erdogan may have even been able to influence some of the unrest. There have been credible reports in recent years about Turkish activism in Israel's Arab communities. For example, in 2018, Israel's *Haaretz* reported that Jordan, Saudi Arabia, and the PA were warning about "growing Turkish activity in East Jerusalem." Senior Jordanian and Palestinian officials stated that Ankara was "extending its influence in the Arab neighborhoods of Jerusalem." According to these officials, "[h]undreds of Turkish citizens became a regular presence in and around the Old City, becoming involved in clashes with police officers during Friday prayers at the Al-Aqsa Mosque." This led to "arrests and deportations of some of the Turkish activists — barring some of them from reentering Israel."[25]

According to a report in *Israel Hayom* that same year, the Turkish Cooperation and Coordination Agency (TIKA) "handed out about $420,000 in $500 checks to east Jerusalem merchants and residents in recent days as a gift for the holy Muslim month of Ramadan." The money was described as a form of "silent" jihad.[26] By 2019, Israel was sufficiently alarmed that it prepared a plan "to bring an end to Turkey's incitement and subversion activities in East Jerusalem."[27]

In 2020, *Israel Hayom* reported that Turkey funds 10 percent of all civil society activities in East Jerusalem.[28] In a separate report in *Middle East Eye*, Israeli authorities ceded that across the country, "under the guise of cultural and humanitarian work, Turkey is promoting the ideology of the Muslim Brotherhood, as well as

Erdogan's grandiose vision of restoring the glory days of the Otto-man Empire."[29]

In December 2020, the Israeli government expressed signif-icant concern surrounding TIKA. *The Media Line* reported that TIKA was operating "in east Jerusalem, the West Bank and the Gaza Strip, pumping millions of dollars into aid, relief, and char-ity projects."[30] Agence France-Presse reported that TIKA claimed to have "restored numerous local homes and shops in an effort to ease the hardships faced by east Jerusalem's Muslim community as a result of Israel's ongoing policy of Judaization." Agence France-Presse further noted, "Ankara has become an active global player on behalf of the Palestinians."[31]

This was an understatement. In a bid for leadership of the Muslim world, Erdogan has thrown his weight behind Hamas.[32] In 2010, Ankara sponsored a flotilla that set out for the Hamas-con-trolled Gaza Strip to break an Israeli-led international blockade. As the flotilla neared Israeli territorial waters, Israeli commandos boarded one of the ships, leading to a confrontation that resulted in ten deaths — all Turkish nationals.[33] Ankara has since refused to let go of the episode, marking its anniversary ever since.[34]

Hamas maintains a significant presence in Turkey. This made headlines in August 2014 when Saleh al-Arouri declared that the group was behind the aforementioned kidnapping and killing of three Israeli teens in the West Bank. That was one of the events that contributed to 2014's grueling 51-day war between Israel and Hamas. Arouri brazenly made his announcement in Istanbul in front of a large crowd that included senior Turkish officials.[35]

The year prior, Israel's Shin Bet had announced the arrest of two Palestinians involved in smuggling money for Hamas from Jordan to the West Bank.[36] During their interrogation, the suspects ceded that some of the money was being smuggled on Arouri's behalf.[37] With increased attention on Arouri, the US Treasury Department designated him as a terrorist in September 2015.[38]

Arouri was not the only Hamas figure Turkey embraced. Hamas financier Bakri Hanifa and Hamas Politburo member Maher Ubeid both found refuge in Turkey. So did convicted Hamas terrorists Mahmoud Attoun, Majed Hassan Ragheb Abu Qteish, Taysir Suleiman, Fahed Sabri Barhan al-Shaludi, Walid Zakariya Abd al-Hadi Aqel, and Musa Muhammad Daud Akari.[39] These are just a few.

In 2017, the Shin Bet arrested Muhammad Murtaja, the Gaza coordinator of TIKA, as he attempted to travel from Gaza to Turkey. Murtaja stood accused of diverting funds to Hamas that were earmarked for charity. He was also believed to have provided sensitive intelligence to the terrorist group, including information about military sites inside Israel.[40]

On the heels of the Murtaja arrest, the Shin Bet announced that Hamas was also working with the flotilla organizers — an organization called the *Insan Hak ve Hurriyetleri ve Insani Yardim Vakfi* (IHH Humanitarian Relief Foundation) with close ties to the Turkish government — to gain access to advanced satellite mapping programs to improve the accuracy of the terror group's rockets. IHH denied these claims.[41]

In 2019, Erdogan boasted on Twitter that he was hosting Saleh al-Arouri and Ismail Haniyeh, both of whom were, and still are, under US sanctions for terrorism.[42] This elicited a surprisingly harsh statement from the State Department — Washington's first-ever official condemnation of Turkey's relations with Hamas, and a marked departure from the warm ties between then-President Donald Trump and Erdogan.[43] The Treasury Department soon followed up with a September 2019 terrorism designation of Zaher Jabarin, a Turkey-based Hamas financier.[44]

Turkey has thus gained significant influence in Gaza, as well as inside Israel's Arab communities. It is a problem that must be dealt with promptly.

However, that is not where Israeli leaders will be focusing their attention in the immediate future. Nurturing the complex culture of coexistence between Arab and Jewish citizens of Israel is where they will need to direct their efforts for some time. That coexistence is something the Israeli government has sought to cultivate over the years. Remarkably, it has been the norm, even amidst multiple rounds of violence with Hamas and other terrorist groups.

Netanyahu, visiting Lod after the first night of the unrest, vowed to bring order back with an "iron fist."[45] But Israel's new leaders surely realize that an iron fist likely will not bring calm in a democracy. In Israel's future, there will be grievances to hear and additional political bargains to make. For the Middle East's sole democracy to remain democratic, this is the only way.

TWELVE
THE OTHER GAZA WARS

What made the unrest on the streets of Israel during the 2021 conflict so notable was that it was such a clear break from the past. While there have always been small surprises in each of the preceding conflicts, there is usually more continuity than change. In fact, close observers of previous Gaza wars can almost sense when a conflict is about to erupt, when the tide of the battle is turning, and when the conflict is about to end. The feel for these conflicts also stems from an understanding of how Hamas has built up its capabilities over the years — always with the help of Iran, among others. In brief, the Gaza wars of today are an accumulation of the experiences and capabilities of the past.

When Hamas took control of the Gaza Strip in 2007, Israel tightened restrictions on the border to prevent the flow of weapons and cash into the territory. The Islamic Republic mounted a concerted effort to help its client. A Hamas spokesman confirmed that Iran "was prepared to cover the entire deficit in the Palestinian budget, and [to do so] continuously." The *Bonyad-e Mostazafan za Janbaza* (Foundation of the Oppressed and War Veterans), a fund associated with Iran's IRGC, reportedly provided significant support.[1] During a visit by Hamas prime minister Ismael Haniyeh to Tehran in December 2006, the regime pledged $250 million — a significant increase over previous years.[2] Iran's support got Washington's attention, with Secretary of State Condoleeza Rice voicing concerns during congressional testimony the next year.[3]

With Iranian assistance, Hamas found its footing. Weapons continued to flow into Gaza through tunnels from Egypt despite Israel's best efforts to prevent them. The tunnels also played a significant role in smuggling goods into the coastal enclave, supplying Gazans with everyday items and even luxury goods.[4] Hamas taxed these goods, padding the group's finances and enabling it to withstand Israeli pressure.[5]

The Israelis had to tread carefully with Egypt. The two countries had peace since 1979, but it was a cold peace. The Gaza smuggling problem was a case in point. Israeli officials reported that the smugglers paid Egyptian police and border guards with "bribes or other incentives for keeping the tunnels open." When the Israelis detonated the tunnels, they often observed smoke and debris coming out of tunnel entrances near Egyptian guard posts.[6] The Egyptians dismissed such allegations. Pushed to their limits, the Israelis sent video footage to Washington in December 2007 that clearly depicted Egyptian policemen helping smugglers.[7]

Israel's desperate move appeared to pay dividends. In a foreign aid bill for fiscal year 2008, Congress agreed to withhold about $100 million in US aid to Egypt unless Cairo could certify that it was doing its part to stop the smuggling.[8] Egyptian intelligence minister Omar Suleiman promised to end the smuggling, saying, "[Y]ou will not hear about it again."[9]

But even with a reduction in smuggling, Hamas rocket fire continued. In late November 2007, the IDF stated, "since June, Palestinians have fired at Israel an average of one Qassam rocket every three hours. More than 200 rockets and mortar shells have been launched since the beginning of November."[10] Meanwhile, advances in local Hamas' rocket production enabled the group to amass larger arsenals. Previously, Qassam rockets had to be launched shortly after they were produced, due to the volatility of the warhead. This explains why the rockets were usually fired at Israel in small numbers. Reports emerged, however, that Hamas could now store its rockets for longer periods of time, meaning the group could potentially assemble a large arsenal before firing salvos into Israel.[11]

Amid continued rocket fire, IDF officials stated bluntly that a military operation in Gaza would be necessary.[12] But after a series of limited incursions into Gaza, Prime Minister Ehud Olmert warned Israel "not to become entangled in operations and costs that are not in proportion to the pressures that we are facing."[13] But the threats were growing. According to reports in October 2007, Hamas had smuggled an estimated 73 tons of explosives into Gaza through the tunnels from Egypt. The group also stockpiled other weapons it confiscated from the PA — many of which had been supplied by the United States.[14]

Better armed than ever, and now better trained, thanks to the regime in Tehran, Hamas began to restructure its military capabilities with tunnels, bunkers, rockets, and more lethal explosives.[15] As analyst Nick Francona noted, Hamas developed a "diversified force capable of controlling domestic challenges and enhancing its capabilities against Israel."[16] Equipped with night-vision goggles, Hamas also had the ability to ambush IDF units as they entered Gaza for limited operations, and could even strike Israeli soldiers on their way out.[17]

In January 2008, amid continued rocket attacks, Israel halved the amount of fuel shipped to Gaza's only electric plant.[18] Gaza residents were forced to live without this basic utility for eight hours a day. The blackout sparked international criticism. One UN official asserted that the punitive measure "cannot be justified, even by those rocket attacks."[19]

However, the criticism was not unanimous. The editor of London-based newspaper *Asharq Al-Awsat* stated that Hamas had "committed a stupid act" by firing rockets into Israel. A PA spokesman stated that the crisis was all the result of Hamas' "insistence on creating an Islamic republic in the Gaza Strip."[20] Franco Frattini, the European commissioner for justice, freedom, and security, stated that the Gaza blackout could not be considered a war crime, as some alleged, given the incessant Qassam rocket fire.[21] It is also worth noting that according to the Fourth Geneva Convention (Article 23), a siege or blockade of an enemy territory can be a legitimate tactic of war.[22]

With no end to the rocket fire in sight, in late February 2008 Israel launched what is now seen as the first in a series of major military "operations" in Gaza. The Israelis do not like to call them wars. Of course, that is exactly what they are. As one senior Israeli military official explained to me, "We call them operations because one day there could be a much bigger war. We want the Israeli population to be prepared for that, and to know the difference."[23]

Operation Warm Winter (also known as Hot Winter) was brief. It lasted only four days. For Israel, the goal was simply to target a handful of Hamas operatives along with the group's rocket production and storage facilities.[24] Such targets would become commonplace in future skirmishes between Israel and Hamas. Still, this was the first time observers witnessed Israel's practice of destroying a large number of pre-approved targets that were deemed legal by IDF lawyers in anticipation of an extended military operation against Hamas in Gaza. IDF targeteers and legal advisors worked together to compile this "target bank" for whenever the next conflict might erupt. By hitting all its pre-approved targets, Israel hoped to significantly weaken Hamas' capabilities in an overwhelming display of force.

Target banks are still a common feature in Israel-Hamas wars today. Israel will typically absorb numerous one-off rocket attacks over a sustained period (so long as they remain contained to Israel's southern sector and do not target the country's populous center or the capital, Jerusalem), while the Shin Bet and the IDF patiently catalogue new military assets being built. When conflict erupts, all those military assets are fair game. They are often struck in rapid fashion.

In 2008, other patterns had emerged that would become familiar in skirmishes well into the future. Hamas always knew it was picking a fight it could not win. Regardless, the group fired off rockets, often described as retribution for a perceived Israeli transgression. Israel's "Code Red" sirens would go off as the IDF tracked rockets flying toward Israeli populations centers. The Israeli civilians within range (mostly the communities close to the Gazan border) generally had only a few seconds to find shelter when rockets were incoming. The more Israel struck Hamas targets, the more Hamas fired back. Gazans suffered the vast majority of deaths and injuries, with Hamas operatives often hiding among the Palestinian population. As *The Jerusalem Post* noted at the time of Operation Warm Winter, then-Defense Minister Ehud Barak was eager for the international community to debate the "legality of this tactic,"[25] now commonly known as "human shields."[26] But the international community rarely weighed in, if ever.

The battle of early 2008 ended with no decisive victory. This, too, would become a familiar theme.

An uneasy calm prevailed after this first round of fighting. Officially, a ceasefire came into effect in June of that year. It held, with some small exceptions, until late December 2008, which marked the beginning of another round. The Israelis called this one Operation Cast Lead.

Cast Lead was also initiated in response to Hamas rocket fire. Once again, Israel's immediate goal was to hit pre-approved targets, such as tunnels, rocket facilities, and other Hamas military sites. Israel initially attempted to neutralize these targets from the air, but a week into the war, the IDF brass decided to send in ground troops. The Israeli troops found booby traps and other deadly surprises waiting for them. The IDF pushed forward under air cover, achieving most of its objectives.[27]

The Israelis took quite a bit of heat from the international community for this war, even as they took great pains to avoid civilian deaths. At one point, Israel paused the fighting to allow aid to flow to the beleaguered residents of Gaza. On day 20, the Israelis struck a building where senior Hamas operatives had been meeting, killing Hamas Interior Minister Said Seyyam. Shortly thereafter, Israel declared an end to the war.[28]

But the war did not end there. The UN Human Rights Council (UNHRC), an organization ironically composed of some of the world's worst human rights abusers, commissioned a report to document alleged Israeli war crimes. The UNHRC tapped Richard Goldstone, a retired judge from the Constitutional Court of

South Africa and former chief prosecutor of the UN international criminal tribunals for Yugoslavia and Rwanda, to lead the investigation. Goldstone, as it happened, was also Jewish, which was likely intended to legitimize a report widely expected to excoriate the Jewish state.

To nobody's surprise, Goldstone's report, published on September 25, 2009, alleged that Israeli soldiers had committed "war crimes" by deliberately attacking civilian targets in Gaza. Remarkably, the report failed to incriminate Hamas for the war crime of firing rockets blindly into Israeli population centers. The report instead made vague references to "Palestinian armed groups."[29] As one Hamas leader boasted, "the report acquits Hamas almost entirely."[30]

The report was undeniably wielded as a weapon of "lawfare" against Israel. It was a clear effort to vilify Israel for defending itself against rocket attacks, as any sovereign nation would. Goldstone later disavowed the report in the pages of *The Washington Post*, stating, "If I had known then what I know now, the Goldstone Report would have been a different document." He went on to state that although Israeli military investigations "have established the validity of some incidents that we investigated in cases involving individual soldiers, they also indicate that civilians were not intentionally targeted as a matter of policy."[31] In other words, the basis of the entire report was undermined by the facts, which the UNHRC generally ignored.

The episode underscored the bias of the Orwellian UNHRC and the media circus that surrounded the sporadic conflicts between Hamas and Israel. However, this would certainly not be the last time that the United Nations would insert itself into this conflict.

In 2009, Hamas set about restocking its rocket arsenal. The US government received multiple reports of Iranian smuggling operations moving rockets from Sudan through Egypt and into

Gaza.[32] In March 2009, reports suggested that Israel conducted at least two airstrikes on Iranian arms shipments traveling to Gaza via Sudan.[33]

Tensions on the Israel-Gaza border flared in 2010[34] and 2011,[35] but these were isolated clashes. Meanwhile, there were multiple indications during this time that Iran was helping Hamas to prepare for the next round of major conflict. In January 2010, a team of Mossad agents carried out a daring assassination in Dubai, killing Mahmoud al-Mabhouh, a senior Hamas liaison to Iran in charge of weapons procurement.[36] In August 2010, the US Treasury Department designated Hushang Allahdad, a senior financial officer of the IRGC Quds Force, who, Treasury noted, "personally oversees distribution of funds to Levant-based terrorist groups and provides financial support for designated terrorist entities including . . . Hamas."[37]

In March 2011, the IDF interdicted a Liberian ship sailing from Turkey toward Egypt, seizing numerous Iranian weapons, including anti-ship missiles, destined for Hamas.[38] The following month, the IDF killed two Hamas operatives involved in weapons procurement, striking their car as they drove near Port Sudan.[39] The State Department that year also designated Hamas operative Muhammad Hisham Muhammad Isma'il Abu Ghazala, noting his extensive links to Iran.[40]

Tehran's support for Hamas plummeted in 2011 after Hamas refused to back the Iranian-allied Assad regime as Syria descended into civil war.[41] It was the first sign of significant divisions between the Islamic Republic and its longtime client. Hamas filled the void with lesser support from Qatar and Turkey. There was hope in Israel and elsewhere that the Islamic Republic's influence in Gaza was waning, but it soon became clear that the regime was still very much in the picture.

War came to Gaza again in 2012. As before, Hamas fired rockets into Israel. Once again, Israel predictably responded with force. However, this time the context was perhaps even more important than the conflict itself.

The story began on the night of October 23, when four Israeli fighter jets screamed across the sky over Khartoum and bombed the Yarmouk weapons factory,[42] which belonged to the IRGC.[43] The weapons Israel targeted — which included Iranian-made Fajr-5 rockets that one Israeli intelligence official described to me as "game changers"[44] — were bound for Hamas in the Gaza Strip. At the time, Sudan was believed to be the key jurisdiction for Iranian weapons smuggled through Egypt, across the Sinai Peninsula, and into Hamas' network of tunnels.

The raid was one of necessity for the Israelis, but its timing was decidedly inconvenient for Washington — less than two weeks before a presidential election. It also took place on a day when 3,500 US troops were in Israel for a joint military exercise known as Austere Challenge.[45]

Somehow, the destruction of the Yarmouk warehouse passed with relatively little media coverage. With officials in Khartoum denying all knowledge, Sudanese social media users struggled to piece together what exactly happened. The headlines worldwide fixated on the US election. Israel, seeking deniability for the attack, probably preferred it that way.

Three weeks later, however, Hamas committed the error of once again firing rockets into southern Israel. Terrorists in Gaza also fired a guided missile at an Israeli Jeep. Without much delay, the Israelis launched Operation Pillar of Defense, dispatching fighter jets, helicopters, and drones to attack pre-approved Hamas military targets throughout the Gaza Strip. The 2012 war was underway.

The most notable target in the early hours of the war was Hamas military commander Ahmed Jabari. Israel released a video of the strike, showing a direct hit on Jabari's car as it rolled down a Gaza street before exploding into a ball of flames.[46] Jabari had ascended through the ranks of Hamas through a process of elimination — literally. The IDF eliminated Salah Shehadeh, the leader of al-Qassam Brigades, Hamas' military wing, in 2002.[47] A few months later, another IDF strike wounded his successor, Mohammed Deif,[48] leaving Jabari, known in Hamas circles as the "Chief of Staff" or the "General," next in line.

Credited with "professionalizing" Hamas' military activities, Jabari had presided over the group's shift away from suicide bombings (primarily due to Israel's separation barrier) toward rocket attacks that reached deeper and deeper into Israeli territory. He also helped mastermind Hamas' violent takeover of Gaza. However, Jabari was perhaps best known for the June 2006 kidnapping of Gilad Shalit.[49] Jabari even allowed himself to be photographed in October 2011 when he delivered the captured Israeli soldier to the Egyptians for transfer to Israel.[50] For him, the photo was a victory lap.

While the Israelis undoubtedly took pride in this high-level assassination, their real concern was Hamas' Fajr-5 rockets. The IDF had destroyed many of them in Yarmouk, but some had found their way into Gaza. This was a red line: The Iranian-made Fajr-5 rockets were known to have powerful payloads and longer ranges, enabling Hamas to strike Israel's largest population centers. When the 2012 war erupted, the Israeli Air Force began methodically striking these rocket sites with pinpoint precision. The Israelis claim to have destroyed most of Hamas' Fajr-5s — about 100 — in the first few days of fighting. Realizing it was "use it or lose it" for these weapons, Hamas scrambled to fire off those that Israel had not hit.[51] Israel's new Iron Dome missile defense system, rolled out the previous year, knocked many Hamas rockets out of the sky. This was the first real test for the anti-missile technology, produced jointly by the United States and Israel.

After Israel appeared to have neutralized most of Hamas' Fajr-5s, Secretary of State Hillary Clinton began pressuring Egyptian President Mohammed Morsi to broker a ceasefire.[52] Morsi's role in this war was hugely significant. The Muslim Brotherhood leader, who had only recently risen to power in the wake of the Arab Spring, stood accused by Israel of running Hamas' "back office" out of Cairo.[53] Tunneling and smuggling were at their peak. There is little doubt that Morsi was part of the effort to smuggle the Iranian Fajr-5s to Gaza. His motivations here were purely ideological. The Muslim Brotherhood sought Israel's demise, even if Egypt had a peace agreement with Israel that Cairo was bound to honor. Tellingly, after Morsi first took office, he held the first senior meeting between Iranian and Egyptian leaders since the Islamic Revolution in 1979.[54]

When all was said and done, the 2012 Gaza war, Operation Pillar of Defense, lasted for eight days. Once again, Israel targeted rocket launchers, production facilities, storage facilities, and other Hamas military targets. Once again, Hamas survived. And once again, Israel came under fire from the international community for defending itself, even as 900 rockets struck Israel.[55] Despite the destruction, nothing substantially changed in Gaza. The stage was set for another round of fighting.

That round came a mere two years later. A prelude to the conflict took place in March 2014, when the IDF intercepted a Panamanian-flagged cargo vessel carrying Iranian-supplied M-302 rockets and other advanced weapons bound for terrorist groups in

Gaza.[56] But war did not arrive until June, after the abduction and murder of three Jewish teens in the West Bank. The operation was planned and directed by Saleh al-Arouri, the West Bank chief of Hamas military activities, then based in Turkey.[57] The murders sent shock waves throughout Israel. In retribution, Jewish extremists abducted Palestinian teenager Mohammed Abu Khdeir and burned him alive. Israeli police ultimately arrested those responsible, but not before outrage spread throughout Arab communities in Jerusalem.[58] Within days of his murder, as IDF forces carried out incursions in the West Bank, a number of violent Palestinian groups were calling for renewed conflict with Israel. The epicenter of the protests, not surprisingly, was the Eastern Jerusalem neighborhood of Shuafat, where Abu Khdeir had lived.

The Israelis had made some efforts in recent years to foster better coexistence with Shuafat. Jerusalem's light rail line, for example, ran through the neighborhood. Shuafat protesters, however, destroyed it in the wake of Abu Khdeir's killing. Other Israeli Arab towns took their cue from Shuafat and erupted violently, as did Palestinian towns in the West Bank. Once again, Hamas fired rocket salvos in an expression of solidarity, to which the IDF responded with airstrikes. Another war was underway.

The 2014 war, which the Israelis dubbed Operation Protective Edge, was one in which Hamas rockets struck deep in Israeli territory, with some falling in and around Jerusalem. Some rockets even threatened Israel's international airport outside Tel Aviv. During the war, one Iranian official boasted that Tehran was "sending rockets and military aid [to Hamas]."[59] Another official bragged that the rockets Hamas was firing were "the blessings of Iran's transfer of technology."[60]

I was on a research trip to Israel that summer when the conflict erupted. I recall eating dinner on a Jerusalem rooftop when sirens began to wail. I scrambled for cover inside. I also recall my departure from the country amidst the ongoing battle. I wondered more than once how our airplane would be able to evade the hurtling rockets. But even before I boarded the plane, I was forced to find a shelter at Ben Gurion airport as Hamas rockets landed dangerously close to the tarmac.

In a bid for calm, Secretary of State John Kerry made a surprise visit to Cairo. Egypt announced a ceasefire, but Hamas balked, claiming it was never even consulted.[61] A halt to the conflict did not appear imminent.

At the time, Kerry's credibility in Israel was not exactly high. The Obama administration was knee-deep in negotiations with Iran over its illicit nuclear program. The United States had already entered the 2013 interim Iran nuclear deal, or Joint Plan of Action, and was providing Tehran with roughly $700 million per month merely to remain at the negotiating table.[62] It was hard for the Israelis to imagine that at least some of those funds were not flowing to Tehran's proxy in Gaza. The Israelis were further alarmed that Washington had left Tehran's support for terrorism off the negotiating table.

The rockets hurtling into Israel had Iranian fingerprints all over them. Hamas' longer-range M-302 and M-75 rockets had been smuggled into Gaza courtesy of Iran. The terror group had also built up its arsenal of shorter-range rockets thanks to Iranian assistance, as the speaker of Iran's parliament, Ali Larijani, boasted.[63] During the 2014 war, the IDF also discovered underground commando tunnels that snaked into Israel territory. They were widely believed to have been built with Iranian assistance.[64]

Amidst this tension, Washington engaged with Qatar and Turkey in a bid to end the conflict.[65] This, too, did not sit well with the Israelis. Doha and Ankara had become outspoken champions of Hamas in recent years. Secretary Kerry sparked a diplomatic storm when he endorsed a Turkish-Qatari ceasefire plan favorable to Hamas.[66] Israel was not the only country to object. Egypt, now under the anti-Islamist leadership of President Abdel Fattah al-Sisi, remained staunchly opposed to any ceasefire deal that would empower Hamas or its patrons in Doha or Ankara.[67]

The very notion that the Obama administration viewed Qatar and Turkey as fair arbiters of this conflict was hard to believe. Doha was a financier of Hamas[68] and provided safe haven for many of the organization's operatives.[69] Turkey had also emerged as one of the world's most strident supporters of Hamas[70] and reportedly donated funds to the group, too.[71] In the end, their bid to strengthen Hamas failed.

The 2014 war lasted 51 days. The IDF reported that Hamas fired nearly 5,000 rockets into Israel during the conflict, with 735 of them intercepted by Iron Dome. Khameinei's foreign affairs advisor Ali Akbar Velayati stated, "Without the help of Iran, [Hamas] could not have obtained these rockets, with such long range and accuracy."[72] The Israelis reported that they destroyed much of the group's terrorist infrastructure. Nonetheless, Hamas remained in power, and it quickly set about rebuilding its capabilities for another round of war.

In December 2014, Hamas' deputy leader Mousa Abu Marzouk reported, "bilateral relations between us and the Islamic Republic of Iran are back on track."[73] The following year, after the signing of the Iran nuclear deal, which granted the regime in Iran billions of dollars in sanctions relief, the Israeli press reported that cash from Tehran was flowing to Gaza.[74] In the years that followed,

Hamas official Saleh al-Arouri visited Iran at least five times. One report in 2018 said Iran was providing the group with $70 million per year.[75]

Despite the boost in funding, Hamas next elected to employ a low-cost form of political warfare against Israel. On March 30, 2018, Hamas launched a series of protests on the Israel-Gaza border, dubbed the "Great March of Return."[76] Gazans were sending flaming balloons across the border into Israeli territory. Hamas was reportedly paying bus companies to send protestors to the border[77] and was even paying children to skip school to attend these marches.[78] Militants then fired at Israel from behind these human shields. Unable to disperse the crowd with tear gas or other crowd-control methods, the IDF sometimes opened fire. This went on sporadically for approximately two years.

Even amid the COVID-19 pandemic in 2020, Hamas urged its supporters to continue sending explosive balloons,[79] while organizing riots at the Israel-Gaza border fence[80] and firing rockets for good measure.[81] Hamas' goal was never to defeat Israel militarily. The terror group and its supporters knew that would not happen. Rather, the goal was to elicit public support for the Palestinian cause and to sow fear among Israelis. It accomplished both objectives.

When I visited the Gaza border on June 22, 2021, Israeli officers told me that the fence activity continues daily. Around "20 or 30 kids" still run to the fence each day. They try to snip some of its links. The officers do not expect this to halt anytime soon.[82]

In the end, there is significant communications value to these activities, even if they do little to advance Hamas' military objectives. The same might be said for many of the group's other tactics. Hamas has always lacked the military means to defeat Israel.

But this does not mean that Hamas' violence cannot help set the table for future achievements. Hamas continues to probe Israel's defenses. With every major escalation, the terror group tests Iron Dome's efficacy against larger numbers of rockets. In fact, in June 2019, Israeli media reported that Iran increased monthly financial support to Hamas by $30 million in exchange for information on Israeli military capabilities.[83] It is unclear whether that arrangement was still in place during the Gaza war of 2021.

THIRTEEN
NORTHERN EXPOSURE

To the extent that Hamas tests Israel's defenses, it does so to the benefit of Iran's more powerful proxy: Hezbollah. The Lebanese terrorist group can unleash hell upon Israel thanks to a massive arsenal of both crude and advanced weapons that Iran has eagerly provided over the years. Israeli war planners are always bracing for the next northern battle. Some voice concerns that, one day, Israel will be forced to fight both Hamas and Hezbollah at the same time — a two-front war.

Throughout the 2021 war in Gaza, there was an eerie quiet to Israel's north. All eyes were on Hezbollah. The group's *raison d'etre* is war with Israel. Yet amid a massive economic and political crisis that had rocked the country — Lebanon was unable to form a government, while debts of more than $93 billion accrued — it seemed like a safe bet that the group would sit out this round.[1] Lebanon simply could not afford another devastating conflict like the one that took place in 2006.[2] The financial fallout was a minimum of $7 billion in property damage,[3] but the total human costs were far greater. As the May 2021 Gaza war raged, Hassan Fakih, vice president of the General Confederation of Lebanese Workers, a major national trade union, warned Hezbollah against "taking the country into total chaos that will wipe out what is left of Lebanon."[4]

Hezbollah seemed to understand the need to abstain. Nonetheless, silence was not guaranteed. Tensions reached new heights on the night of May 13, when three rockets were fired from Lebanon. Fortunately for all involved, all three projectiles landed in the Mediterranean Sea.[5] The rockets were reportedly launched from the Qlaileh area, near Lebanon's southern coast.[6] On May 17, another six rockets were fired into Israeli airspace from the Shebaa Farms border area. All landed in Lebanese territory.[7] On May 19, four more projectiles were fired from a location near the city of Tyre, prompting sirens to sound in Israel. Iron Dome knocked one of them out of the sky. Another landed in an uninhabited area, and two more splashed into the Mediterranean. Israel fired artillery in response — a rather muted reaction.[8]

The Lebanese Armed Forces (LAF), as part of an investigation that they had virtually no choice but to conduct, reportedly found empty rocket launchers where projectiles had been fired.[9] In all three cases, the culprits were believed to be Palestinians from the refugee camps in Lebanon, where for years Palestinians have been living symbols of the unfulfilled dreams of the Palestinian national project. Hezbollah denied any connection. In fact, reports suggested that Hezbollah was cooperative in the investigators who ultimately concluded that the culprits were "close to the Muslim Brotherhood."[10]

For Israel, no matter who was responsible, a potential second front in Lebanon was a major concern. Hezbollah had stockpiled an estimated 150,000 rockets over the years, thanks to Iranian largesse. The group's fighters had also gained significant experience fighting in Syria alongside the Iranians, the Assad regime, and Russian forces. Yet Israel's most significant concerns revolved around Hezbollah's project to acquire precision-guided munitions (PGMs) from Iran.

The War Between Wars that Israel has waged in Syria against Iran and its proxies in recent years, as outlined in chapter nine, largely centers on the smuggling of PGMs. As early as 2013, in not-for-attribution conversations, Israeli officials spoke euphemistically about the need to carry out such strikes, noting that they were targeting "game-changing weapons" that Iran was transferring to its proxies amid the chaos of Syria's civil war. Since 2018, the Israelis have become much more specific. Their targets are PGMs.

In decades past, Israel was blessed with ill-equipped enemies. More recently, the efforts of Iranian proxies such as Hamas, Hezbollah, and PIJ have been mitigated by Iron Dome. Iron Dome's success rate is well known, but it has been boosted by the fact that Israel's foes have been firing unguided, or "dumb," rockets. Without GPS or target-acquisition capabilities, many of these rockets miss their intended targets. When Iron Dome's radar detects a rocket and the battle management and weapon control system determines that the projectile is not going to strike a target of value, operators decline to expend a valuable interceptor, permitting the rocket to fall harmlessly into an uninhabited space.

With PGMs, however, Iran's proxies could potentially evade Iron Dome while striking within five to ten yards of their intended targets. The regime in Iran thus began working overtime in 2013 to stand up a program to enable its proxies to convert their dumb rockets into smart ones. In a 2018 interview with Iran's *Tasnim News Agency*, the IRGC Aerospace Force commander, General Amir-Ali Hajizadeh, recounted how in 2009 he presented the Iranian leadership with a plan to modernize the country's missile program. Supreme Leader Khamenei overruled his entire plan and ordered him to focus solely on the development of PGMs.[11] Hezbollah's leader, Hassan Nasrallah, has since boasted about the importance of this project to his organization and to the broader "Axis of Resistance."[12]

The PGM project remains a top priority for the regime. Even after the January 2020 assassination of IRGC-Quds Force commander Major General Qassem Soleimani,[13] who was widely known to be a champion of the project, PGM development was believed to have continued under deputy Quds Force commander Mohammed Hijazi until he died, reportedly of natural causes, in 2021.[14]

Whole PGMs are difficult to transfer now that Israel is fully aware of the Iranian project. Hezbollah has therefore worked to convert unguided rockets (what some Israeli officials have described to me as "statistical" rockets) into PGMs. The process is both simple and complicated. It is simple because all it takes are tail fins, a circuit board, and the right software. One former Israeli official estimated that an entire PGM-making kit might cost $15,000 per munition. However, the process is also complicated because dismantling a rocket, retrofitting it with precision-guided technology, and then reassembling it are dangerous and requires knowledge and infrastructure that Iran's low-tech proxies generally lacked.

With Iran's help, Hezbollah is working hard to bridge that gap. That explains why the Israelis have struck so many targets in Syria in recent years. They have been patrolling the smuggling routes from Iran to Syria to Lebanon to halt the transfer of PGMs, PGM parts, or other related technology.[15]

Israel has also targeted PGMs inside Lebanon. In August 2019, an Israeli drone strike reportedly targeted a solid fuel production facility in Lebanon, setting back Hezbollah's PGM production by an estimated one year.[16] It was the first time the IDF had operated inside Lebanon in several years, marking a dramatic break from the unspoken rules of the game — that Israel could freely strike PGMs in Syria, but Lebanon was off-limits. The following year, the IDF exposed three new PGM sites in Lebanon.[17] Hezbollah denied the reports, but on a tour the group granted to journalists at one of the sites, it inadvertently revealed machinery that was used to manufacture the weapons.[18]

Iran's PGM efforts have continued despite Israel's intelligence dominance and increasingly aggressive operations to counter the program. Both sides understand that when enough PGMs reach the hands of Israel's enemies, the effect will indeed be game-changing. It is for this reason that IDF Chief of Staff Aviv Kochavi identified the PGM threat to Israel as second only to Iran's nuclear program.[19]

The PGM threat to Israel is manifold. First, PGM accuracy will force Israel to use far more Iron Dome interceptors than it currently deploys. This is because the number of errant launches will plummet, forcing Israel to try to neutralize nearly every projectile that is launched. Each Tamir interceptor costs roughly $100,000.[20] Thus, defending Israel could become much more expensive. Moreover, Iron Dome could eventually run out of interceptors if tens of thousands of rockets are fired during a prolonged conflict.

More worrying, with enough PGMs fired at the same target, some may get through. In the future, if the intended target is the chemical plant in Haifa, the *Kiriya* (Israel's defense headquarters) in Tel Aviv, Ben Gurion International Airport, the Dimona nuclear facility, or a Tel Aviv high-rise office building, the results could be catastrophic. As Nagel told me during one of our many conversations during the COVID-19 lockdown of 2020, "with enough PGMs, the impact on certain targets could be close to the impact of a nuclear weapon."

Currently, the Israelis believe that Hezbollah is the only Iranian proxy group on its borders that possesses Iranian PGMs. Most officials will not say how many PGMs Hezbollah has. Initially, Israelis were saying "dozens,"[21] but I have heard "several hundred" in my not-for-attribution conversations. Those numbers will grow as Hezbollah continues to work feverishly on this project.

Targeting PGMs will become even more complicated for Israel in the future. The regime in Iran is not only working assiduously to obscure their transportation and assembly, but also is devising ways to store them under homes, schools, hospitals, apartment buildings, refugee camps, and other heavily populated civilian infrastructure. In other words, Hezbollah, like Hamas, is using the illegal tactic of human shields. Dealing with this deadly tactic will likely become even more challenging for the Israeli military in the near future. When the time comes, the decision to strike these weapons on the ground will be excruciating for the IDF. Just as Hezbollah and its Iranian backers have planned it, every strike will create immense public-relations pressure for Israel as images of injured or dead civilians fill the television screens and Twitter feeds of news consumers worldwide.

Theoretically, there are two organizations in Lebanon that could avert this crisis. The reality is that neither will. The first is the American-funded Lebanese Armed Forces (LAF). Though Lebanon is thoroughly dominated by Hezbollah, the United States continues to look to the LAF as a counterbalance to the Iranian proxy — and it is still not entirely clear what that means. The United Nations also embraces this odd logic, with dangerous consequences. In 2006, the UN Security Council passed Resolution 1701, calling on Lebanon to disarm Hezbollah. Yet for years, the LAF has looked the other way while Iran smuggled PGMs and PGM parts into Lebanon.[22] The LAF also was somehow unaware that Hezbollah spent an estimated two years digging a massive system of subterranean cross-border attack tunnels into Israel.[23]

As my colleague Tony Badran has repeatedly noted, the problem is not the LAF's capabilities. The problem is the LAF's collusion. In one telling example, Israel in 2019 exposed a Hezbollah PGM facility in eastern Lebanon. The site was a short drive away from a LAF base where the United States has delivered equipment, including ScanEagle reconnaissance drones. The base also hosts the US- and UK-funded Land Border Training Center, designed to help the LAF secure Lebanon's porous border. Hezbollah, with Iran's assistance, built a PGM facility next door.[24]

The other actor in Lebanon that should be halting the PGM program is the UN Interim Force in Lebanon (UNIFIL). It was first created in the 1970s to halt terrorist activity in the country. UNIFIL's mandate expanded greatly in 2006 after the war between Hezbollah and Israel. Nonetheless, the organization has utterly failed to halt the smuggling of weapons into Lebanon, even in the limited territory defined in its mandate. It barely pretends to try. No steps have been taken to strengthen its capabilities or to redefine its mandate more aggressively. In short, UNIFIL epitomizes the failure of the UN system.[25] Some Israeli officials still defend the organization, primarily because it affords the IDF opportunities to engage directly with their Lebanese counterparts. The value of that, particularly as Lebanon unravels, is questionable.

A third actor also may have the ability to avert or at least stem this crisis, but it is a long shot. Russia has a significant presence in Syria, giving the Russians a front row seat to the PGM smuggling operation. Israel, in recent years, mounted an effort to convince the Russians to usher the Iranians out of Syria, explaining how the PGM project is deeply destabilizing for the region. Israeli officials have repeatedly told Putin and his top aides that so long as the PGM threat continues, and so long as Iran violates Israel's red lines in Syria and Lebanon, Israeli airstrikes will continue. There will be no stability in Syria, leaving Russia's investment there at risk. Thus far, and rather predictably, the Russians have done little. Though, to their credit, they do stand aside while Israel takes care of its business.

As I observed the rocket fire out of Lebanon during the 2021 Gaza war, it dawned on me that Hamas might have been firing those rockets in a bid to draw Lebanon into the conflict.

In June 2017, the Israelis sent a letter to the United Nations, accusing Hamas of "colluding with Hezbollah and its sponsor in Tehran to expand its malicious activities. . . to areas within Lebanon." A subsequent letter dated May 11, 2018, expressed additional concerns. When I was visiting Israel that summer, a contact of mine at the Foreign Ministry in Jerusalem gave me a copy of that letter.

The document was not classified. But it was also not widely circulated for reasons that were not clear to me. I did not know what to do with it, so it sat in my office for nearly three years. When the rockets were fired from Lebanon during the May 2021 conflict, I dug it out. (See appendix.) The letter's contents were eye-opening. Israel's ambassador to the United Nations, Danny Dannon, alleged military cooperation between Iran, Hezbollah, and Hamas in Lebanon:

> Some of this cooperation has been publicized in pre-announced meetings of high-ranking operatives and statements of mutual support. It is led by Saleh al-Arouri, the Lebanon-based deputy head of Hamas' Politburo, and Saeed Izadi, head of the Palestinian Branch of the Iranian al-Quds Force, both of whom have made no attempt to conceal the growing coordination between

Iran, Hezbollah, and Hamas. Furthermore, Iran has publicly declared its commitment to increase its support for Hamas. Iranian military leader, Qassem Soleimani, has even gone as far as to say that all of this country's means and resources are at Hamas' disposal, without precondition, to be used for aggression against Israel.

In addition to their publicly known relationship, Hamas has been building its own military force covertly in Lebanon. Hamas has recruited and trained hundreds of fighters, mostly men of Palestinian origin, and plans to recruit thousands more who will comprise a force that will operate on Hamas' behalf in Lebanon. At the direction of Hamas operative Majid Hader, Hamas has assembled infrastructure in Lebanon ready to manufacture its own missiles and UAVs to add to its war arsenal and increase its offensive capabilities.

The goal of Hamas' activities, both overt and covert, is not just to gain an additional front from which Hamas could launch terrorist attacks against Israel's innocent civilians. Hamas also intends to use its armed force and growing arsenal of rockets to pull Lebanon into conflict with Israel. This intention increases the possibility of a conflict that could engulf the entire Middle East.[26]

That same year, Israeli analyst Yossi Melman outlined some of this in an article he penned for *The Jerusalem Post*. He noted that in 2017, Shin Bet chief Nadav Argaman warned publicly, "Hamas was trying to build a 'post' in South Lebanon."[27] The Kuwaiti newspaper *Al-Seyassah* published a piece around this time, suggesting that Hamas' goal was much bigger than simply creating a "post." The

Lebanese press picked up on the story. The piece alleged that Hamas intended to drag Lebanon into a future Hamas-Israel conflict, forcing Israel to fight on two fronts.[28]

In the months that followed the war, several additional rocket salvos were fired out of Lebanon. Hezbollah took credit for only one of those attacks — the first acknowledged attack by the group in 15 years.[29] Was Hamas behind the others? Or was it isolated Palestinian militants from Lebanon's refugee camps? More importantly, has Iran helped Hamas establish a more formidable military presence in Lebanon? It will be important to answer these questions before the next round of fighting in Gaza erupts.

FOURTEEN
FOREIGN FIGHTER

May 23, 2021, was a Sunday. I remember this because it was the first weekend after the 11-day Gaza war. For the previous week and a half, I had been watching the news around the clock, writing articles, and briefing reporters in more than a dozen countries. So when Egypt brokered a ceasefire between Hamas and Israel, I unplugged. But that Sunday, I received a phone call from Tom Joscelyn, one of the editors of *FDD's Long War Journal*, or *LWJ*. Suddenly, I was back to work.

LWJ is a project of my think tank, the Foundation for Defense of Democracies. For more than a decade, *LWJ* has produced no-nonsense reporting in the highly politicized field of terrorism studies. The team, led by Joscelyn and Bill Roggio (the founder of *LWJ*), had for years been calling balls and strikes on US counterterrorism operations against al-Qaeda, the Islamic State, and other terrorist groups in the Middle East and nearby regions. Their reporting often conflicted with the official statements of US government officials, but I cannot recall a time when they were forced to print a retraction. Not one.

In 2020, amidst the pandemic, FDD's management made the somewhat controversial decision to fund a new position at *LWJ*. We agreed that it was time to branch out a little by looking at Iran-backed terrorist groups. After all, Iran was financing, arming, and training proxies in Gaza, Lebanon, Syria, Iraq, Yemen, and beyond. Not enough deep domain experts were reporting on the daily operations of these groups. So we hired Joe Truzman, a young analyst who had a keen eye for open-source reporting — primarily on Twitter — relating to these groups.

When Joscelyn called me that Sunday, he told me that Truzman had a big scoop: A 33-year-old American citizen had gone to fight for Hamas in Gaza and was subsequently killed in an Israeli airstrike during the May 2021 war. The *LWJ* team shared their sourcing and sought my assurances that we would back the piece. *LWJ* soon ran it. They were the first to break the story.[1]

The specifics of the story were important. An American citizen named Osama al-Zebda joined the Izz ad-Din al-Qassam Brigades, the "armed wing" of Hamas. An official confirmed to Truzman that al-Zebda had been on a US terrorist watch list and was killed by an Israeli airstrike on May 12. His 64-year-old father, Jamal al-Zebda, was also killed in the strike.[2]

During the war, amidst Israel's targeting of rocket launchers and other key military assets, the IDF also conducted a series of airstrikes to neutralize leaders and commanders of militant factions in Gaza. Multiple commanders and mid-level Hamas militants were reportedly killed by IDF airstrikes during the operation.[3] The Zebda men were among the targets.

As the *LWJ* team worked to nail down the facts of the story, Truzman found a 1989 research paper on aerodynamics written by a man named Jamal al-Zebda at the Virginia Polytechnic Institute and State University.[4] This suggested that the father had likely been based in the United States. While the team could not independently verify if this was the same Jamal al-Zebda, the IDF website suggested they were on the right track. The website described Jamal al-Zebda as a "senior member of Hamas' research and development division," noting that he held a "PhD in Mechanical Engineering, specializing in aerodynamics."[5] According to one Palestinian expert, Jamal al-Zebda was an important target for Israel due to his scientific expertise.[6]

On May 12, pictures of the Zebda men began circulating on Palestinian social media. The father and son were described as "martyrs."[7] One post from May 19, written by Osama al-Zebda's wife, Yosra Aklouk, claimed he had American citizenship.[8] She told ABC News that her husband had lived in the United States for five years.[9] "My husband, who is of American nationality, knew that the shortest way to God is to sacrifice his spirit, mind, time, and money for the sake of Allah and his religion," Aklouk wrote on Facebook.[10]

Hamas formally acknowledged Osama al-Zebda's death and that he belonged to the terror organization,[11] referring to him as a "commander."[12] Family members described Osama al-Zebda as a "military man" and confirmed that both he and his father were rocket engineers.[13] The State Department also confirmed Osama al-Zebda's death. "We are aware of reports of a U.S. citizen killed in Gaza," a department spokesperson told ABC News. "Due to privacy considerations, we have no further comment."[14]

According to ABC, the Zebda men lived in the United Arab Emirates for a time. The father returned to Gaza in 1994 to help Hamas develop its rocket arsenal. The Palestinian Information Center (PIC), a Hamas-affiliated website, noted that Jamal al-Zebda had joined al-Qassam Brigades in 2006 and helped the terrorist group develop more powerful warheads for its rockets using locally accessible materials. An Israeli military official added that Jamal al-Zebda was a senior member of Hamas' R&D division who worked on weapons projects that were "developed and intended to harm Israeli citizens." The PIC also noted that Jamal had survived an Israeli assassination attempt in 2012 but provided no further details.[15]

In the aftermath of the war, Hamas leader Yahya Sinwar emerged from his bunker to address the surviving members of Hamas as well as Gaza's population. Dressed in a white button-down shirt and brandishing an AK-47 rifle, Sinwar hoisted a child onto his shoulder. The child was wearing camouflage and a green "al-Qassam Brigades" headband.[16] The child was Osama al-Zebda's son.[17] Whether he liked it or not, he had become the poster child of the 2021 Gaza war.

The Zebda episode was a reminder that Hamas is not just a local violent group. It is a global terrorist organization. The group has sent its members to study military technology in foreign educational institutions worldwide. In 2018, for example, Fadi al-Batsh, an engineer and Hamas member, was assassinated by the Israeli Mossad in Malaysia. According to reports at the time, the man was studying to help Hamas develop rocket technology.[18] He may have even negotiated a Hamas arms deal with North Korea.[19]

Malaysia, it should be noted, has long been an important jurisdiction for Hamas. In 2012, at least ten Hamas members traveled to Malaysia to train for cross-border attacks against Israel.[20] In a West Bank raid in 2014, Israel captured Majdi Mafarja, who admitted to training in message encryption and computer hacking for Hamas in Malaysia.[21] In 2015, Israeli authorities alleged that a group of Palestinian students had been sent to Malaysia back in 2010 to learn how to use hang gliders to infiltrate Israel for an attack. This came after the Israeli security services arrested Waseem Qawasmeh, a 24-year-old student who had studied in Malaysia. He was charged with belonging to Hamas and receiving funding from the terror group.[22]

The Zebda story was also a reminder that multiple Americans have gone off to join foreign terrorist organizations. Doing so is illegal under US law. That did not stop Adam Gadahn (an al-Qaeda leader killed in a US drone strike),[23] Anwar al-Awlaki (an al-Qaeda in the Arabian Peninsula leader killed in a US drone strike),[24] John Georgelas (an Islamic State propagandist killed in Syria),[25] or John Walker Lindh (captured while fighting for the Taliban).[26] There will undoubtedly be more.

FIFTEEN
EGYPT'S THANKLESS CEASEFIRE

There were other important stories that should have grabbed bigger headlines during the 2021 Gaza war. The role of Egypt was among them.

In the wake of the 2011 Arab Spring, when Egypt was under the leadership of Muslim Brotherhood figure Mohammed Morsi, Hamas was more flush with cash and weapons than it probably had ever been. Morsi was president for just the blink of an eye — from June 30, 2012, to July 3, 2013. Yet his time in office was hugely significant for Israel. On a phone call in 2013, one senior Israeli official called Cairo the "back office of Hamas." The official indicated to me that elements of the Brotherhood's financial network were bankrolling Hamas even as Egypt's economy cratered.[1] Egypt was so central to Hamas' operations that the movement in 2013 held a round of internal elections in the Egyptian capital.[2]

In the weeks after Morsi's dramatic ouster by the Egyptian military in July 2013, the new regime froze the accounts of at least 14 senior Brotherhood figures,[3] including at least one significant contributor to Hamas' coffers, a senior Israeli security official told me in a not-for-attribution conversation.

However, the new regime of President Abdel Fattah al-Sisi was not satisfied with merely freezing accounts. The Sisi regime went on to destroy more than 1,639 subterranean smuggling tunnels connecting Egypt to Gaza.[4] The crackdown made bulk cash smuggling — the primary way Hamas filled its coffers — exceedingly difficult. Cairo's anti-tunnel campaign also depleted the tax revenues of the Hamas government; the group had reportedly collected at least $365 million in taxes each year from the tunnel trade.[5] Ala al-Rafati, Hamas' economy minister, estimated that Egypt's disruption of these tunnel operations cost the terror group $230 million annually — about one-tenth of Gaza's gross domestic product.[6] And that was before hundreds of additional tunnels were destroyed.

All of this came at a horrendous time for Hamas. Until 2012, the faction relied heavily on Iran and Syria for financial support. The carnage of civil war in Syria prompted Hamas to reconsider these relationships. The Sunni Palestinian group simply could not maintain its credibility among Palestinians if it stood by the Islamic Republic and the Assad regime as they killed Sunnis and Palestinians by the thousands.[7] The group began to look for support from other patrons, namely Qatar and Turkey.

Egypt's crackdown on the tunnels did not stem from love for Israel. True, Egypt had enjoyed peace with Israel since 1979. However, theirs was a cold peace. For Sisi, the goal was to stabilize the Sinai Peninsula, and to blunt the influence of Iran and the Muslim Brotherhood. Over time, however, it became clear that the Sisi regime and Israel had even more in common. The two countries also sought to counter the growth of the Islamic State in the Sinai

Peninsula.[8] They also cooperated together with Greece and Cyprus on Eastern Mediterranean energy.[9] The relationship between Egypt's strongman and Prime Minister Netanyahu quickly evolved. The two allowed themselves to be photographed together.[10] They were often seen smiling — a marked shift from the cool and transactional relationship between former Egyptian President Hosni Mubarak and prior Israeli prime ministers.

After the 2014 Gaza conflict, Egypt thrust itself into the role of broker. Admittedly, Egypt has long mediated between Israel and the Palestinians on a range of political issues over the years. However, given the Sisi regime's anti-Brotherhood and anti-Iran leanings, its neutrality is debatable. Still, Cairo was uniquely qualified to work as a go-between for Hamas and Israel during times of tension. The Egyptians genuinely sought to reduce tensions to prevent war, and to ease certain restrictions to ensure better lives for the people of Gaza. Israel was often willing to make concessions if Egypt requested them, so long as Hamas was not firing rockets or discernibly smuggling in new weapons for the next round of conflict.

In recent years, both Egypt and Israel warily allowed Qatar, an unabashed patron of Hamas, to play a role in this process. The Qataris had the deep pockets to help make up for shortfalls in the Gaza Strip. During times of economic stress, Qatar repeatedly offered to help fund specific projects or to pay the salaries of Hamas government officials. Never mind that Qatari assistance came in the form of suitcases full of cash.[11] For seven years, this strange arrangement appeared to pay dividends. Calm prevailed. Neither the Israelis nor the Egyptians appeared particularly thrilled about working with Doha given its sordid history of terrorism finance. Yet they were willing to hold their noses so long as the threat of war was contained.

In 2021, the streak ended. Qatari cash was no longer able to contain Hamas, and the terrorist group provoked a war with Israel. As analyst Haisam Hassanein noted, Cairo immediately got to work in an effort to shape the outcome of the conflict. He notes that Egypt did not "want to see Hamas succeed. But for similar reasons, [Cairo did not] want Hamas' allies — [Egypt's] sworn enemies Iran, Turkey, and Qatar — to gain even more influence in Gaza."[12]

Even before the fighting broke out, amidst the drama of Sheikh Jarrah and the Temple Mount, Egypt positioned itself as the center of gravity for negotiations. Egyptian mediators attempted to engage in de-escalation talks with Hamas and Israel. The Egyptians reached out to solicit support from the Biden administration, which until then had expressed zero interest in engaging with Cairo. This reluctance stemmed from the Obama administration's experience with Egypt, which overlapped with the counter-revolution that overthrew Morsi and brought Sisi to power in 2013. The Obama team, many of whom were now serving in the Biden administration, viewed the Sisi regime as anti-democratic owing to the heavy hand it took against the Brotherhood government. The Biden White House did not exactly jump at the opportunity to re-engage.

When the 2021 war erupted, Egypt began working with Hamas, Israel, and the PA in a bid to restore calm. One Egyptian official told me that the Egyptians shuttled back and forth between rooms at a hotel in Cairo, working tirelessly to bridge the gaps between the three sides.[13]

While war raged, Egyptian diplomats were working the phones, speaking with officials from the United Nations,[14] the PA,[15] Saudi Arabia,[16] and others. To the chagrin of officials in Jerusalem, Egypt's rhetoric was often deeply critical of Israel, much like that of almost every other Arab state in the region. This did not stop Israel from working with the Sisi regime, however. The Israelis likely understood that such rhetoric, even if not always truthful or fair, would help Cairo gain the trust of Hamas and other regional players during the Gaza crisis.

In the first days of the conflict, Egyptian officials engaged with Arab foreign ministers[17] and European officials.[18] During one call with Israeli Foreign Minister Gabi Ashkenazi, Egyptian Foreign Minister Sameh Shoukry emphasized Cairo's desire to see the warring parties settle their differences by diplomatic means.[19] Israel, for its part, conveyed that it could not discuss diplomatic concessions while Hamas was firing thousands of rockets.[20]

On May 13, Egypt sent delegations to both Gaza and Tel Aviv. Cairo proposed a three-hour pause to allow negotiations to gain steam. According to press reports, the Egyptians went to Gaza first but were told by Hamas military leader Saleh al-Arouri that the group would not abide. The Egyptians were also in touch with external Hamas leader Ismail Haniyeh.[21]

Undeterred, on May 13 and 14, Shoukry worked the phones with diplomats from Russia,[22] Tunisia,[23] and Jordan.[24] Cairo continued to float a temporary ceasefire, with this one suggested to last until the end of Ramadan. Still fending off Hamas rockets and other threats, the Israelis declined.[25]

On May 15, Shoukry spoke with diplomats from Saudi Arabia[26] and Pakistan,[27] updating them on Egypt's progress — or lack thereof. The Egyptians on that day also opened their border with Gaza to allow ambulances to enter the territory and evacuate the injured.[28]

On May 16, the Egyptian ambassador to Ramallah met with Palestinian Prime Minster Mohammed Shtayyeh. The PA had little leverage in the crisis, but the Egyptians still felt it was important to include the West Bank government in the process, even if it was a marginal player.[29]

That day, Shoukry also addressed the UN Security Council.[30] He called on the international community to "shoulder its responsibility to bring an end to the conflict and undertake efforts to deescalate the situation so that everyone can take a deep breath and think about the causes." He asserted those causes stemmed from "a climate of tensions perpetuated over years of systematic regression and the undermining of efforts to achieve peace in the region."[31]

Shoukry also spoke with US Secretary of State Antony Blinken, in a sign that US-Egypt ties were warming as a result of Cairo's efforts.[32] Shoukry then spoke with the Qatari,[33] Greek, and Dutch foreign ministers.[34] Greece's role was particularly intriguing in light of the fact that Greece, Egypt, and Israel had grown closer in recent years thanks to shared concerns about security in the Eastern Mediterranean, largely due to Turkish aggression.[35]

On May 17, Sisi met with French President Emmanuel Macron in Paris.[36] Macron, in recent years, had increasingly worked to assert French leadership of the European Union, filling the void left by Brexit and a financially and politically weakened Germany. The following day, the two leaders participated in a three-way summit with Jordan, aimed at bringing the conflict to an end.[37]

Meanwhile, Egypt was working hard to bring humanitarian aid to Gaza. The Sisi regime sent an estimated $900,000 in medicine and medical supplies to Gaza in 26 trucks.[38] Cairo also announced it would provide $500 million for Gaza's reconstruction.[39]

By May 18, Israeli television was reporting that a ceasefire was imminent. In apparent confirmation of this, Shoukry appeared on CNN to discuss the ceasefire efforts.[40] The pace of rocket fire out of Gaza had undeniably abated. The Israeli response was also less fierce.

The ceasefire was slated to take effect at 2:00 a.m. on May 21.[41] The Israeli security cabinet agreed to its terms. Hamas agreed as well. The Egyptians also made sure to include the PA in the discussion.[42] In fact, this was the beginning of an effort on the part of Egypt and the United States, among others, to begin to strengthen (to the extent they could) the PA.

After the ceasefire took hold, President Joe Biden held an official call with Sisi. It was the first time that the two men had spoken since Biden took office in January.[43] Readouts from both countries conveyed that the two leaders discussed the ceasefire and vowed to keep in close touch. UN Secretary General Antonio Guterres also spoke to Sisi that day.[44]

Back in Washington, Biden addressed the American people. He credited Egypt for its efforts but, remarkably, also appeared to be taking a victory lap for the ceasefire.

> Over the last 11 days, I spoke with the [Israeli] Prime Minister six times. I've also spoken with President Abbas of the Palestinian Authority more than once in part of our intense diplomatic engagement.
>
> And I want to also thank the Secretary of State, the Secretary of Defense, our National Security Advisor, and everyone on our team for their incredible efforts to bring this about — this outcome that we're about to see.
>
> You know, we've held intensive high-level discussions, hour by hour, literally — Egypt, the Palestinian Authority, and other Middle Eastern countries — with an aim of avoiding the sort of prolonged conflict we've seen in previous years when the hostilities have broken out.

I extend my sincere gratitude to President Al Sisi and the senior Egyptian officials who played a critical role in this diplomacy...

My administration will continue our quiet and relentless diplomacy toward that end. I believe we have a genuine opportunity to make progress, and I'm committed to working for it.[45]

The American president claimed that his administration had engaged on more than 80 occasions with regional stakeholders.[46] With that, two crises concluded. The Gaza war was over. And Egypt, by giving Biden center stage, also appeared to have negotiated its way out of isolation.

On May 24, Sisi received another call from Biden. They spoke about the ceasefire along with a range of other issues related to Egyptian national security — Ethiopia, Libya, and even Egyptian human rights.[47] Two days later, Blinken visited Cairo as part of a regional tour. He met with Sisi and Shoukry to discuss ways to build upon the quiet.[48]

The Egyptians soon embarked on a new effort to broker a longer-term calm. On the one hand, it was a thankless job with little prospect of success. On the other hand, Egypt was now viewed as a friend of the White House again. This was a status that Cairo did not wish to lose.

SIXTEEN
BIDEN'S TOUGH TALK

President Abdel Fattah al-Sisi was not the only Middle Eastern leader to get the cold shoulder from President Joe Biden. One month into the new American president's term, Biden had not called Prime Minister Benjamin Netanyahu. On the one hand, the silence was odd given the longstanding alliance between Israel and the United States. On the other, Netanyahu was merely the acting prime minister after four rounds of inconclusive elections in Israel. The embattled prime minister was heading into another round of elections in March, and the American president justifiably wanted to steer clear of domestic Israeli politics.

Moreover, it was not as if the two countries were not cooperating. Plenty of senior officials downstream in the US bureaucracy were engaging with their Israeli counterparts. Secretary of State Antony Blinken spoke with Israeli Foreign Minister Gabi Ashkenazi.[1] National Security Adviser Jake Sullivan spoke to Meir Ben Shabbat, Netanyahu's national security advisor.[2] Many other American bureaucrats were working with their counterparts in Jerusalem, too. The US-Israel relationship is both wide and deep.[3]

But the silence at the top was a sign of lingering mistrust from the bad old days of acrimony between the Netanyahu government and the Biden officials who previously served in the Obama administration. Those tensions reached a zenith with the Obama administration's decision to pursue an ill-advised deal with Iran in 2015 that yielded huge financial perks to the Islamic Republic in exchange for weak and temporary restrictions on its nuclear program.[4] US-Israel tensions flared further when Obama lowered the American diplomatic shield at Turtle Bay in the waning days of his presidency, allowing the UN Security Council to pass a one-sided resolution that effectively upended previous US-Israel understandings about Middle East peace and denied Israel's very heritage in Jerusalem.[5]

Whatever his reasons, Biden's delay in calling Netanyahu was a clear deviation from the norm. President Bill Clinton called Prime Minister Yitzhak Rabin on January 23, 1993, and hosted Rabin less than two months later.[6] President George W. Bush called Prime Minister Ariel Sharon on February 6, 2001, the day Sharon was elected prime minister.[7] President Barack Obama spoke with Prime Minister Ehud Olmert on January 21, 2009,[8] then called Netanyahu on April 1, the day after the latter was sworn in as prime minister.[9] President Donald Trump spoke with Netanyahu on January 22[10] and hosted his Israeli counterpart at the White House the following month.[11]

At the time, some believed Biden just had more pressing agenda items on this desk. This was certainly not wrong. Biden was dealing with a global pandemic, an uncertain economy, and the fractured Washington politics that had led to an assault on the United States Capitol Building on January 6, 2021, prompting security officials to wrap the Capitol in concertina wire. However, if Biden had, in fact, decided to keep the focus at home, how exactly did he make time for calls with Russian President Vladimir Putin,[12] Chinese leader Xi Jinping,[13] Canadian Prime Minister Justin Trudeau,[14] Mexican President Andres Manuel Lopez Obrador,[15] UK Prime Minister Boris Johnson,[16] and others? Perhaps Biden made time for foreign-policy issues on America's immediate borders (Canada and Mexico), great power competition (Russia and China), and repairing transatlantic alliances (the United Kingdom) after four years of Trump administration policies that strained those ties. That certainly would explain it.

Here is what did not make sense: The Biden administration issued multiple statements about its intent to return to the highly controversial 2015 Iran nuclear deal, or JCPOA.[17] Biden and Blinken tapped controversial figure Rob Malley as the envoy to try to resurrect that agreement.[18] That appointment was one of several unmistakable signs that the Middle East remained a priority for the Biden White House. This was a policy that clearly impacted Israel, America's most valuable ally in the region.

So why not engage with the Israeli prime minister? During the lead-up to the 2015 nuclear deal, the Israelis emerged as the most effective and outspoken critics of the Iran deal. From public statements to private meetings, the Netanyahu government was relentless in its opposition. This was not surprising given that Israel is within range of Iran's large and growing arsenal of ballistic and cruise missiles, which the JCPOA did not address. Also, Iran has been perfectly honest about the fact that it seeks the destruction of the Jewish state.[19]

Israel was certainly not the only critic of the deal. The JCPOA will go down as one of the most controversial foreign-policy initiatives in modern American history, both for its generous sanctions relief to the world's foremost state sponsor of terrorism and for its "sunset" clauses that granted Iran permission to ultimately return to the illicit nuclear activity that Tehran never admitted it was pursuing in the first place.[20] The deal provoked harsh criticism from Republicans (and some Democrats) in America and national security hawks worldwide. The Gulf Arab states — notably the United Arab Emirates, Saudi Arabia, and Bahrain — also steadfastly opposed the JCPOA.

With the Iran deal now back on the table in 2021, this rather severe policy disagreement between Israel's prime minister and America's new president was set to pick up right where it left off. Netanyahu was probably better armed this time with proof that Iran did not deserve sanctions relief.[21] The 2018 Mossad raid on the Iranian nuclear warehouse yielded ample evidence of the Islamic Republic's previous and potentially ongoing efforts to develop a nuclear weapon — something the Islamic Republic denied throughout the US-led negotiations that resulted in the JCPOA.[22]

Biden was trying to avoid controversy early on in his presidency. He was elected to be a healer and a uniter. With the JCPOA as a foreign policy priority, however, there was no way for him to avoid a confrontation with opponents of the deal, and certainly not Israel. The longer Biden waited to engage, the more his silence could be construed as signaling a deeper problem with Israel. Critics were already deriding his foreign policy as "Obama's third term."[23]

On February 17, Biden finally called Netanyahu. The two leaders chatted for an hour, and the readout suggested that the tone was friendly and warm.[24] This was really no surprise. After all, the two leaders had known one another for 40 years. As a senator, Biden had been an unwavering friend of the Jewish state. But storm clouds were gathering; the Iran issue loomed large. The Israelis were not simply concerned that Biden would lift the crippling sanctions imposed by the previous administration when it withdrew from the JCPOA. They were also worried that sanctions relief would trickle down to Iran's terrorist proxies once the funding began to flow. Biden undoubtedly grasped this. He may even have been sympathetic to Israel's concerns. However, the domestic politics in America, with Democrats looking to overturn a wide range of President Donald Trump's policies, gave Biden little choice but to pursue the nuclear deal.

In the spring of 2021, the Biden administration and Israel made a good-faith effort to isolate their disagreement over the Iran nuclear deal from the range of other issues that have traditionally bound the two countries in a warm alliance. The Israelis informed the administration that they would oppose a return to the deal and would continue to do what was necessary to address Iranian security threats — a clear nod to Israel's ongoing War Between Wars. The administration seemed fine with that, so long as Israel did not air its disagreements in public.

When the rocket salvos out of Gaza began, Biden made it clear that he supported the Israelis, citing their right to defend themselves.[25] When it became apparent that the conflict was not going to end any time soon, the White House dispatched Deputy Assistant Secretary of State Hady Amr to the region.[26] Amr was one of the administration's first figures to be named to the Middle East portfolio. However, the more senior administration positions remained vacant, including assistant secretary of state and ambassador to Israel. How much Amr could achieve was an open question. Diplomatic protocol dictates that Amr, a relatively low-ranking official, would not enjoy access to Israel's top decision makers. It seemed clear that the leaders of the two countries, primarily through their national security advisors Jake Sullivan and Meir Ben Shabbat, would be dealing with the major issues.

Early on in the conflict, Biden had a call with Netanyahu, after which a White House readout said the American president "reiterated his firm support for Israel's right to defend itself against indiscriminate rocket attacks."[27] In a separate statement, the White House noted that Biden "expressed his support for a cease-fire and discussed US engagement with Egypt and other partners toward that end." Notably, he did not demand that Israel end its response to Hamas' rocket barrage.[28] The president also blocked several resolutions at the UN Security Council that would have censured Israel.[29] By all accounts, despite some tense moments stemming from the IDF attack on the Hamas Metro system, and even amidst the controversy surrounding Israel's strike on the Al-Jalaa building, the president stood by America's embattled ally.

By the end of the war, a handful of hard-left Democrats were openly voicing frustration with Biden's policy.[30] In their view, Trump had been too supportive of Israel during his time in office. These self-described progressives were hoping to reverse that policy, among others.

Biden's policy probably came under the heaviest fire from Representative Rashida Tlaib (D-MI), a Palestinian-American. On May 17, she told MSNBC television viewers that Biden's rhetoric was insufficient: "You don't hear the words 'Palestinians deserve human rights, that Palestinians deserve to exist, that Palestinians deserve to live freely, that children need to be safe and secure.'" Tlaib criticized "the hypocrisy of us saying that we need to be stewards of human rights, except for Palestinians," adding, "I hope that my president, our president, speaks up and speaks truth about what exactly is happening, because I know [officials in the White House] know." The congresswoman accused Biden of "taking orders" from Netanyahu, stating that "passive language" from the White House was "enabling" Israel's government. She urged Biden to "speak out against this violence in a very aggressive way that holds Netanyahu and his leadership accountable."[31]

Tlaib and Biden had a rather dramatic exchange on a tarmac in Detroit before a May 18 political rally in Dearborn, Michigan. The conversation was reportedly tense, with Tlaib pushing Biden to punish Israel. During the rally, Biden told her, "I admire your intellect, I admire your passion, and I admire your concern for so many other people. . .You're a fighter, and God thank you for being a fighter." He promised to ensure that Tlaib's family in the West Bank remained safe.[32]

Tlaib was not alone. Her colleague from New York, Representative Alexandria Ocasio-Cortez (D-NY), called Israel an "apartheid state," earning her headlines. She urged tougher American policies against Israel.[33] Representative Ilhan Omar (D-MN) likened Israel to terrorist groups for its airstrikes in Gaza, sparking outrage among centrists, not to mention the American right.[34] Representative Cori Bush (D-MO) attempted to tie Gaza to the Black Lives Matter movement, stating, "The fight for Black lives and the fight for Palestinian liberation are interconnected. We oppose our money going to fund militarized policing, occupation, and systems of violent oppression and trauma. We are anti-war. We are anti-occupation. And we are anti-apartheid. Period."[35] Senator Bernie Sanders (I-VT) also weighed in, tweeting: "The devastation in Gaza is unconscionable. We must urge an immediate ceasefire. The killing of Palestinians and Israelis must end. We must also take a hard look at nearly $4 billion a year in military aid to Israel. It is illegal for US aid to support human rights violations."[36]

The rhetoric of these legislators and a handful of others was reminiscent of another member of Congress, Paul Findley, who represented Illinois' 20th district from 1961 to 1983 and passed away in 2019. In the late 1970s, at the height of the PLO's global terrorism campaign, Findley emerged as a vociferous proponent of the movement and a harsh critic of Israel. He called himself "Arafat's best friend in Congress."[37] Findley's anti-Israeli rhetoric was not exactly a ticket to success given the overwhelming support Israel enjoyed in Congress, not to mention on Main Street America. In 1982, he lost his seat to Richard Durbin.[38] Not surprisingly, Findley blamed his defeat on the "Israel lobby." In 1985, he authored a screed titled *They Dare to Speak Out: People and Institutions Confront Israel's Lobby.*[39]

Findley was, in essence, the godfather of the vitriol exhibited during the Gaza war. He was the original member of what has now been described as the "Hamas Caucus" in Congress. Of course, there are significant differences between then and now. Today's toxic and polarized political atmosphere in Washington grants the most outrageous political flamethrowers an outsized megaphone. This stands in stark contrast to the political norms of the 1960s and 1970s, which called for more decorum among our politicians, even if American politics had become more unwieldly relative to the generations prior. Social media — something hardly conceivable during Findley's days in office — is partly to blame today. Twitter and Facebook have completely transformed the way politicians engage on issues and relate to their constituents. Rather than avoiding conflict, legislators now run toward political feuds on these and other platforms. The Hamas Caucus of today understands that expressing overt animosity toward Israel comes at little cost.[40]

Biden clearly understood that his left flank was a problem. Even if he wanted to support America's ally in a war it did not start, against an Iranian proxy that sought nothing less than its destruction, the president had to play politics. As the 2021 Gaza war dragged on, Biden began to talk tough to Israel. However, a careful examination of the timing of this rhetoric reveals that the toughest talk came only after the Egyptian-brokered ceasefire was reported on Israeli television. With roughly two days until the ceasefire was to take effect, the American president had a blank check to cash. He could call upon the Israelis to halt their operations in Gaza, with the full knowledge that they had already agreed to do so.

On May 19, in the fourth conversation between the two leaders since the crisis erupted, Biden told Netanyahu that he expected a "significant de-escalation" in Gaza, demanding a "path to a cease-fire."[41] According to one leaked report (presumably by a White House official looking to convey that the president was getting tough with Israel), Biden told Netanyahu that he was "done kidding around," telling the Israeli leader it was time to end the operation.[42] News reports suggested that ties were strained between the two leaders, reminding readers that the two had squared off during a 2010 Biden visit to the region as Israel approved construction in territory that Palestinians sought to include in a future state.[43] I received a number of phone calls on this manufactured controversy from journalists digesting off-the-record White House comments.

From Israel's perspective, however, Biden's tough talk was not a problem. The reality was that he gave the IDF exactly what it needed: the political cover to neutralize Hamas' military assets. As my FDD colleague Bradley Bowman and journalist Seth Frantzman noted, the IDF aimed to "force the terror groups to take longer to reconstitute forces, render them less effective in killing civilians in the next conflict, and make them think twice before starting the next missile barrage at all."[44] Biden seemed to understand this. In retrospect, the American president handled the Hamas Caucus with the expertise that only someone with four decades of experience in Washington could wield.

The drama was not quite over, however. Days after the end of the battle, Senator Sanders introduced a bill to block a US arms sale replenishing precision-guided munitions and Iron Dome interceptors Israel had used during the war.[45] "At a moment when US-made bombs are devastating Gaza, and killing women and children, we cannot simply let another huge arms sale go through without even a congressional debate," Sanders said. He was rebuked by Senator Jim Risch (R-ID) and Representative Michael McCaul (R-TX), the top Republicans on the foreign relations committees in the Senate and House. They called on Biden to "draw a firm line that the United States will stand with Israel and other allies in their hour of need."[46]

Ultimately, Sanders' bid failed. "There is no shift in my commitment, the commitment to the security of Israel, period," Biden later told reporters.[47] But the intent of Sanders' initiative was shocking. It ran counter to his stated goal of preventing future bloodshed. The interceptors had saved thousands of Israeli lives over the years. Without them, the IDF would have had little choice but to respond with overwhelming force to deadly strikes on Israeli population centers. At the same time, precision-guided munitions enabled Israel to strike Hamas military targets with accuracy, minimizing collateral damage. Without these weapons, Israel would need to deploy less precise weapons that would leave greater damage in their wake. Sanders thus appeared to be advocating for an uglier war between Hamas and Israel in the future.

For Omar, the drama did not end, either. Amid a rash of antisemitic attacks on the streets of America, the congresswoman continued to take heat from her own Democratic colleagues in Congress for her acerbic comments about Israel, equating the embattled democracy with the Taliban.[48] Ultimately, Omar walked back her comments on Twitter.[49] But the episode, which continued well after the Gaza war was over, was a clear sign that the Democratic Party was divided between supporters of the longstanding US-Israel alliance and the small but vociferous Hamas Caucus.[50] Republicans were, not surprisingly, even more harsh in response to Omar's comments, with a handful of Republican members calling for her removal from the House Foreign Affairs Committee.[51]

The debate on Capitol Hill over the Gaza war is far from settled. In fact, it erupted again in September. As is the case with many other policy issues, Congress is fractured. For Israel, this is not good news. In one conversation I had with an official at the Israeli Ministry of Foreign Affairs, I heard concerns about keeping Israel's longstanding friendship with America a bipartisan value. For decades, both parties have embraced the alliance. However, in this new age of angry American politics and the hyper-partisanship often seen on social media, the Israelis feel that the sands are shifting. While the center is still holding for now, anti-Israel politicians have undeniably found their voices. They are growing louder.

SEVENTEEN
UNRWA COMES CLEAN

One interesting debate for Congress in the aftermath of the 2021 Gaza war will surround America's support for one of the most controversial UN agencies in history: the United Nations Relief and Works Agency for Palestine Refugees in the Near East, or UNRWA.

UNRWA was established shortly after Israel's War of Independence, or what the Palestinians call the *Nakba* (the "Catastrophe"). The war began after the UN General Assembly voted in 1947 to partition the British Mandate in Palestine into two states, one Arab and one Jewish. When Israel declared independence, five Arab armies invaded, attempting to destroy the fledgling state. Israel did not want the war. It was a nascent country of Holocaust survivors and refugees from conflicts around the world. Surrounded and outnumbered, the Israelis somehow won the war.

As a result of the war, some 700,000 to 800,000 Palestinians were displaced. The United Nations created UNRWA in 1949 to care for this population.[1] What was odd in retrospect: The agency was dedicated solely to Palestinian Arab refugees. Somehow, UNRWA was never folded into the Office of the UN High Commissioner for

Refugees, the agency responsible for resettling every other refugee population in the world.

UNRWA soon became a key component of the Arab world's anti-Israel narrative. The Arabs claimed that due to the creation of Israel, millions of Palestinians were trapped as refugees, living in destitution, and yearning to return home. Until these people realized their "right of return," the Arab world insisted, the Middle East would never see peace. There was no talk of resettlement.

Even as UNRWA began to take funds from the international community to address the needs of refugees in Arab states such as Jordan, Lebanon, and Iraq, Israel quietly absorbed 800,000 Jewish refugees who were exiled from Arab states.[2] The Israelis never asked for UN assistance in absorbing their refugees.

Over time, America somehow allowed itself to become UNRWA's leading donor. From 1950 to 2018, American taxpayers contributed more than $6 billion (not accounting for inflation) even as legislators from both parties raised concerns about the agency. UNRWA's most egregious wrongdoings have been reported in Gaza, particularly after the Hamas takeover in 2007. The agency has increasingly appeared to function as a partner to the terrorist group.

Over the years, UNRWA employees have moonlighted as terrorists.[3] Hamas has used UNRWA schools as human shields to store and even fire rockets at Israel.[4] Meanwhile, concerns in Congress have mounted over waste, fraud, and abuse.[5]

For years, UNRWA stonewalled congressional investigations into its distribution of textbooks that promote hatred and incitement against Israel and Jews.[6] In 2018, the Trump administration suspended funding to the agency, citing its vitriolic textbooks.[7] After repeated denials, UNRWA's chief finally acknowledged in 2021 that there was a problem.[8] There really was not much to debate. The agency's curricula refer to Israel as the "enemy," endorse "martyr-dom," and assert that "Jihad is the road to glory."[9]

UNRWA's corruption runs even deeper. The agency today claims 5.6 million people as refugees. That number is difficult to grasp. If there were 800,000 refugees in 1948, how could that number have grown seven-fold while the population in question aged and died?[10] This is mathematically impossible. Yet it is part of how the agency does business — with a definition of refugees that includes descendants and ensures that numbers multiply, thereby guaranteeing that the issue will never be solved.[11] The UN bureaucracy understands this, and it has never demanded reform.

In 2012, then-Senator Mark Kirk of Illinois tried to get to the bottom of UNRWA's dubious statistics. His amendment to an annual spending bill demanded an estimate of people receiving UNRWA services who were personally displaced by the 1948 war.[12] The Obama administration delivered a classified answer in 2015. Subsequent advocates for reform, including US Ambassador to the United Nations Nikki Haley, also pushed for public answers, but to no avail.[13] The State Department guarded that secret up until the very end of the Trump administration.

On January 14, as the Trump administration was set to stand aside for the new Biden team, outgoing Secretary of State Mike Pompeo ended the secrecy. He tweeted, "UNRWA is not a refugee agency; it's estimated <200,000 Arabs displaced in 1948 are still alive and most others are not refugees by any rational criteria."[14] He followed up this tweet with one more: "Taxpayers deserve basic truths: most Palestinians under UNRWA's jurisdiction aren't refugees, and UNRWA is a hurdle to peace. America supports peace and Palestinian human rights; UNRWA supports neither. It's time to end UNRWA's mandate."[15]

In so doing, Pompeo confirmed that out of the more than 5 million people identified as "Palestinian refugees" by UNRWA, fewer than 200,000 (a mere 5 percent of its registered aid recipients) meet the internationally recognized criteria for refugee status.[16] The revelation was not a shock. The numbers never added up. In fact, the number of Palestinians still alive today that meet the criteria for refugee status might be fewer than 30,000, according to some conversations I have had with experts in both the United States and Israel. This was the first time, however, that a high-ranking US official exposed the raw numbers. Until then, one administration after another, Democrat and Republican, had enabled UNRWA to perpetuate its fiction.

UNRWA's fiction does not just waste money. As Pompeo noted, it also poses a significant obstacle to peace. The UN High Commissioner for Refugees, which covers every other refugee on the planet, has a mandate to seek "durable solutions" for refugees under its care, whether through voluntary repatriation, local integration, or third-country resettlement. UNRWA, however, has no such mandate. The agency acknowledges that it "has no authority to seek lasting durable solutions for refugees," including resettlement in third countries.[17]

As a result, generation after generation of Palestinians — millions of people — are doomed to remain in refugee purgatory, stuck between a new life and the "right of return" promised by radical factions intent on fighting unending wars with Israel.[18] Even Palestinian leaders privately recognize that this "right of return" is unrealistic.[19] But it remains a key sticking point in Israeli-Palestinian negotiations. In this way, rather than helping to solve the problem, UNRWA exacerbates it.

Yet in April 2021, just weeks before the Gaza war, President Biden restored US funding to the agency.[20] The president never justified the move. He never explained why America should support more than 5 million people through a refugee agency if fewer than 200,000 of them are actual refugees. Moreover, he never explained why the State Department's refugee bureau would oversee UNRWA if most of the individuals on its registry are not refugees.

For years, my colleague Richard Goldberg, who worked for Kirk on the Hill and then later for the Trump White House, has advocated a shake-up. The goal is not to zero out US assistance for the Palestinian populations currently supported by UNRWA. Rather, Congress and the administration need to work with regional actors to find bilateral solutions. America can work with the countries that currently host UNRWA operations to shift the funds and ensure direct assistance for destitute Palestinians. But as Goldberg and I noted in *The Wall Street Journal* in February 2021, right now "there are no technical teams from the U.S. Agency for International Development or other federal agencies designing programs, projects, or budgets to help Palestinians registered with UNRWA achieve economic independence. In other words, there are no plans to improve their lives. That needs to change."[21]

We also argued, "American oversight of the UN must also change. When the U.S. contributes to UN agencies, it often takes a seat on the board to exercise basic oversight. UNRWA, however, has no board of governors and no oversight."[22]

The urgent need for reform and oversight became increasingly obvious in the wake of the 2021 Gaza war. The drama began when Matthias Schmale, UNRWA's director of operations in Gaza, told Israel's Channel 12 that IDF operations during the war were carried out with "sophistication" and "precision."²³ In so doing, he seemed to confirm that Israel operated within the bounds of international law during the war. Schmale also noted, to the surprise of the Israeli anchor interviewing him, that "[d]uring the 11 days of war, we did not run out of . . . medical supplies, food, or water." Finally, Schmale admitted that UNRWA "cannot work in a place like Gaza without coordinating with the local authorities [Hamas]; that's true for any autocratic regime of this nature."²⁴

Schmale's interview was nothing short of shocking. In one fell swoop, he acknowledged that Israel had taken pains to avoid collateral damage, that it helped ensure the flow of aid to Gaza even as rockets were being fired upon Israeli civilians, and that UNRWA was actively coordinating with Hamas — a terrorist group pursuant to the laws of most Western countries that support his agency. To no one's surprise, Hamas authorities soon declared Schmale *persona non grata* in the Gaza Strip.²⁵

But the controversy did not end there. On June 4, the agency issued a statement asserting that the Israeli Air Force had conducted airstrikes on an UNRWA school in Gaza between May 13 and 15. While noting that nobody was killed or injured, the agency chided Israel for attacking a UN installation. However, the statement also went on to note something very damning to Hamas and to UNRWA itself.

> While investigating how to secure the building from the missile, a detailed assessment on 31 May 2021 revealed what appears to be a cavity and a possible tunnel, at the location of the missile strike. The depth of the cavity is approximately 7.5 meters below the surface of the school. UNRWA discovered the existence of a possible tunnel in the context of the investigation of the fired

missile. There is no indication of the existence of any entry or exit points for the tunnel within the premises.

UNRWA condemns the existence and potential use by Palestinian armed groups of such tunnels underneath its schools in the strongest possible terms. It is unacceptable that students and staff be placed at risk in such a way.

UNRWA demands that all parties desist from any activities or conduct that put beneficiaries and staff at risk and undermine the ability of UNRWA staff to provide assistance to Palestine refugees in safety and security. . . Letters of protest regarding this incident have been sent to both parties.[26]

After years of Israeli accusations that were repeatedly denied, UNRWA had finally admitted that one of its schools was being used as a human shield for Hamas military tunnels. In August, the agency announced that it was investigating reports that ten staffers were promoting hatred and Hamas propaganda.[27] Days later, UNRWA complained that Hamas was preventing UN bomb disposal units from inspecting a school under which commando tunnels had been built.[28] At this point, there is no denying that UNRWA has a Hamas problem.

Awkwardly, these revelations came just as the international effort was underway to provide hundreds of millions of dollars to reconstruct the Gaza Strip. UNRWA was set to receive significant funds to that end. Could the organization find ways to bypass Hamas?[29] My former FDD colleague Julia Schulman was not convinced. Writing for *The National Interest*, she noted that UNRWA "doesn't consider Gaza's violent extremist groups to be terrorist organizations. Not even Hamas." She called on "Congress to ensure that aid doesn't flow to Palestinian terrorist groups, by holding both the State Department and the United Nations to account."[30]

Will Congress take those steps? If the Hamas Caucus has anything to say about it, probably not. Thankfully, the center of gravity in Congress remains clear-eyed about Hamas and other terrorist groups — at least for now. One can only hope that Washington will take steps to prevent Hamas military infrastructure from being rebuilt.

EIGHTEEN
REGIONAL PEACE BECKONS

Beyond reforming UNRWA, additional progress toward peace can be made if America continues to promote normalization between Israel and its Arab neighbors. Significant strides have already been made in that direction. In 1978, Israel made peace with Egypt. In 1994, Israel signed a peace agreement with Jordan. Then came the Abraham Accords in August and September 2020. The first two countries to sign were the United Arab Emirates and Bahrain. Sudan and Morocco followed soon thereafter.[1] With these four deals, a rare sense of optimism washed over the Middle East. Even amidst a devastating year marked by the COVID-19 crisis, the Trump administration had somehow persuaded these Arab states to end more than 70 years of needless hostility toward Israel.

Many in Israel believed that these agreements signaled that the Arab world had given up on the Palestinian cause. The Israelis hoped that their new allies might convey tough love to the Palestinians in both the West Bank and Gaza, with the message that it is time to end their longstanding conflict with Israel. The Israelis hoped that the Arab states would tell both Hamas and Fatah that their calls to conquer Israel must be seen for what they are: unrealistic, even reckless. The Israelis hoped that the Arab states might even help dismantle UNRWA.

Perhaps that was too optimistic. The decision to normalize relations with Israel meant that these countries were less inclined to view the Palestinian issue as a priority than in years past. This did not mean that they would renounce Palestinian nationalism or slaughter some of the movement's sacred cows. These Arab states were simply tired of letting the issue dominate their political and economic agendas, particularly when so many other challenges and threats beckoned.

In addition to the very clear and tangible benefits of security, intelligence, and economic cooperation with Israel, these states also hoped the very act of strengthening ties between the Arab states and Israel could help push the two-state agenda forward. The more countries that de-emphasized historical Palestinian claims and narratives on the path to normalizing with Israel, the more the Palestinians would likely feel the pressure to negotiate and compromise. At the same time, the more Israel drew closer to Arab states, the more Israel would value their advice on the Palestinian issue.

In past bouts of violence stemming from the Arab-Israeli conflict, many Arab leaders deliberately or inadvertently enabled Palestinian intransigence. They reflexively lashed out at Israel with populist statements that resonated among their people but rarely contributed to the cause of peace or coexistence. Worse, Arab leaders ignored a core cause of the violence. They ignored Iran's role as the primary state sponsor of the terrorist groups that targeted Israel.

In fact, the threat from Iran was an important reason why the four Arab states (with the possible exception of Morocco) decided to engage in diplomacy with Israel in 2020. The United Arab Emirates and Bahrain, in particular, had grown increasingly alarmed over Iran's pursuit of nuclear weapons, not to mention its support for terrorism across the Middle East. Sudan, after four decades of Iranian manipulation that earned Khartoum a US designation as a State Sponsor of Terrorism in 1993, had only recently experienced a change in leadership and decided to rejoin the international community.[2] These countries looked to Israel, the country with the strongest military capabilities in the Middle East, as an important ally to counter the region's foremost destabilizing force.

Hamas predictably did not appreciate these developments. In a direct shot at the United Arab Emirates and Bahrain just before the war erupted, Khaled Meshal, Hamas' former Politburo chief and current diaspora director, called countries that normalized with Israel "worthless scum," adding that they had "lost their conscience" and no longer belong to the Islamic nation.[3] Some UAE officials were defiant. Notably, Lieutenant General Dhai Khalfan Tamim of the Dubai police department said Hamas could "go to Iran and let them help you. Go to hell."[4]

With the Gaza war of 2021, these new diplomatic relations faced a significant test. Nevertheless, as one senior Emirati official stated during a July briefing, "they did not fail."[5]

At the onset of the crisis, all four countries — the United Arab Emirates, Bahrain, Morocco, and Sudan — criticized Israel. Khartoum rebuked Israeli moves as "coercive action." Abu Dhabi called on Israel to "take responsibility for de-escalation" at the Al-Aqsa Mosque. Morocco's King Mohammed VI noted that Israeli "violations" could "fuel tensions." Bahrain punched the hardest, calling upon the Israeli government "to stop these rejected provocations against the people of Jerusalem."[6]

Gulf states that were widely believed to be considering diplomatic ties with Israel also weighed in. Saudi Arabia condemned

Israel's "flagrant violations" during the war and called on Israel to end its "dangerous escalation."[7] Oman, which hosted Israeli Prime Minister Benjamin Netanyahu in 2018,[8] also rebuked Israel, stating that the sultanate "salutes the resilience of the Palestinian people and their legitimate struggle and calls for achieving peace based on international legitimacy and a two-state solution."[9]

Kuwait, a country known for its rather strident parliamentary rhetoric against Israel but also seen as a possible candidate for normalization, initially took a relatively mild stance but later issued a second, tougher statement following a public outcry.[10] Kuwaitis subsequently staged a sit-in outside parliament to voice their support for the Palestinians, chanting "no to normalization" with the Jewish state.[11]

The visuals of Israeli airstrikes in Gaza certainly elicited a visceral reaction from many Arab observers, including those who supported normalization. Some Arab contacts of mine from the Gulf expressed anger over some of Israel's social media messaging during the war. In particular, they found one tweet objectionable because it cited the Quran to justify Israel's military response against Hamas.[12]

All this underscored that change does not happen rapidly in the Middle East. Official change may have come quickly with the signing of the Abraham Accords. That did not mean, however, that attitudes about the Palestinian-Israeli conflict itself were going to change overnight.

What was more disconcerting: The Arab states barely criticized Iran for providing Hamas with the rockets, training, cash, and other assistance that the terror group required to prepare for the May 2021 conflict. If these Arab states had normalized relations with Israel as a means to counter Iran and its proxies, they had an odd way of showing it.

For Saudi Arabia and the United Arab Emirates, the silence was especially puzzling. Iran was not their only concern. Both view Hamas with utter disdain because it is a splinter faction of the Muslim Brotherhood.[13] Riyadh and Abu Dhabi both designated the Muslim Brotherhood as a terrorist organization in 2014.[14] Hamas' relationship with Qatar did not help matters. The tiny Gulf emirate's neighbors had singled it out over the previous four years for supporting terrorism.[15]

In the end, the silence of the Gulf states regarding Iranian support for Hamas most likely stemmed from their fears of provoking anti-government or pro-Hamas sentiments at home. They may even have feared rejuvenating domestic extremist groups that had recently been dormant but likely have not disappeared. This would explain why the Arab regimes in places such as Morocco, Bahrain, and Sudan tolerated or even encouraged protests.[16] Across these protests, the rhetoric was vehemently anti-Israel and supportive of the Palestinians. Still, in a potentially positive sign, overt support for Hamas was not prominent.

Interestingly, a dichotomy emerged online. The hashtag "Jerusalem is my cause" trended on Moroccan social media.[17] But in the United Arab Emirates and Saudi Arabia, the governments appeared to be trying to cool flaring tempers, with the hashtag "Palestine is not our cause" trending in both countries.[18] It appeared to be an effort to defend the normalization agreements signed by the United Arab Emirates and Bahrain. In not-for-attribution conversations I had with diplomats from these countries after the conflict subsided, it was apparent that the Gulf Arab leaders were pleased to see the Israeli-Palestinian issue recede.

A particularly positive message came out of the United Arab Emirates. Ali al-Nuaimi, the chairman of the defense affairs, interior, and foreign relations committee of the UAE Federal National

Council, published an article in *Newsweek* after the war. In the piece, he asserted that the "Palestinian people's rights and hopes have been hijacked by Hamas to serve an Iranian agenda." He called upon the rest of the region to work together to sideline Iran and its proxies.[19]

Bahrain's foreign minister also had a positive message, which he shared with the American Jewish Committee in June. "Hopefully, the people of the region can see the benefits, and, in particular, the Israelis and Palestinians can see the benefit of the peace," he said. For Bahrainis, he said, "the most important benefit is that the values of the Bahrainis are being really recognized. We are sending the message from a small nation, saying that peace is the way forward." He concluded, "We need the international community to convince Iran that it cannot prosper by trying to subvert and undermine other countries."[20]

In one troubling sign from Morocco, however, the country's Islamist prime minister hosted Hamas leader Ismael Haniyeh in Rabat in mid-June.[21] Still, a Moroccan official told me after the conflict that the country was trying to get back to the business of normalization with Israel.[22] Although the prime minister had sent a letter of support to Hamas during the war, the kingdom would not permit him to do so on official letterhead. Instead, he was forced to use the Islamist Justice and Development Party's letterhead.[23] The overtures to Hamas did little to dissuade Israel from pursuing deeper ties with Rabat. In August, Yair Lapid, Israel's new foreign minister, visited the country, where he signed three separate agreements, and opened full diplomatic ties between the two countries.[24]

For its part, the Sudanese government officially welcomed the end of the war.[25] During the conflict, the president of Sudan's transitional Sovereignty Council asserted that "normalization has nothing to do with Palestinians' right to create their own state," stressing that the Israel-Sudan normalization agreement represented "a reconciliation with the international community which includes Israel."[26] After the war, he also boldly declared that Sudan had ruled out resuming ties with Iran, noting that his country viewed the Islamic Republic as a "security threat."[27]

The war demonstrated that the Palestinian issue is still an emotional one for the Arabs. The Arab world has decidedly not given up on Palestinian nationalism. At the same time, the new diplomatic relations between Israel and four Arab states weathered the storm.

NINETEEN
IRAN LOOMS

On September 9, 2015, the Obama administration's Treasury Department designated four Hamas financial facilitators and a company controlled by one of them. It was part of Treasury's ongoing efforts to combat terrorism finance through targeted financial sanctions. Included in the designation was Saleh al-Arouri, the head of Hamas' military operations in the West Bank, who was also heavily involved in the organization's fundraising.[1] The announcement of the Treasury action revealed quite a bit about Arouri's operations over the years. It also included new information about Hamas' relationship with Iran.

Specifically, the press release noted that a Saudi-based Hamas financier named Mahir Jawad Yunis Salah had "overseen the transfer of tens of millions of dollars from Iran to Saudi Arabia to fund the Izzedine al-Qassam Brigades and Hamas activity in Gaza."[2]

The timing of the designation was perhaps the most notable thing about it. The announcement came less than two months after the Obama administration had agreed to the 2015 Iran nuclear deal, or JCPOA. The United States was set to enter into the agreement in October of that year, with no small amount of controversy. During the deal's negotiations, which began in 2013, the United States provided roughly $700 million per month to keep Iran at the negotiating table.[3] The 2015 deal would also provide Iran with billions more in sanctions relief. In other words, Washington was about to provide the world's most prolific state sponsor of terrorism with a significant financial windfall.

In the years between the 2013 interim nuclear deal and the finalized agreement, there were ample signs of Iranian assistance to Hamas. In 2013, a former IRGC officer serving as speaker of Iran's parliament met with Imad al-Alami,[4] the terror group's representative to Tehran and a key figure in procuring funds and weapons for Hamas.[5] The US Treasury Department had designated Alami in 2003 for his role as a senior Hamas leader.[6]

The following year, in a letter regarding that year's Gaza conflict, Major General Qassem Soleimani, the commander of the IRGC's expeditionary Quds Force who was killed in a 2020 US air strike, described the leaders of Hamas as "my dear brothers" and reaffirmed Iran's support for the group.[7] Iran was widely identified as an important source of support for Hamas during that war.

After the JCPOA was finalized and implemented, the Obama administration sent Iran $400 million in cash in January 2016, along with another $1.3 billion later that year.[8] All told, the Islamic Republic was conservatively estimated to have reaped $100 billion in direct sanctions relief and other concessions.[9] And that does not even include the tens of billions of dollars in indirect sanctions relief granted through the lifting or waiving of sanctions that enabled the Islamic Republic to re-enter energy and commercial markets.

The JCPOA's end result was certainly not a permanent halt to Tehran's nuclear program. As my colleague Mark Dubowitz observed, the deal granted Iran "patient pathways" to nuclear weapons. Key restrictions were designed to fade away. Meanwhile, the regime could expand its missile program, fortify its regional position, and buttress its economy against future American pressure. Dubowitz has for years warned of the JCPOA's "lethal end state," in which future US administrations and Israeli governments will have to confront a much more dangerous Iran.[10]

That is not all. Thanks to the deal, Iran was able to increase its ability to fund terrorism worldwide. That is what made Treasury's September 2015 designation of Hamas financiers so strange. As the JCPOA opened the financial floodgates to Iran, the targeted sanctions seemed like a fool's errand.

At the time, I tried but failed to confirm with contacts inside the US government that funds were flowing to Hamas. The best I could do was confirm that Iran had sent funds to Yemen's Houthi rebels, another terrorist proxy of Iran.[11] This was just an indication of how American sanctions relief would make it easier for Iran to fund other violent groups around the region.

However, Iran's windfall was fleeting. The funds stopped flowing in 2018 when Trump unilaterally withdrew from the JCPOA.[12] It was hard to gauge exactly how much terrorism infrastructure Iran was able to underwrite during the two years the JCPOA was in force. It was even harder to zero in on the support to Hamas. Until 2019, that is.

In August 2019, the Treasury Department issued another terrorism designation, this time targeting "financial facilitators responsible for moving tens of millions of dollars between Iran's Islamic Revolutionary Guard Corps-Quds Force (IRGC-QF) and

HAMAS's operational arm, the Izz-Al-Din Al-Qassam Brigades in Gaza." A key figure in all of this was Muhammed Sarur, who served as a "middle-man between the IRGC-QF and HAMAS and worked with Hezbollah operatives to ensure funds were provided to the Izz-Al-Din Al-Qassam Brigades." But one line in the announcement was particularly important. Treasury noted that "in the past four years, the IRGC-QF transferred over U.S. $200 million dollars to the Izz-Al-Din Al-Qassam Brigades."[13]

In short, Iran remained an important patron for the terrorist group. It was not particularly hard to understand that Iran, if given more cash, would continue to fund Hamas in Gaza. In fact, in May 2020, Iran's supreme leader stated, "Iran realized Palestinian fighters' only problem was lack of access to weapons. With divine guidance and assistance, we planned, and the balance of power has been transformed in Palestine, and today the Gaza Strip can stand against the aggression of the Zionist enemy and defeat it."[14] A few months later, Israel seized a $4 million payment facilitated by Gaza businessman Zuhir Shamalach, who was attempting to funnel the money from Iran to Hamas.[15]

Heading into the Gaza war of 2021, relations between Israel and the United States were once again tense. Biden had hired many of the key figures from the 2015 JCPOA negotiations, looking to re-enter the deal.[16] The Israelis were unabashedly opposed to the JCPOA, as they had been the first time around. Their reason: America's role in the renewed deal would again include billions of dollars in sanctions relief for the Islamic Republic, in exchange for only temporary nuclear concessions.

Worse still from Israel's perspective, the administration was weighing the possibility of removing terrorism sanctions against Iran to provide additional incentives for the Islamic Republic to re-enter the deal. Such a move — ignoring the evidence that originally resulted in those terrorism designations — would be tantamount to a permanent green light to terror financiers in Iran and beyond.[17]

The very fact that these considerations were on the table as Israel battled Hamas for 11 days in May undermined the notion that Washington could play a productive role in charting the future of Gaza-Israel ties. In fact, if the United States rejoined the Iran deal, there was no denying that Washington would be funding both parties in a future conflict. With one hand, the United States would be providing $3.8 billion per year to Israel, primarily in military assistance. With the other, America would be providing tens or even hundreds of billions of dollars in financial incentives and sanctions relief to Hamas' most important financial patron.[18]

During the 2021 Gaza war, Iran did not try to hide its patronage of Hamas and other terrorist groups. The regime's supreme leader openly cheered on Hamas.[19] General Esmail Qaani of the IRGC's Quds Force called Hamas leader Ismail Haniyeh to offer moral support.[20] Qaani also lauded Hamas military chief Mohammed Deif, calling him a "living martyr."[21] After the ceasefire, Haniyeh thanked "the Islamic Republic of Iran, [which] did not hold back with money, weapons and technical support."[22] An IRGC statement warned that "in the future the Zionists can expect to endure deadly blows from within the occupied territories."[23]

Iran's fingerprints were certainly seen on weaponry throughout the May 2021 conflict. A rocket variant fired by PIJ, the Badr-3, was identified as being of Iranian origin. In fact, a PIJ spokesman, in announcing the use of the rocket, thanked "the Axis of Resistance, headed by the Islamic Republic of Iran, which has been generous with us in every aspect."[24] In addition, Hamas' aerial[25] and underwater[26] drones were believed to be of Iranian origin. The tunnels in the Hamas Metro were also suspected to have been built with significant Iranian financial or even technical assistance.[27]

Yet one month after the Gaza war ended, Biden administration officials were in Vienna negotiating with regime officials, working hard to convince the Islamic Republic to resume compliance with the JCPOA. The administration warned that Iran was getting dangerously close to a nuclear weapon.[28] White House officials insisted that the deal was the best way to curb these nuclear ambitions. Curiously, the Biden administration said little about how the deal might impact the Islamic Republic's ability to support terrorism.

With negotiations in limbo, Iranian president Hassan Rouhani left office, making way for Ebrahim Raisi. In August, Hamas dispatched Politburo chief Ismail Haniyeh to attend the inauguration of the new Iranian president.[29] In a meeting that included Hezbollah and other Iranian-backed terrorist groups, Raisi vowed his country's continued support.[30]

The Iran debate has raged in Washington and around the Middle East for the better part of a decade. Iran continues to advance its nuclear ambitions. Sometimes it walks slowly. Sometimes it sprints. Throughout the entire saga, it has always supported terrorist groups. These proxies, along with the nuclear program, constitute core elements of the regime's hegemonic design on the Middle East. The Islamic Republic seeks to control the territory stretching from its own borders, through Iraq and Syria, and on to the Mediterranean coastline. Hamas is part of this plan. So is the destruction of Israel. The United States has not seriously addressed any of this amid many rounds of diplomacy.

This context is crucial to understanding the intermittent wars that erupt in Gaza. To be sure, the Palestinian desire to establish an independent state also plays a role. However, to ignore Iran's regional designs and patronage of terrorist groups is to ignore the most important aspect of a conflict that Washington says it hopes to end.

CONCLUSION

Sitting in the office of a senior IDF official on June 20, I looked out over the bustling city of Tel Aviv. It was hard to believe that a month had passed since the war had ended. The country was back to normal. There was a new government in place, led by Prime Minster Naftali Bennett. With hospitalizations on the rise, he appeared more concerned with the Delta variant of the coronavirus than the recent Gaza war. Hamas seemed like a distant memory.

In the *Kiriya*, Israel's defense ministry building, security officials were wrestling once again with the question of Iran. Between the nuclear negotiations and the WBW, officials had their hands full. When the moment was right, I finally asked my interlocutor for his assessment of the Gaza war. Without hesitation, he admitted that although Israel achieved nearly all its military objectives, Hamas had "exploited the moment strategically."[1]

He offered five specific ways the group did so. First, the group walked away from the conflict after generating the impression that it had defended the Al-Aqsa Mosque. Second, because of this perception, Hamas succeeded in making the conflict a religious one. Third, Hamas was able to effectively erase Mahmoud Abbas and the PA from the Palestinian-Israeli equation. Fourth, Hamas was able to ride the wave of the Arab-Israeli riots, making it seem as if Arab-Israelis were more connected to the violent extremist group than to the sovereign state that granted them the rights and citizenship that they had long enjoyed — albeit with reservations. Finally, Hamas was able to put Israel's center — the region around Tel Aviv — under more rocket fire than ever before.[2]

Some might debate this assessment. However, even one of these achievements would constitute a significant win for Hamas. "It was a win for us tactically," the official said. "But it was a loss strategically. Strategic communications is our weakest point."[3]

Looking to the future, my interlocutor noted that there will almost certainly be future Hamas technological advances that will challenge Israel. These include PGMs, cruise missiles with a "depleted trajectory" that hug the ground, more advanced drones, and other high-tech weaponry that Iran is expected to provide.[4] In other words, the Gaza wars will get nastier over time.

Two days later, after a dusty tour of the Gaza border area, I found myself sitting in the war room at IDF Southern Command. It was eerily quiet. I was briefed by a young officer whose job is to stand watch, monitoring the reports of Hamas activity that pour in from across the Israeli bureaucracy. The silence of the room was interrupted only occasionally by a brief siren indicating activity close to the high-tech barrier. She seemed not even to notice.

She told me that during the run-up to the war, in marked contrast to the silence of the room during my visit, the room was packed with personnel and the system was blinking red. The many television screens and computers organized in pods across the room, now turned off, were all switched on, with dozens of officers tracking an astounding array of imminent threats. The woman said that two days before the conflict, they could clearly discern that violence would soon erupt.[5] The highly efficient and digital nature of the room was what struck me most. The Israelis, at least for now, have the threats out of Gaza down to a science. They derive no joy from this. It is simply a matter of need, perhaps even survival.

This became even more clear to me as I sat down with Eliezer Toledano for dinner that evening. Todelano is the general in charge of the Southern Command. He underscored that Gaza is a "lost district" of the PA. In fact, most people forget that the PA took control of Gaza and Jericho first before expanding its authority to other parts of the West Bank, pursuant to the Oslo Accords.[6] Today, the PA still tries to claim sovereignty there, but Palestinian President Mahmoud Abbas cannot step foot in the territory, for fear of violence against him.

Toledano noted that there are five problems (Israeli officials apparently like to make lists of five) that make Gaza a terrible conundrum: Terror, internal divisions, a civilian crisis, the diversion of international aid toward terrorism, and the territory's undesirability among the other regional players.[7] This last point is vital to underscore. Nobody wants Gaza. Egypt occupied the territory during the 1948–1949 Arab-Israeli war. Then Egypt lost it to Israel in 1967. After two intifadas and numerous other challenges, Israel quit the territory in 2005 with the hope of handing it over to a future Palestinian state. Hamas forcibly conquered the enclave in 2007 and has since invested little in its development to benefit the suffering population. Instead, the terror group has turned the territory into a perpetual battleground for conflict with Israel.

Despite its utter undesirability, Gaza holds real importance for the Middle East. First and foremost, it has become part of the

Islamic Republic's hegemonic designs on the region. It will be important to remove Iran's influence from this territory as part of a broader policy to minimize the influence of the world's foremost state sponsor of terrorism across the region. Nuclear diplomacy that yields Tehran massive sanctions relief is certainly not the answer. Yet this is exactly the policy that the Biden administration was determined to pursue. Should it continue down this path, more intense violence in the Gaza Strip is a foregone conclusion.

But Iran is not the only malign influence on this territory. The Muslim Brotherhood's top patrons, Qatar and Turkey (along with Malaysia to a lesser extent), see an opportunity to extend their influence in Gaza. This must also be countered. Currently, the United States has a policy of looking the other way. Turkey remains in the NATO tent, with no prospects of being removed. Qatar maintains the largest US airbase in the Middle East, affording Doha significant leverage with the Pentagon. As a result, this issue is never aired publicly. It is not even clear that it is discussed privately.

Right now, the only Arab actors actively trying to mitigate Iranian, Turkish, and Qatari influence in Gaza are Egypt and the United Arab Emirates. Both are better alternatives to the current malign influences in Gaza. However, their strategy is not particularly well-coordinated. Moreover, both countries have adopted a soft-power approach, which will not easily undermine Hamas anytime soon.

Gaza also carries obvious significance for the Palestinian national project. After a somewhat promising decade in the 1990s, that project collapsed. The demise of the peace process in 2000 was only part of the problem. Hamas' military takeover of Gaza signaled an end to Palestinian political unity, rendering the territory a breakaway republic that has made it impossible to proceed with diplomatic efforts to achieve a two-state solution. The PA, in its current weakened state, has zero chance of retaking Gaza. It simply lacks the political credibility (evidenced by growing anti-PA protests in the month following the war), and its military capabilities, even with American training, are no match for the brutality and zeal of Iran-backed Hamas.

If anything, under the current circumstances, a three-state solution (Israel, the West Bank under the PA, and Hamas-controlled Gaza) appears to be the only path forward. Such a scenario, with Hamas in a continuous state of war with Israel, will not offer much of a future for the Palestinian national project. If anything, it all but guarantees that the Palestinian-Israeli conflict will continue to limp along, with no diplomatic solution in sight.

There are some who suggest that Hamas might someday moderate. A peace deal, they say, is the aspirin for this headache. However, Hamas has yet to indicate a willingness to reverse course on its *raison d'etre*: the destruction of Israel. So long as Hamas holds fast to its charter and continues diverting international assistance to finance rockets, drones, tunnels, and military training, one should expect no change.

The lack of prospects for change in Gaza portends poorly for the security of the surrounding Middle Eastern countries, apart from Israel, such as Egypt, Jordan, and Lebanon. Despite some encouraging developments in regional diplomacy in recent years, Hamas keeps the Middle East simmering on a low flame every day, with the possibility of conflagration at any time. As the United States looks to pivot toward a policy of countering revisionist powers such as Russia and China, putting the war against terrorism in the rearview mirror, the Gaza problem will remain.

For some in Washington, and certainly for the Hamas Caucus, it may be easy to saddle Israel with the blame. For others, it may be tempting to ask Israel to simply solve this problem. Neither approach makes sense. Israel cannot easily find a political solution. If it could, it would have done so already. Nor can it ignore the military provocations of Hamas and other terrorist groups. When the country comes under assault, no fewer than nine million people rely on the IDF to neutralize those threats. Nor can Israel simply lift the restrictions that it currently has in place to limit the increasingly lethal weaponry, supplied mostly by Tehran, that continues to flow into this Hamas-controlled territory. The Israeli people rely on the IDF to ensure that Hamas fails to acquire the means to mount a significant threat.

It would be wonderful if the United Nations could step in. However, the US-led international order is under significant strain. The United Nations is buckling under the weight of Chinese and Russian malign influence. The UN Human Rights Council, not to mention UNRWA, is interested only in vilifying the Israelis for conflicts that they do not initiate but to which they ultimately have no choice but to respond.

It would also be heartening if the pragmatic Arab states could provide economic, diplomatic, or other assistance. On that front, Israel's new peace partners in the United Arab Emirates, Bahrain, Sudan, and Morocco would be ideal candidates. However, convincing these countries to commit to fixing Gaza is no small feat. It is unclear how motivated they are to engage. After all, Hamas currently sees them as traitors. Moreover, their goals in normalizing with Israel were to work with Israel to counter the region's bad actors and to boost their own economies. Solving one of the world's thorniest conflicts is probably low on their list of priorities.

As of this writing, the only country willing to engage seriously appears to be Egypt. After successfully brokering an end to the May 2021 conflict, Cairo set about working to establish a more permanent solution. However, Egypt has a tough road ahead. The United States remains engaged, albeit without the focus or zest of previous administrations, along with a host of European and Arab nations with disparate regional goals.

Egyptian diplomats are now shuttling back and forth between Hamas and Israel to reach a long-term ceasefire.

Israel wants the terror group to end its rocket fire and return the Israeli citizens and remains of fallen Israeli soldiers still in Hamas' hands. The Israelis also want a better system for the provision of aid, to prevent Hamas from using the incoming material for military means.

Hamas, for its part, wants fewer restrictions — hoping to better arm itself for the next round of violence. The group also refuses to allow the issue of prisoners and the remains of fallen soldiers to be connected to the negotiations surrounding a more permanent ceasefire.

Unfortunately, even if Egypt successfully brokers a deal, whatever is agreed upon will almost certainly not hold. Hamas exists to fight Israel. The group's patrons provide funds and other assistance for exactly that reason. War will unfortunately come again.

With few, if any, other options available, the problem falls back on the shoulders of Israel, which is forced to defend itself, time and again. This does not mean that Israel should be given a green light to lay waste to the Gaza Strip. In speaking with a wide range of government and military officials over the last two decades, I have never found that to be Israel's objective. But it does not back down from defending itself. The Israelis should be given all the appropriate military tools needed to neutralize the threats faced from Gaza. This includes assistance on Iron Dome as well as Israel's barrier and perhaps the AI systems that have helped Israel identify and neutralize threats while minimizing collateral damage. Precision-guided munitions, which Israel purchases from the United States, are also important.

To put it another way, America's policy should be one of support for an embattled ally that has consistently gone out of its way both to shorten the length of its conflicts with a brutal terrorist organization and to minimize casualties among the beleaguered Gazan population. Israel does this on its own accord, despite the unjust excoriation from the international community, not to mention the often one-sided coverage of the media and, more recently, the bombastic statements of certain members of Congress. Fortunately, American foreign policy is already geared to support Israel's "qualitative military edge" against its foes in the region. It will be important to sustain this policy, particularly amidst some of the unpredictable shifts occurring in American politics, not to mention the international system.

The fourth Gaza war was the latest installment in a longer conflict that lamentably is likely to continue for many years to come. It was not an extension of the Arab-Israeli conflict. If anything, that conflict is shrinking. Nor was it a typical flare-up in the Palestinian-Israeli conflict. Israel's wars with Hamas are very distinct from the uneasy but pragmatic relations that currently exist between the PA and Israel.

Gaza is now ground zero in a proxy conflict. It is part of a bigger battle between Israel and Iran, along with other determined foes. When conflicts erupt on this small patch of land, journalists and analysts too often offer quick takes or "click bait." But the reporting and analysis require a greater appreciation for the history and political dynamics of a complex region that is too often reduced to the false binary of Israelis vs. Palestinians. The wars in Gaza are far more complex. American policymakers and reporters must come to terms with this, particularly as the United States attempts to exit the Middle East.

This is undeniably a moment of flux for US policymakers. The failed wars of Iraq and Afghanistan have led decision makers and the broader American public to advocate for quitting the entire region. Admittedly, Washington has every reason to pivot away. Two tough decades of failed interventionist policies yielded little for the United States. We have lost thousands of lives and trillions of dollars trying to fix systems that may well be broken beyond repair. These failures have prompted some in Washington to want to negotiate a permanent exit. The effort to re-start the nuclear deal with Iran is a flawed attempt, among several, to leave and not look back. The broader strategy, if one can call it that, is to ignore the malign actors in the region in the hope that they will ignore America in return.

If the United States is to pivot out of the Middle East success-fully, it must conduct a clear-eyed assessment of what can still be achieved with the help of trusted partners. This will require Wash-ington to rely on allies that uphold US interests and are willing to fight for them even when politicos in Washington are not. For that reason alone, Israel remains a valued partner. The country has a unique combination of Western values and advanced military capa-bilities that will ultimately win wars, and also help US warfighters on future battlefields.

In looking back at the history of Israel's battles with Hamas, the country deserves US support. After seven decades of war, Israel continues to fight with restraint — time and again. And it does so with the knowledge that its enemies seek nothing less than its complete destruction.

Policymakers in Washington must remember that Hamas is a persistent threat to regional stability, and the politics of Gaza are a Gordian knot. These are well-armed terrorists who flagrantly violate the laws of war while receiving weapons, cash, and training from state sponsors who cheer for the decline of the American-led world order. This does not mean that Washington must support every Israeli action taken against them. However, it should be clear by now that until a solution arrives, Israel must do what any other country in the world would do: Protect its own.

APPENDIX

AMBASSADOR DANNY DANON
PERMANENT REPRESENTATIVE OF ISRAEL
TO THE UNITED NATIONS

השגריר דני דנון
הנציג הקבוע
של ישראל לאומות המאוחדות

H.E. Ms. Joanna Wronecka
President of the Security Council
United Nations
New York

11 May 2018

Excellency,

I am writing to inform you, once again, of ominous developments that continue to plague our region.

I wish to draw your attention to the strengthening of ties between two internationally recognized terrorist organizations, Hamas and Hezbollah, the Iranian proxy. As I informed you in my letter sent 27 June 2017, Hamas has been colluding with Hezbollah and its sponsor in Tehran to expand its malicious activities beyond Gaza, Judea and Samaria to areas within Lebanon.

The increasing cooperation between Hamas, Hezbollah and Iran constitutes a major threat not only to Israel but to the stability and security of the entire region.

Some of this cooperation has been publicized in pre-announced meetings of high-ranking operatives and statements of mutual support. It is led by Saleh al-Arouri, the Lebanon-based deputy head of Hamas' Politburo, and Saeed Izadi, head of the Palestinian Branch of the Iranian al-Quds Force, both of whom have made no attempt to conceal the growing coordination between Iran, Hezbollah, and Hamas. Furthermore, Iran has publicly declared its commitment to increase its support for Hamas. Iranian military leader, Qassem Soleimani, has even gone as far as to say that all of his country's means and resources are at Hamas' disposal, without precondition, to be used for aggression against Israel.

In addition to their publicly known relationship, Hamas has been building its own military force covertly in Lebanon. Hamas has recruited and trained hundreds of fighters, mostly men of Palestinian origin, and plans to recruit thousands more who will comprise a force that will operate on Hamas' behalf in Lebanon. At the direction of Hamas operative Majid Hader, Hamas has assembled infrastructure in Lebanon ready to manufacture its own missiles and UAVs to add to its war arsenal and increase its offensive capabilities.

The goal of Hamas' activities, both overt and covert, is not just to gain an additional front from which Hamas could launch terrorist attacks against Israel's innocent civilians. Hamas also intends to use its armed force and growing arsenal of rockets to pull Lebanon into conflict with Israel. This intention increases the possibility of a conflict that could engulf the entire Middle East.

AMBASSADOR DANNY DANON
PERMANENT REPRESENTATIVE OF ISRAEL
TO THE UNITED NATIONS

השגריר דני דנון
הנציג הקבוע
של ישראל לאומות המאוחדות

Despite the fact that multiple media outlets have exposed key elements of Hamas' covert activities in recent months, the State of Lebanon has done nothing to combat this additional terrorist entity operating in its territory.

Not only is the Lebanese government neglecting to fulfill its obligations under Security Council Resolutions 1701 and 1559, it is also in flagrant violation of them, legitimizing Hamas and Hezbollah's activities as a result. In light of these developments, the United Nations must remain vigilant to ensure the safety of our region and ensure that all the relevant Security Council resolutions are strictly enforced.

I should be grateful if you would have this letter distributed as an official document of the Security Council. I wish to inform you that an identical letter has been sent to H.E. Mr. António Guterres, Secretary-General of the United Nations.

Please accept, Excellency, the assurance of my highest consideration.

Sincerely,

Danny Danon
Ambassador
Permanent Representative

800 SECOND AVENUE, NEW YORK, NY 10017 ● TEL. (212) 499-5510 ● FAX: (212) 499-5515 ● AMBASSADOR@NEWYORK.MFA.GOV.IL

ENDNOTES

INTRODUCTION

1   The U.S. State Department first designated Hamas as a "Foreign Terrorist Organization" in 1997. See: U.S. Department of State, Bureau of Counterterrorism, "Foreign Terrorist Organizations," accessed July 8, 2021. https://www.state.gov/foreign-terrorist-organizations

2   See: Dennis Ross, *Doomed to Succeed: The U.S.-Israel Relationship from Truman to Obama* (NYC: Farrar, Straus and Giroux, 2015).

3   Sammy Westfall, "Indiscriminate Hamas Rocket Attacks on Israel Are War Crimes, Human Rights Watch Says," *The Washington Post*, August 12, 2021, https://www.washingtonpost.com/world/2021/08/12/hamas-rockets-war-crimes/

4   "Gaza Death Toll 212 with 61 kids, 35 women, 16 elderly killed in Israeli Strikes," *Al Bawaba* (Jordan), May 18, 2021. https://www.albawaba.com/news/gaza-death-toll-212-61-kids-35-women-16-elderly-killed-israeli-strikes-1428047

5   This is "back of the envelop" math. Israel sometimes fires two interceptors at rockets aimed at the Tel Aviv area, or other major population centers, and it declines to fire any at rockets projected to land in uninhabited spaces. I assess that that roughly one interceptor per rocket was deployed, based on conversations I had with Israeli officials.

6   World Bank Group, European Union, and United Nations, "Gaza Rapid Damage and Needs Assessment," June 2021. https://unsco.unmissions.org/sites/default/files/gaza_rapid_damage_and_needs_assessment_july_2021_1.pdf

CHAPTER ONE | NO SINGLE SPARK

1 Bradley Bowman and Joe Truzman, "Tehran's Terror Proxies in Gaza Escalate Attacks on Israeli Civilians," *Foundation for Defense of Democracies*, May 14, 2021. https://www.fdd.org/analysis/2021/05/14/tehrans-terror-proxies-escalate-attacks

2 Michael J. Armstrong, "Gaza's enhanced rocket technology challenges Israel's defences," *The Conversation*, May 17, 2021. https://theconversation.com/gazas-enhanced-rocket-technology-challenges-israels-defences-160853

3 Noga Tarnopolsky, "U.S. closes consulate in Jerusalem that served as the de facto embassy to Palestinians," *Los Angeles Times*, March 4, 2019. https://www.latimes.com/world/la-fg-israel-us-consulate-20190304-story.html

4 Avi Bell and Eugene Kontorovich, "Almost Nothing You've Heard About Evictions in Jerusalem Is True," *The Wall Street Journal*, May 14, 2021. https://www.wsj.com/articles/almost-nothing-youve-heard-about-evictions-in-jerusalem-is-true-11621019410

5 "From TikTok to Temple Mount Clashes: 28 Days of Violence in Jerusalem," *Haaretz* (Israel), May 10, 2021. https://www.haaretz.com/israel-news/.premium.HIGHLIGHT.TIMELINE-from-tiktok-to-riots-a-timeline-of-recent-israeli-palestinian-violence-1.9787700

6 Daniel Siryoti and Efrat Forsher, "17 police officers, 200 Palestinians injured in Temple Mount riots," *Israel Hayom* (Israel), May 8, 2021. https://www.israelhayom.com/2021/05/08/17-police-officers-200-palestinians-injured-in-temple-mount-riots

7 "Tree catches fire outside Jerusalem's al Aqsa mosque, no damage to mosque," *Reuters*, May 10, 2021. https://www.reuters.com/article/us-israel-palestinians-mosque-fire-idCAKBN2CR24V

8 Patrick Kingsley and Isabel Kershner, "After Raid on Aqsa Mosque, Rockets From Gaza and Israeli Airstrikes," *The New York Times*, May 10, 2021. https://www.nytimes.com/2021/05/10/world/middleeast/jerusalem-protests-aqsa-palestinians.html

9 Ibid.

10 Nidal al-Mughrabi and Jeffrey Heller, "Jerusalem violence leads to rockets, air strikes," *Reuters*, May 10, 2021. https://www.reuters.com/world/asia-pacific/violence-erupts-al-aqsa-mosque-israel-marks-jerusalem-day-2021-05-10

11 Patrick Kingsley and Isabel Kershner, "After Raid on Aqsa Mosque, Rockets From Gaza and Israeli Airstrikes," *The New York Times*, May 10, 2021. https://www.nytimes.com/2021/05/10/world/middleeast/jerusalem-protests-aqsa-palestinians.html

12   Luke Hurst, "Sheikh Jarrah: A Small Neighbourhood Making a Big Impact in the Gaza Conflict," *EuroNews* (France), May 20, 2021, https://www.euronews.com/2021/05/20/sheikh-jarrah-a-small-neighbourhood-making-a-big-impact-in-the-gaza-conflict

13   "Iran's Top Commander: Zionists to Come to Senses by Resistance Front," *Fars News Agency* (Iran), April 25, 2021. https://www.farsnews.ir/en/news/14000205000407/Iran%E2%80%99s-Tp-Cmmander-Ziniss-Cme-Senses-by-Resisance-Frn

14   Farnaz Fassihi, "Iran, A Longtime backer of Hamas, Cheers Attacks on Israel," *The New York Times*, May 23, 2021, https://www.nytimes.com/2021/05/23/world/middleeast/iran-israel.html

15   Interview with IDF Southern Command, Mahaneh Ra'im, June 22, 2021.

16   Jonathan Schanzer and David May, "Sheikh Jarrah is the latest 'single point of failure' fiction," *The Jerusalem Post* (Israel), May 18, 2021. https://www.jpost.com/opinion/sheikh-jarrah-is-the-latest-single-point-of-failure-fiction-opinion-668470

17   Suzanne Goldenberg, "Rioting as Sharon visits Islam holy site," *The Guardian* (UK), September 28, 2000. https://www.theguardian.com/world/2000/sep/29/israel

18   "Second Intifada," *Wikipedia*, https://en.wikipedia.org/wiki/Second_Intifada

19   Marcy Oster, "Yasser Arafat planned the second intifada, his widow says," *Jewish Telegraphic Agency*, December 31, 2012. https://www.jta.org/2012/12/31/israel/yasser-arafat-planned-the-second-intifada-his-widow-says

20   Jonathan D. Halevi, "The Palestinian Authority's Responsibility for the Outbreak of the Second Intifada: Its Own Damning Testimony," *Jerusalem Center for Public Affairs*, February 20, 2013. https://jcpa.org/article/the-palestinian-authoritys-responsibility-for-the-outbreak-of-the-second-intifada-its-own-damning-testimony

21   Douglas J. Feith, "The Hebron Riots of 1929: Consequences and Lesson," *Hudson Institute*, August 27, 2019. https://www.hudson.org/research/16088-the-hebron-riots-of-1929-consequences-and-lesson

22   David G. Dalin and John F. Rothmann, *Icon of Evil: Hitler's Mufti and the Rise of Radical Islam* (NYC: Random House, 2008), pages 26–32.

23   "ICC opens 'war crimes' investigation in West Bank and Gaza," *BBC News* (UK), March 3, 2021. https://www.bbc.com/news/world-middle-east-56249927

24   Sunniva Rose, "Shebaa Farms: Why Hezbollah uses Israel's occupation of a tiny strip of land to justify its arsenal," *The National* (UAE), May 6, 2019. https://www.thenationalnews.com/world/mena/shebaa-farms-why-hezbollah-uses-israel-s-occupation-of-a-tiny-strip-of-land-to-justify-its-arsenal-1.857998

CHAPTER TWO | THE ORIGINS OF HAMAS

1   Literally, "shaking off."

2   Mark Tessler, *A History of the Israeli-Palestinian Conflict* (Bloomington, IN: Indiana University Press, 1994), pages 678–679.

3   Michel Jubran and Laura Drake, "The Islamic Fundamentalist Movement in the West Bank and Gaza Strip," *Middle East Policy*, Volume 2, Number 2, 1993, page 7. Available at: https://onlinelibrary.wiley.com/doi/10.1111/j.1475-4967.1993.tb00068.x

4   Ben Lynfield, "Hamas Plans Rally to Mark its Birthday," *United Press International*, December 13, 1994. https://www.upi.com/Archives/1994/12/13/Hamas-plans-rally-to-mark-its-birthday/4504787294800

5   Azzam Tamimi, *Hamas: A History From Within* (Northampton, MA: Olive Branch Press, 2007), page 53.

6   Matthew Levitt, *Hamas: Politics, Charity and Terrorism in the Service of Jihad* (New Haven, CT: Yale University Press, 2006), page 24.

7   Michel Jubran and Laura Drake, "The Islamic Fundamentalist Movement in the West Bank and Gaza Strip," *Middle East Policy*, Volume 2, Number 2, 1993, page 7. Available at: https://onlinelibrary.wiley.com/doi/10.1111/j.1475-4967.1993.tb00068.x

8   "Hamas Charter Totally Rejects Israel and Zionism – 1988," Center for Israel Education, https://israeled.org/hamas-charter-totally-rejects-israel-and-zionism/

9   "Palestine National Council: The Palestinian National Charter (July 1968)," The Philos Project, https://philosproject.org/wp-content/uploads/2020/09/The-Palestinian-National-Charter.theisraelarabreader.pdf

10   Mark Tessler, *A History of the Israeli-Palestinian Conflict* (Bloomington, IN: Indiana University Press, 1994), page 722.

11   Hamas, "Hamas operations -The Glory Record," accessed August 4, 2021. Archived version available at: https://web.archive.org/web/19990826061916/http://www.palestine-info.net/hamas/index.htm

12   Zaki Chehab, *Inside Hamas: The Untold Story of the Militant Islamic Movement* (NYC: Nation Books, 2007), page 15.

13   Sean Durns, "1989 and the rise of Hamas," *The Jerusalem Post* (Israel), December 22, 2019. https://www.jpost.com/opinion/1989-and-the-rise-of-hamas-611745

14   Zaki Chehab, *Inside Hamas: The Untold Story of the Militant Islamic Movement* (NYC: Nation Books, 2007), page 41.

15   Anoushiravan Ehteshami and Raymond A. Hinnebush, *Syria and Iran: Middle Powers in a Penetrated Regional System* (NYC: Routledge, 1997), pages 43 and 185.

16   Elie Rekhess, "The Terrorist Connection – Iran, the Islamic Jihad and Hamas," *Justice*, Vol. 5, May 1995, https://fas.org/irp/world/para/docs/950500.htm

17   J. Millard Burr and Robert O. Collins, *Sudan in Turmoil: Hasan al-Turabi and the Islamist State* (Princeton, NJ: Markus Winer Publishers, 2010), page 85.

18   Meir Hatina, *Islam and Salvation in Palestine*, Dayan Center Papers Number 127 (Tel Aviv: The Moshe Dayan Center for Middle Eastern and African Studies, 2001), page 83.

19   For more, see: Ezzedeen Al-Qassam Brigades Information Office, "Ezzedeen Al-Qassam Brigades," accessed July 8, 2021. https://en.alqassam.ps/page/1

20   Azzam Tamimi, *Hamas: A History From Within* (Northampton, MA: Olive Branch Press, 2007), page 75.

21   J. Millard Burr and Robert O. Collins, *Sudan in Turmoil: Hasan al-Turabi and the Islamist State* (Princeton, NJ: Markus Winer Publishers, 2010), page 85.

22   Zaki Chehab, *Inside Hamas: The Untold Story of the Militant Islamic Movement* (NYC: Nation Books, 2007), page 142.

23   See: E. O'Ballance, *Islamic Fundamentalist Terrorism* (Basingstoke: Macmillan Press, 1996), page 133.

24   Clyde Haberman, "Israel Expels 400 From Occupied Lands; Lebanese Deploy to Bar Entry of Palestinians," *The New York Times*, December 18, 1992. https://www.nytimes.com/1992/12/18/world/israel-expels-400-occupied-lands-lebanese-deploy-bar-entry-palestinians.html

25   Rafael D. Frankel, "Israel troubled that war in Lebanon drove its enemies closer," *The Christian Science Monitor*, September 22, 2006. https://www.csmonitor.com/2006/0922/p01s04-wome.html

26   Zaki Chehab, *Inside Hamas: The Untold Story of the Militant Islamic Movement* (NYC: Nation Books, 2007), pages 129–130.

27   Yohanan Ramati, "Islamic Fundamentalism Gaining," *Midstream*, Volume 39, Number 2, February/March 1993, page 2.

28   Anoushiravan Ehteshami and Raymond A. Hinnebush, *Syria and Iran: Middle Powers in a Penetrated Regional System* (NYC: Routledge, 1997), page 188.

29   "Israel-PLO Mutual Recognition Letters," Center for Israel Education, https://israeled.org/resources/documents/israel-plo-mutual-recognition-letters/

30   Samih K. Farsoun and Christina E. Zacharia, *Palestine and the Palestinians* (Boulder, CO: Westview Press, 1997), page 196.

31   Anoushiravan Ehteshami and Raymond A. Hinnebush, *Syria and Iran: Middle Powers in a Penetrated Regional System* (NYC: Routledge, 1997), page 218.

32   Iran and Hezbollah were behind the April 1983 suicide bombing that killed 60 at the U.S. Embassy in Beirut. The following October, a suicide truck bomb, also believed to be the work of Iran and Hezbollah, struck the U.S. Marine Corps barracks in Lebanon, killing 241. See: Israeli Ministry of Foreign Affairs, "173. Foreign Minister Peres's Statement on the Murders in Afula, 6 April 1994," Volume 13–14, April 6, 1994. https://mfa.gov.il/MFA/ForeignPolicy/MFADocuments/Yearbook9/Pages/173%20Foreign%20Minister%20Peres-s%20Statement%20on%20the%20Murd.aspx

33   Matthew Levitt, "The Origins of Hezbollah," *The Atlantic*, October 3, 2013. https://www.theatlantic.com/international/archive/2013/10/the-origins-of-hezbollah/280809

34   Zaki Chehab, *Inside Hamas: The Untold Story of the Militant Islamic Movement* (NYC: Nation Books, 2007), page 142.

35   "The Nobel Peace Prize 1994," *The Nobel Foundation*, accessed July 8, 2021. https://www.nobelprize.org/prizes/peace/1994/summary

36   Israeli Ministry of Foreign Affairs, "Fatal Terrorist Attacks in Israel (Sept 1993-1999)," September 24, 2000. https://www.mfa.gov.il/mfa/foreignpolicy/terrorism/palestinian/pages/fatal%20terrorist%20attacks%20in%20israel%20since%20the%20dop%20-s.aspx

37   U.S. Department of the Treasury, Press Release, "Treasury Targets Facilitators Moving Millions to Hamas in Gaza," August 29, 2019. https://home.treasury.gov/news/press-releases/sm761

38   Zaki Chehab, *Inside Hamas: The Untold Story of the Militant Islamic Movement* (NYC: Nation Books, 2007), pages 113–114 and 224.

39   Azzam Tamimi, *Hamas: A History From Within* (Northampton, MA: Olive Branch Press, 2007), page 89.

40   Anoushiravan Ehteshami and Raymond A. Hinnebush, *Syria and Iran: Middle Powers in a Penetrated Regional System* (NYC: Routledge, 1997), page 190.

41   Maria do Ceu Pinto, "Some US concerns regarding Islamist and Middle Eastern terrorism," *Terrorism and Political Violence*, Volume 11, Number 3, Fall 1999, pages 88–89. Available at: https://www.tandfonline.com/doi/abs/10.1080/09546559908427517

42   Paul McGeough, "The Botched Assassination Attempt That Binds Israel and Gaza's Warring Leaders," *Vanity Fair*, July 18, 2014. https://www.vanityfair.com/news/politics/2014/07/netanyahu-mishal-gaza-israel

43   U.S. Department of the Treasury, Press Release, "Treasury Targets Facilitators Moving Millions to Hamas in Gaza," August 29, 2019. https://home.treasury.gov/news/press-releases/sm761

44   Ely Karmon, "Hamas' Terrorism Strategy: Operational Limitations and Political Restraints," *Middle East Review of International Affairs*, Volume 4, Number 1, March 4, 2000, pages 1–2. https://ciaotest.cc.columbia.edu/olj/meria/meria00_kae01.html

45   Azzam Tamimi, *Hamas: Unwritten Chapters* (London: Hurst and Company, 2007), page 113.

46   Ray Takeyh, *Guardians of the Revolution: Iran and the World in the Age of the Ayatollahs* (NYC: Oxford University Press, 2009), page 174.

47   Matthew Levitt, *Hamas: Politics, Charity and Terrorism in the Service of Jihad* (New Haven, CT: Yale University Press, 2006), page 172.

48   Ely Karmon, "Hamas' Terrorism Strategy: Operational Limitations and Political Restraints," *Middle East Review of International Affairs*, Volume 4, Number 1, March 4, 2000, page 5.

49   U.S. Department of State, Office of the Secretary of State, Office of the Coordinator for Counterterrorism, "Patterns of Global Terrorism 1999," April 2000. https://fas.org/irp/threat/terror_99/1999index.html

50   Reuven Paz, "Hamas's Lessons from Lebanon," *The Washington Institute for Near East Policy*, May 25, 2000. https://www.washingtoninstitute.org/pdf/view/9692/en

51   Matthew Levitt, *Hamas: Politics, Charity and Terrorism in the Service of Jihad* (New Haven, CT: Yale University Press, 2006), page 172.

52   David Schenker, "Palestinian Fictions—Yasser Arafat Stands Alone as the Undisputed Leader of the Palestinian Authority and the Palestinians," *World and I*, Volume 16, Number 11, November 2001, page 26. (Accessed via Lexis Nexis)

CHAPTER THREE | THE HAMAS UNDERGROUND

1   Interview with IDF Southern Command, Mahaneh Ra'im, June 22, 2021.

2   @SBHendrix, "from IDF last two hours: 12:17: 'IDF air and ground troops are currently attacking in the Gaza Strip.' 1:26: '*Official IDF Statement* There are ground troops in Gaza.' 2:13: 'Clarification: there are currently no IDF ground troops inside the Gaza Strip,' *Twitter*, May 13, 2021. https://twitter.com/SBHendrix/status/1392985783313870853?s=20

3   Israeli Ministry of Foreign Affairs, "Two soldiers killed, one missing in
        Kerem Shalom terror attack, "June 25, 2006. https://www.mfa.gov.il/mfa/
        pressroom/2006/pages/two%20soldiers%20killed%20one%20missing%20
        in%20kerem%20shalom%20terror%20attack%2025-jun-2006.aspx

4   Michal Zippori, Paul Colsey, and Kareem Khadder, "After 5 years in
        captivity, Shalit is back home," *CNN*, October 18, 2011. https://www.cnn.
        com/2011/10/18/world/meast/israel-prisoner-swap/index.html

5   Tobias Siegal, "Knesset holds discussion on return of bodies of Oron Shaul,
        Hadar Goldin," *The Jerusalem Post* (Israel), January 27, 2021. https://www.
        jpost.com/israel-news/knesset-holds-discussion-on-return-of-bodies-of-
        oron-shaul-hadar-goldin-656911

6   @washingtonpost, "Israeli troops have entered the Gaza Strip as conflict
        with Palestinians escalates, Israeli military says," *Twitter*, May 13, 2021.
        https://twitter.com/washingtonpost/status/1392973938150498309?s=20

7   Felicia Schwartz, "Israel Begins Ground Operations Against Hamas in
        Gaza," *The Wall Street Journal*, May 13, 2021. https://www.wsj.com/articles/
        israel-steps-up-airstrikes-against-hamas-in-gaza-tries-to-contain-violence-
        at-home-11620900941?mod=hp_lead_pos5

8   Yaron Steinbuch, "How Israel used a tweet to lure militants to their
        doom in terror tunnels," *New York Post*, May 14, 2021. https://nypost.
        com/2021/05/14/how-one-idf-tweet-led-to-false-reports-of-gaza-ground-
        attack

9   See video at: Israel Defense Forces, "IDF strike on a Hamas terror tunnel
        located underneath a school and in close proximity to civilian buildings,"
        May 13, 2021. https://idfanc.activetrail.biz/ANC13052021.2; Israel
        Defense Forces, May 13, 2021. https://spokesperson.gincher.net/releases/
        wA_slEoMpLjnee-lZEKuf

10   Tovah Lazaroff and Anna Ahronheim, "Security cabinet meets as pressure
        mounts on Israel to end Gaza operation," *The Jerusalem Post* (Israel), May
        16, 2021. https://www.jpost.com/arab-israeli-conflict/israel-keeps-up-
        pressure-on-hamas-with-non-stop-bombings-of-gaza-668170

11   Judah Ari Gross, "IDF: Overnight bombardment targeted Hamas' tunnel
        network under Gaza city," *The Times of Israel* (Israel), May 14, 2021. https://
        www.timesofisrael.com/idf-overnight-bombardment-targeted-hamass-
        tunnel-network-under-gaza-city

12   Seth J. Frantzman, "How Israel Targeted Hamas Underground (And
        What It Could Do Next)," *The National Interest*, June 2, 2021. https://
        nationalinterest.org/blog/buzz/how-israel-targeted-hamas-underground-
        and-what-it-could-do-next-186662

13   Yaron Steinbuch, "Israeli military video shows scope of airstrikes
        against Hamas tunnels," *New York Post*, May 18, 2021. https://nypost.
        com/2021/05/19/israeli-military-video-shows-airstrikes-on-hamas-tunnels

14   Orde F. Kittrie, *Lawfare: Law as a Weapon of War* (Oxford, UK: Oxford University Press), 2016.

15   Orde F. Kittrie, "Help NATO by Holding Hamas Accountable for Terrorist War Crimes," *The National Interest*, May 19, 2021. https://nationalinterest.org/feature/help-nato-holding-hamas-accountable-terrorist-war-crimes-185581

16   Sanctioning the Use of Civilians as Defenseless Shields Act, Pub. L. 115-348, 132 Stat. 5055–5058, codified as amended at 50 U.S.C. §1701. https://www.congress.gov/115/plaws/publ348/PLAW-115publ348.pdf

17   "Gaza's Deadly Night: How Israeli Airstrikes Killed 44 people," *The New York Times*, June 24, 2021. https://www.nytimes.com/video/world/middleeast/100000007787471/israel-airstrikes-gaza.html

18   "This is how Israel destroys Hamas terror tunnels—Watch," *The Jerusalem Post* (Israel), May 15, 2021. https://www.jpost.com/arab-israeli-conflict/watch-this-is-how-israel-destroys-hamas-terror-tunnels-668261

19   Ryan Pickrell, "Israel says it has destroyed more than 60 miles of a vast Hamas tunnel network called the 'Metro,'" *Business Insider*, May 20, 2021. https://www.businessinsider.com/israel-gaza-strikes-destroy-hamas-tunnel-network-2021-5; Israel Defense Forces, "IDF Destroys Hamas 'Metro' Terror Tunnels," *YouTube*, May 19, 2021. https://www.youtube.com/watch?v=YqaauZN-M1o

20   Sharon Wrobel, "Report: Hamas, Islamic Jihad Still Have Enough Rockets to Wage Months-Long Clashes With Israel," *The Algemeiner*, June 8, 2021. https://www.algemeiner.com/2021/06/08/report-hamas-islamic-jihad-still-have-enough-rockets-to-wage-months-long-clashes-with-israel

21   Ahmed Abu Amer, "Hamas downplays damage to tunnel network," *Al-Monitor*, May 21, 2021. https://www.al-monitor.com/originals/2021/05/hamas-downplays-damage-tunnel-network

22   Israel Defense Forces, "IDF strike on a Hamas terror tunnel located underneath a school and in close proximity to civilian buildings," May 13, 2021. https://idfanc.activetrail.biz/ANC13052021.2

23   Israel Defense Forces, "First Week Summary: Operation Guardian of the Walls," May 16, 2021. https://www.idf.il/en/articles/defense-and-security/israel-under-fire

24   @IDF, "Hamas is using children as human shields. Hamas has been using a school—in close proximity to civilian buildings including a hospital—to hide a terror tunnel. We neutralized the terror tunnel so that Hamas can no longer hide behind innocent children." *Twitter*, May 13, 2021. https://twitter.com/IDF/status/1392727848721559552?s=20

25   David M. Halbfinger, "A Press Corp Deceived, and the Gaza Invasion That Wasn't," *The New York Times*, May 14, 2021. https://www.nytimes.com/2021/05/14/world/middleeast/israel-gaza-disinformation.html

26   @SBHendrix, "from IDF last two hours: 12:17: 'IDF air and ground troops are currently attacking in the Gaza Strip.' 1:26: "*Official IDF Statement* There are ground troops in Gaza.' 2:13: 'Clarification: there are currently no IDF ground troops inside the Gaza Strip,'" *Twitter*, May 13, 2021. https://twitter.com/SBHendrix/status/1392985783313870853?s=20

27   David M. Halbfinger, "A Press Corp Deceived, and the Gaza Invasion That Wasn't," *The New York Times*, May 14, 2021. https://www.nytimes.com/2021/05/14/world/middleeast/israel-gaza-disinformation.html

CHAPTER FOUR | AL-JALAA TOWER

1   Yaakov Katz, "The AP tower: How the IDF messed up explaining why it attacked in Gaza," *The Jerusalem Post* (Israel), May 23, 2021. https://www.jpost.com/opinion/the-ap-tower-the-anatomy-of-an-idf-diplomatic-mishap-comment-668711

2   Amy Goodman, "Gaza Journalist: Israel Is Deliberately Targeting the Media by Bombing AP & Al Jazeera Offices," *Democracy Now*, May 17, 2021. https://www.democracynow.org/2021/5/17/israeli_bombing_gaza_media_building

3   "'Give us 10 minutes:' How Israel bombed a Gaza media tower," *Al Jazeera* (Qatar), May 15, 2021. https://www.aljazeera.com/news/2021/5/15/give-us-10-minutes-how-israel-bombed-gaza-media-tower

4   Lahav Harkov, "Israel showed US 'smoking gun' on Hamas in AP office tower, officials say," *The Jerusalem Post* (Israel), May 17, 2021. https://www.jpost.com/israel-news/israel-showed-us-smoking-gun-on-hamas-in-ap-office-tower-officials-say-668303

5   Michael N. Schmitt, "Legal Protection of the Media in Armed Conflict: Gaza," *United States Military Academy's Lieber Institute for Law & Warfare*, May 18, 2021, https://lieber.westpoint.edu/legal-protection-media-armed-conflict-gaza/

6   @amnesty, "We're calling on US to intervene bilaterally & as UN Security Council member to end cycle of impunity & violations in Israel/OPT by publicly denouncing war crimes & other serious violations including illegal settlement expansion, blockade of Gaza, dispossession of Palestinians," *Twitter*, May 15, 2021. https://twitter.com/amnesty/status/1393546386151444489

7   Yaron Steinbuch, "AP slammed for claiming it was unaware of Hamas presence," *New York Post*, May 17, 2021. https://nypost.com/2021/05/17/ap-slammed-for-claiming-it-was-unaware-of-hamas-presence/

8   Israel Defense Forces, Press Release, "Information regarding the IDF strike on the al-Jalaa building," May 15, 2021. https://idfanc.activetrail.biz/ANC0806202101

9   Jacob Magid, "UN General Assembly to meet on Gaza as US blocks 3rd Security Council statement," *The Times of Israel* (Israel), May 17, 2021. https://www.timesofisrael.com/un-general-assembly-to-meet-on-gaza-as-us-blocks-3rd-security-council-resolution

10   The White House, Readout, "Readout of President Joseph R. Biden, Jr. Call with Prime Minister Benjamin Netanyahu of Israel," May 15, 2021. https://www.whitehouse.gov/briefing-room/statements-releases/2021/05/15/readout-of-president-joseph-r-biden-jr-call-with-prime-minister-benjamin-netanyahu-of-israel-3

11   Lahav Harkov, "Israel showed US 'smoking gun' on Hamas in AP office tower, officials say," *The Jerusalem Post* (Israel), May 17, 2021. https://www.jpost.com/israel-news/israel-showed-us-smoking-gun-on-hamas-in-ap-office-tower-officials-say-668303

12   @netanyahu, "שוחחתי בטלפון עם נשיא ארה״ב ג׳ו ביידן ועדכנתי אותו בהתפתחויות ובפעולות שישראל נקטה ומתכוונת לבצע. הודיתי לו על התמיכה הבלתי מסויגת של ארה״ב בזכות שלנו להגן על עצמנו.. [I spoke on the phone with US President Joe Biden and updated him on developments and actions that Israel has taken and intends to take. I thanked him for his unreserved US support for our right to defend ourselves.]" *Twitter*, May 15, 2021. https://twitter.com/netanyahu/status/1393616093353291776

13   Lahav Harkov, "Israel showed US 'smoking gun' on Hamas in AP office tower, officials say," *The Jerusalem Post* (Israel), May 17, 2021. https://www.jpost.com/israel-news/israel-showed-us-smoking-gun-on-hamas-in-ap-office-tower-officials-say-668303

14   Yaron Steinbuch, "AP slammed for claiming it was unaware of Hamas presence," *New York Post*, May 17, 2021. https://nypost.com/2021/05/17/ap-slammed-for-claiming-it-was-unaware-of-hamas-presence/

15   U.S. Department of State, Office of the Spokesperson, Readout, "Secretary Blinken's Call with Gary Pruitt, President and CEO of the Associated Press," May 15, 2021. https://www.state.gov/secretary-blinkens-call-with-gary-pruitt-president-and-ceo-of-the-associated-press

16   @PressSec, "We have communicated directly to the Israelis that ensuring the safety and security of journalists and independent media is a paramount responsibility," *Twitter*, May 15, 2021. https://twitter.com/PressSec/status/1393577210964058115

17   Laila Al-Arian, "My Grandfather Bought a Home in Gaza With His Savings. An Israeli Airstrike Destroyed It," *The New York Times*, May 20, 2021. https://www.nytimes.com/2021/05/20/opinion/gaza-airstrike-apartment-building.html

18   *United States v. Sami Amin Al-Arian, et al.*, 8:03-cr-00077. (M.D. Fla., filed February 19, 2003). https://fas.org/irp/ops/ci/al-arian_indict_022003.pdf

19   U.S. Department of Justice, Press Release, "Sami Al-Arian Pleads Guilty To Conspiracy To Provide Services To Palestinian Islamic Jihad," April 17, 2006. https://www.justice.gov/archive/opa/pr/2006/April/06_crm_221.html

20   Stephen M. Flatow, "Old terrorists do not die, they just move to Turkey," *Jewish News Syndicate*, August 25, 2020. https://www.jns.org/opinion/old-terrorists-do-not-die-they-just-move-to-turkey

21   Jonathan Schanzer and Michael Argosh, "Lying Down with Dogs," *Foreign Policy*, August 20, 2014. https://foreignpolicy.com/2014/08/20/lying-down-with-dogs

22   @fahrettinaltun, "İsrail katliamlarına ve savaş suçu işlemeye devam ediyor. Gazze'de Associated Press ve Al Jazeera ofislerini hedef alan işgalci İsrail, basın özgürlüğüne de darbe vuruyor. Katliamlarını gizleyebilmek için basın merkezlerini vuran İsrail'in bu alçak saldırılarını lanetliyorum. [Israel continues to commit massacres and war crimes. By targeting the Associated Press and Al Jazeera offices in Gaza, the occupying Israel is also dealing a blow to the freedom of the press. I condemn these vile attacks of Israel, which hit the press centers in order to hide their massacres.]" *Twitter*, May 15, 2021. https://twitter.com/fahrettinaltun/status/1393554333640364034

23   Aykan Erdemir and Merve Tahiroglu, "The Islamist Takeover of Turkish Media," *Digital Dictators: Media, Authoritarianism, and America's New Challenge*, Ed. Ilan Berman (Lanham, MD: Rowman & Littlefield, 2018), pages 53–76.

24   Yasser Abu Wazna and Bill Bostock, "Owner of AP tower destroyed in Israeli airstrike in Gaza says he saw no evidence of Hamas in the building," *Business Insider*, May 21, 2021. https://www.businessinsider.com/owner-of-ap-tower-gaza-no-evidence-of-hamas-2021-5

25   Jacob Miller, "Erdan: Ground operation in Gaza was alternative to strike that hit AP offices," *Jewish Insider*, June 10, 2021. https://jewishinsider.com/2021/06/gilad-erdan-israel-strike-ap-building-gaza/?fbclid=IwAR1lLr6M6-ON2k6RDA1eh0wspN-rgsI6XE90PIlDk81iyY87WkxId_dzawY); Ambassador Gilad Erdan, *Remarks Delivered at Event Hosted by the Democratic Majority for Israel*, June 9, 2021. https://otter.ai/u/2r-yURnbyNfzryhYV6TeB92os4I

26   Ron Kampeas, "Hamas was developing technology to jam Iron Dome system in bombed AP building, Israel says," *Jewish Telegraphic Agency*, June 8, 2021. https://www.jta.org/quick-reads/hamas-was-developing-technology-to-jam-iron-dome-system-in-bombed-ap-building-israel-says

27   @TVietor08, "Last thought on this...I'm sure Hamas offices were in that building & that they purposefully co-locate operations with civilians. But that is not a new problem. And if the IDF wants to claim that the military effort is targeted, precise, etc...then you shouldn't hit that building," *Twitter*, May 15, 2021. https://twitter.com/TVietor08/status/1393588056054136835

28   Joseph Wulfsohn, "Former Obama aide says he 'talked to people' who worked in Gaza media building knowing Hamas had office space," *Fox News*, May 17, 2021. https://www.foxnews.com/media/tommy-vietor-israel-gaza-hamas

29   Matti Friedman, "Falling for Hamas's Split-Screen Fallacy," *The New York Times*, May 16, 2018. https://www.nytimes.com/2018/05/16/opinion/hamas-israel-media-protests.html

30   Matti Friedman, "What the Media Gets Wrong About Israel," *The Atlantic*, November 30, 2014. https://www.theatlantic.com/international/archive/2014/11/how-the-media-makes-the-israel-story/383262

31   Mark Lavie, "Matti Friedman hits back at AP, and so do I," *Broken Spring Blog*, September 19, 2014. https://brokenspring.wordpress.com/2014/09/19/matti-friedman-hits-back-at-ap-and-so-do-i

32   Associated Press, Statement, "AP statement on meeting with Israeli ambassador," June 8, 2021. https://blog.ap.org/announcements/ap-statement-on-meeting-with-israeli-ambassador

33   Lahav Harkov, "Israel showed US 'smoking gun' on Hamas in AP office tower, officials say," *The Jerusalem Post* (Israel), May 17, 2021. https://www.jpost.com/israel-news/israel-showed-us-smoking-gun-on-hamas-in-ap-office-tower-officials-say-668303

34   Louay Y. Bahry, "The New Arab Media Phenomenon: Qatar's Al-Jazeera," *Middle East Policy Council*, Volume VIII, Number 2, summer 2001. https://mepc.org/journal/new-arab-media-phenomenon-qatars-al-jazeera

35   "Qaradawi: The top advocate of suicide bombings," *Al Arabiya* (Saudi Arabia), June 9, 2017. https://english.alarabiya.net/News/middle-east/2017/06/09/The-reasons-Qaradawi-on-the-top-of-Egypt-s-most-wanted-list

36   Christopher M. Blanchard, "Qatar: Background and U.S. Relations," *Congressional Research Service*, June 6, 2012, page 5. https://www.everycrsreport.com/files/20120606_RL31718_ba79d91db17af18d337d3c2ebbce5a7aed539eb9.pdf

37   "Qatar Seen Bankrolling Hamas," *The Washington Times*, March 5, 2008. http://www.washingtontimes.com/news/2008/mar/05/qatar-seen-bankrolling-hamas/?page=all

38   "Hamas, Qatar to sign 250 million USD deal to rebuild Gaza,"
      Xinhua News Agency (China), February 26, 2012. http://en.people.
      cn/90777/7740684.html

39   "Official: Qatar to open office to oversee Gaza reconstruction," *Ma'an News
      Agency* (West Bank), August 27, 2012. http://www.maannews.net/eng/
      ViewDetails.aspx?ID=514177

40   Jodi Rudoren, "Qatar's Emir Visits Gaza, Pledging $400 Million To
      Hamas," *The New York Times*, October 23, 2012. http://www.nytimes.
      com/2012/10/24/world/middleeast/pledging-400-million-qatari-emir-
      makes-historic-visit-to-gaza-strip.html?_r=0

41   Under Secretary for Terrorism and Financial Intelligence David Cohen,
      U.S. Department of the Treasury, "Remarks of Under Secretary for
      Terrorism and Financial Intelligence David Cohen Before The Center
      for a New American Security on 'Confronting New Threats in Terrorist
      Financing,'" March 4, 2014. http://www.treasury.gov/press-center/press-
      releases/Pages/jl2308.aspx

42   Allen Fromherz, *Qatar: A Modern History* (Washington, DC: Georgetown
      University Press, 2012), page 104.

43   "مبعدو صفقة تبادل حركة حماس وإسرائيل] Those sent into exile under the
      Hamas-Israel exchange deal]," *Wafa* (West Bank), January 10, 2011. https://
      info.wafa.ps/ar_page.aspx?id=9155

44   Fares Akram, "Hamas Leader Abandons Longtime Base In Damascus," *The
      New York Times*, January 27, 2012. http://www.nytimes.com/2012/01/28/
      world/middleeast/khaled-meshal-the-leader-of-hamas-vacates-damascus.
      html?_r=0

45   Anna Ahronheim and Khaled Abu Toameh, "U.S. offers $5m. reward for
      the capture of Hamas leader Saleh al-Arouri," *The Jerusalem Post* (Israel),
      November 14, 2018. https://www.jpost.com/middle-east/us-department-of-
      state-offers-rewards-for-info-on-hamas-and-hezbollah-571882

46   Interview with U.S. and British diplomats, Doha, Qatar, August 31, 2013.

47   David Andrew Weinberg, Oren Adaki, and Grant Rumley, "The Problem
      with Al Jazeera," *The National Interest*, September 10, 2014. https://
      nationalinterest.org/feature/the-problem-al-jazeera-11239

48   @DavidAWeinberg, "#Hamas reportedly moved #Qatar news
      conference to Sheraton b/c InterContinental backed out, 'Jewish lobby'
      blamed:" *Twitter*, May 1, 2017. https://twitter.com/DavidAWeinberg/
      status/859070966722437120

49   "Former Mossad chief says Qatari payments to Hamas got 'out of control,'"
      The Times of Israel (Israel), June 8, 2021. https://www.timesofisrael.com/
      former-mossad-chief-says-qatari-payments-to-hamas-got-out-of-control

50   "Families of Israeli terror victims suing Qatari banks for compensation," *Ynet* (Israel), June 9, 2021. https://www.ynetnews.com/article/S1159y0qu

51   John Hannah, "Qatar Needs to Do Its Part," *Foreign Policy*, May 22, 2017. https://foreignpolicy.com/2017/05/22/qatar-needs-to-do-its-part

52   Wolf Blitzer, "Are U.S. Troops Losing Ground in Iraq?; Al-Sadr in Coalition Crosshairs," *CNN*, April 12, 2004. http://edition.cnn.com/TRANSCRIPTS/0404/12/wbr.00.html

53   James Dobbins, Seth G. Jones, Benjamin Runkle, and Siddharth Mohandas, *Occupying Iraq: A History of the Coalition Provisional Authority* (Santa Monica, CA: RAND Corporation, 2009), page 191. https://www.rand.org/content/dam/rand/pubs/monographs/2009/RAND_MG847.pdf

54   "Al Jazeera Timeline," *Pew Research Center*, August 22, 2006. https://www.journalism.org/2006/08/22/al-jazeera-timeline

55   Samy Magdy and Josef Federman, "Qatar Pledges $500 million for postwar construction in Gaza," *Associated Press*, May 26, 2021. https://abcnews.go.com/International/wireStory/blinken-heads-egypt-shore-gaza-cease-fire-efforts-77910095

56   @galberger, "על הקטרי זירה אל-ג'זירה לערוץ הוקרה תעודת מעניקים בעזה חמאס בכירי מידי התעודה את מקבל דחדוח ואיל בעזה הערוץ נציג החומות שומר מבצע של מופתי סיקור רעל_זה_קטר# אל-חיה, ח'ליל אל סינוואר, יחיא של סגנו [Senior Hamas officials in Gaza present a certificate of appreciation to the Qatari al-Jazeera channel for exemplary coverage of Operation Guardian of the Walls, the channel's representative in Gaza and Wael Dahdouh receives the certificate from Yahya Sinwar's deputy, Khalil al-Haya]," *Twitter*, June 8, 2021. https://twitter.com/galberger/status/1402339837609394183?s=20

CHAPTER FIVE | THE COLLAPSE OF PEACE, A NEW WAR

1   Wye River Memorandum, Wye River, Maryland, October 23, 1998. https://www.un.org/unispal/document/auto-insert-176306

2   U.S. Department of State, Bureau of Counterterrorism, "Executive Order 13224," accessed June 21, 2021. https://www.state.gov/executive-order-13224. See also: U.S. Department of the Treasury, Press Release, "Treasury Targets Facilitators Moving Millions to HAMAS in Gaza," August 29, 2019. https://home.treasury.gov/news/press-releases/sm761

3   "Text of President Bush's 2002 State of the Union Address," *The Washington Post*, January 29, 2002. https://www.washingtonpost.com/wp-srv/onpolitics/transcripts/sou012902.htm

4   Matthew Levitt, *Hamas: Politics, Charity and Terrorism in the Service of Jihad* (New Haven, CT: Yale University Press, 2006), page 46.

5   Beverly Milton-Edwards and Stephen Farrell, *Hamas: The Islamic Resistance Movement* (Cambridge, UK: Polity Press, 2010), page 93.

6   Israeli Ministry of Foreign Affairs, "Passover suicide bombing at Park Hotel in Netanya," March 27, 2002. https://mfa.gov.il/MFA/MFA-Archive/2002/Pages/Passover%20suicide%20bombing%20at%20Park%20Hotel%20in%20Netanya.aspx

7   "Israel arrests suspects in university bombing," *CNN*, August 21, 2002. https://www.cnn.com/2002/WORLD/meast/08/21/mideast

8   "Bush snubs Arafat on 'terrorists,'" *CNN*, November 9, 2001. http://www.cnn.com/2001/WORLD/meast/11/09/gen.mideast.bush/

9   "Hamas Rejects Offer to Join Cabinet," *Associated Press*, June 3, 2002. (Accessed via Lexis Nexis)

10   U.S. Department of State, Bureau of Public Affairs, "Roadmap for Peace in the Middle East: Israeli/Palestinian Reciprocal Action, Quartet Support," July 16, 2003. https://2001-2009.state.gov/r/pa/ei/rls/22520.htm

11   Israeli Ministry of Foreign Affairs, "Suicide bombing of No 20 Egged bus in Kiryat Menahem—Jerusalem," October 2, 2000. https://mfa.gov.il/MFA/MFA-Archive/2000/Pages/Suicide%20bombing%20of%20No%2020%20Egged%20bus%20in%20Kiryat%20Menah.asp

12   "Erased In A Moment: Suicide Bombing Attacks Against Israeli Civilians," *Human Rights Watch*, October 15, 2002. https://www.hrw.org/report/2002/10/15/erased-moment/suicide-bombing-attacks-against-israeli-civilians

13   Israeli Ministry of Foreign Affairs, "Palestinian Terrorism- Photos- January 22-27- 2002," January 22, 2002. https://mfa.gov.il/MFA/MFA-Archive/2002/Pages/Palestinian%20Terrorism-%20Photos%20-%20January%2022-27-%20200.aspx

14   "Hamas Leader Killed in Israeli Air Strike," *PBS*, March 22, 2004. https://www.pbs.org/newshour/politics/middle_east-jan-june04-mideast_03-22

15   Greg Myre, "In Loss of Leaders, Hamas Discovers a Renewed Strength," *The New York Times*, April 25, 2004. https://www.nytimes.com/2004/04/25/world/in-loss-of-leaders-hamas-discovers-a-renewed-strength.html

16   John Ward Anderson and Molly Moore, "Palestinians Throng Militant's Funeral," *The Washington Post*, August 23, 2003. https://www.washingtonpost.com/archive/politics/2003/08/23/palestinians-throng-militants-funeral/273196b5-23d7-4312-a6e4-058b9bf45d60/

17   Reena Ninan, "Dr. Terror: An Interview with Hamas Leader Mahmoud Zahar," *Fox News*, December 5, 2007.https://www.foxnews.com/story/an-interview-with-hamas-leader-mahmoud-zahar

18   Greg Myre, "In Loss of Leaders, Hamas Discovers a Renewed Strength," *The New York Times*, April 25, 2004. https://www.nytimes.com/2004/04/25/world/in-loss-of-leaders-hamas-discovers-a-renewed-strength.html

19   Ezzedeen Al-Qassam Brigades Information Office, "Abu Obaida, the English Spokesman, Answers Important Questions About the Brigades," December 5, 2007. Archived version available at: https://web.archive.org/web/20090119214519/www.alqassam.ps/english/?action=showinet&inid=17

20   For more, see: Eben Kaplan, "Profile of Khaled Meshal (aka Khalid Meshaal, Khaleed Mash'al)," *Council on Foreign Relations*, July 13, 2006. https://www.cfr.org/backgrounder/profile-khaled-meshal-aka-khalid-meshaal-khaleed-mashal

21   Matthew Levitt, *Hamas: Politics, Charity and Terrorism in the Service of Jihad* (New Haven, CT: Yale University Press, 2006), page 174.

22   Jennifer Siegel, "Carter Book Slaps Israel With 'Apartheid' Tag, Provides Ammo to GOP," *The Forward*, October 17, 2006. https://forward.com/news/5918/carter-book-slaps-israel-with-apartheid-tag/

23   Israeli Ministry of Foreign of Affairs, "Saving Lives: Israel's Anti-Terrorist Fence," January 2004, page 20. https://mfa.gov.il/MFA_Graphics/MFA%20Gallery/Documents/savinglives.pdf

24   See: David Makovsky, *Engagement Through Disengagement: Gaza and the Potential for Renewed Israeli-Palestinian Peacemaking* (Washington, DC: The Washington Institute for Near East Policy, 2005).

25   *Beit Sourik Village Council v. The Government of Israel*, HCJ 2056/04 (HCJ, June 30, 2004). https://versa.cardozo.yu.edu/sites/default/files/upload/opinions/Beit%20Sourik%20Village%20Council%20v.%20Government%20of%20Israel_0.pdf

26   Gad Lior, "Cost of Border Fences, Underground Barrier, Reaches NIS 6bn," *Ynet* (Israel), January 30, 2018, https://www.ynetnews.com/articles/0,7340,L-5078348,00.html

27   Doron Almog, "Tunnel-Vision in Gaza," *Middle East Quarterly*, Volume 11, Number 3, summer 2004, pages 3–11. http://www.meforum.org/article/630

28   Interview with retired Israeli military official, Washington, DC, October 15, 2003.

29   Kevin Frayer, "Gaza Tunnel Smugglers Grow Under Hamas," *Associated Press*, August 14, 2007. http://www.washingtonpost.com/wp-dyn/content/article/2007/08/14/AR2007081400721_2.html

30   "Israel Destroys Palestinian Tunnels Into Israel," *CNN*, November 13, 2003. http://edition.cnn.com/TRANSCRIPTS/0311/13/i_ins.00.html

31   Interview with retired Israeli military official, Washington, DC, October 15, 2003.

32   Matthew Levitt, *Hamas: Politics, Charity, and Terrorism in the Service of Jihad* (New Haven, CT: Yale University Press, 2006), page 6.

33   Luke Baker, "Shadow of Israel's Pullout from Gaza Hangs Heavy 10 Years On," *Reuters*, August 10, 2015, https://www.reuters.com/article/us-israel-gaza-disengagement-insight/shadow-of-israels-pullout-from-gaza-hangs-heavy-10-years-on-idUSKCN0QF1QQ20150810

34   The text of the speech can be found at: "Ariel Sharon Administration: Speech First Describing Gaza 'Disengagement Plan,'" *Jewish Virtual Library*, December 18, 2003. http://www.jewishvirtuallibrary.org/jsource/Peace/sharon_1203.html

35   Zaki Chehab, *Inside Hamas: The Untold Story of the Militant Islamic Movement* (NYC: Nation Books, 2007), page 52.

36   Beverly Milton-Edwards and Stephen Farrell, *Hamas: The Islamic Resistance Movement* (Cambridge, UK: Polity Press, 2010), page 133.

CHAPTER SIX | FIREBALLS IN THE SKY

1   See, for example: "The Guardian view on... a futile war in Gaza," *The Guardian* (UK), July 21, 2014. https://www.theguardian.com/commentisfree/2014/jul/21/guardian-view-futile-war-gaza

2   "Tank belonging to Eilat-Ashkelon oil pipeline on fire after rocket hit," *The Times of Israel* (Israel), May 11, 2021. https://www.timesofisrael.com/liveblog_entry/tank-belonging-to-eilat-ashkelon-oil-pipeline-on-fire-after-rocket-hit

3   "Israeli energy pipeline hit in Gaza rocket attack - Israel's Channel 12 TV," *Reuters*, May 11, 2021. https://news.trust.org/item/20210511182434-pb886

4   "Europe Asia Pipeline Co. Ltd.," *Europe Asia Pipeline Company*, accessed July 14, 2021. https://www.eapc.com

5   Elza Turner and Eklavya Gupte, "Israel's EAPC clarifies that rocket attack did not hit its terminal," *S&P Global*, May 17, 2021. https://www.spglobal.com/platts/en/market-insights/latest-news/oil/051721-israels-eapc-clarifies-that-rocket-attack-did-not-hit-its-terminal

6   Briefing by IDF officer on Israel-Gaza border, June 22, 2021.

7   Tom O'Connor, "Hamas Targets Israel Nuclear Site, Oil Line to Arab World as Conflict Death Toll Rises," *Newsweek*, May 12, 2021. https://www.newsweek.com/hamas-targets-israel-nuclear-site-oil-line-arab-world-conflict-death-toll-rises-1590880

8   "Israeli energy pipeline hit as Iron Dome fails to intercept missile," *Daily Sabah* (Turkey), May 11, 2021. https://www.dailysabah.com/world/mid-east/israeli-energy-pipeline-hit-as-iron-dome-fails-to-intercept-missile

9   Briefing by IDF officer on Gaza border, June 22, 2021.

10   Caleb Adebayo, "The Israeli-Palestine conflict and its impact on energy security," *Nairametrics*, May 24, 2021. https://nairametrics.com/2021/05/22/the-israeli-palestine-conflict-and-its-impact-on-energy-security

11   Email correspondence with Dr. Brenda Shaffer, July 6–7, 2020.

12   Tom O'Connor, "Hamas Targets Israel Nuclear Site, Oil Line to Arab World as Conflict Death Toll Rises," *Newsweek*, May 12, 2021. https://www.newsweek.com/hamas-targets-israel-nuclear-site-oil-line-arab-world-conflict-death-toll-rises-1590880

13   "Hamas condemns UAE for dealing with Israel," *The Times of Israel* (Israel), August 13, 2020. https://www.timesofisrael.com/liveblog_entry/hamas-condemns-uae-for-dealing-with-israel

14   Zev Stub, "Fire continues to blaze at Ashkelon's Trans-Israel pipeline – background," *The Jerusalem Post* (Israel), May 12, 2021. https://www.jpost.com/arab-israeli-conflict/gaza-news/fire-continues-to-blaze-at-ashkelons-trans-israel-pipeline-background-667954

15   "Swiss court backs Iran in decades-old oil row with Israel," *Reuters*, August 11, 2016. https://www.reuters.com/article/us-iran-israel-court/swiss-court-backs-iran-in-decades-old-oil-row-with-israel-idUSKCN10M12F

16   See, for example: "Hamas Targets Israeli Oil and Nuclear Facilities With Rocket Attacks," *Oil Price*, May 14, 2021. https://oilprice.com/Geopolitics/Middle-East/Hamas-Targets-Israeli-Oil-And-Nuclear-Facilities-With-Rocket-Attacks.html; @MEMRIReports, "Israeli Nuclear Facility Destroyed by a Missile Attack in an Iranian Animated Video Posted on an IRGC Telegram Account on the Occasion of "Jerusalem Day" #Iran #JCPOA #QudsDay #dimona," *Twitter*, May 9, 2021. https://twitter.com/MEMRIReports/status/1391291378240528386

17   Tamar Pileggi, "Nasrallah threatens to bomb chemical facility, kill thousands of Israelis," *The Times of Israel* (Israel), February 16, 2016. https://www.timesofisrael.com/nasrallah-threatens-to-bomb-chemical-plants-kill-thousands-of-israelis

CHAPTER SEVEN | A WAR IGNORED

1   Jonathan Schanzer, *Hamas vs Fatah: The Struggle for Palestine* (NYC: Palgrave Macmillan, 2009).

2   For more, see: "Special Public Opinion Poll on the Upcoming Palestinian Elections," *Palestinian Center for Policy and Survey Research*, January 1, 2006. http://www.pcpsr.org/en/node/476

3   Mark Dubowitz and Roberta Bonazzi, "Jihad TV in Europe," *The Wall Street Journal*, February 18, 2009, https://www.wsj.com/articles/SB123490878778903321

4   "Hamas landslide shakes Mideast," *CNN*, January 26, 2006. http://www.cnn.com/2006/WORLD/meast/01/26/palestinian.election.1604/index.html

5   Scott Wilson, "Hamas Sweeps Palestinian Elections, Complicating Peace Efforts in Mideast," *The Washington Post*, January 27, 2006. https://www.washingtonpost.com/archive/politics/2006/01/27/hamas-sweeps-palestinian-elections-complicating-peace-efforts-in-mideast/8a4a4412-5f9b-4583-8607-51c7dd3781f4

6   Robert Satloff, "Hobbling Hamas: Moving beyond the U.S. Policy of Three No's," *The Weekly Standard*, April 3, 2006. https://www.washingtoninstitute.org/policy-analysis/hobbling-hamas-moving-beyond-us-policy-three-nos

7   Scott Wilson, "Hamas Sweeps Palestinian Elections, Complicating Peace Efforts in Mideast," *The Washington Post*, January 27, 2006. https://www.washingtonpost.com/archive/politics/2006/01/27/hamas-sweeps-palestinian-elections-complicating-peace-efforts-in-mideast/8a4a4412-5f9b-4583-8607-51c7dd3781f4

8   "Black Pages in the Absence of Justice: Report on Bloody Fighting in the Gaza Strip from 7 to 14 June 2007," *Palestinian Centre for Human Rights*, October 2007, pages 11–12. Available at: https://reliefweb.int/sites/reliefweb.int/files/resources/5510713891F8DB1FC125736F00462458-Full_Report.pdf

9   "Operation Summer Rains," *GlobalSecurity.org*, accessed July 14, 2021. http://www.globalsecurity.org/military/world/war/intifada2_summer-rains.htm

10   Amos Harel and Avi Issacharoff, *34 Days: Israel, Hezbollah and the War in Lebanon* (NYC: Palgrave Macmillan, 2008).

11   "Abbas calls for early Palestinian poll," *ABC News* (Australia), December 16, 2006. https://www.abc.net.au/news/2006-12-16/abbas-calls-for-early-palestinian-poll/2155576

12   "Black Pages in the Absence of Justice: Report on the Bloody Fighting in the Gaza Strip from 7 to 17 June 2007," *Palestinian Centre for Human Rights*, October 2007. Available at: https://reliefweb.int/sites/reliefweb.int/files/resources/5510713891F8DB1FC125736F00462458-Full_Report.pdf

13   "Text of Palestinians' Mecca Agreement," *Agence France-Presse*, February 9, 2007. (Accessed via Lexis Nexis)

14   Bruce Riedel, "Battle for Gaza: Hamas Jumped, Provoked, and Pushed," *Brookings Institution*, August 16, 2007. https://www.brookings.edu/opinions/battle-for-gaza-hamas-jumped-provoked-and-pushed

15   Khaled Abu Toameh, "PA Fears UN May Order All Aid Workers Out of Lawless Gaza," *The Jerusalem Post* (Israel), April 5, 2007. Archived version available at: https://web.archive.org/web/20070408054307/https://www.jpost.com/servlet/Satellite?cid=1173879257822&pagename=JPost%2FJPArticle%2FShowFull

16   Sarah El Deeb, "Fatah, Hamas Truce Follows More Israeli Attacks," *Associated Press*, May 19, 2007. https://www.thestar.com/news/2007/05/19/fatah_hamas_truce_follows_more_israeli_attacks.html

17   Bruce Riedel, "Battle for Gaza: Hamas Jumped, Provoked, and Pushed," *Brookings Institution*, August 16, 2007. https://www.brookings.edu/opinions/battle-for-gaza-hamas-jumped-provoked-and-pushed

18   Steven Erlanger, "Hamas Seizes Broad Control in Gaza Strip," *The New York Times*, June 14, 2007. www.nytimes.com/2007/06/14/world/middleeast/14mideast.html

19   "Black Pages in the Absence of Justice: Report on Bloody Fighting in the Gaza Strip from 7 to 14 June 2007," *Palestinian Centre for Human Rights*, October 2007. Available at: https://reliefweb.int/report/occupied-palestinian-territory/black-pages-absence-justice-report-bloody-fighting-gaza-stripf

20   "Occupied Palestinian Territories Torn Apart By Factional Strife," *Amnesty International*, October 23, 2007. Pages 29–33. https://www.amnesty.org/en/documents/MDE21/020/2007/en/

21   "Black Pages in the Absence of Justice: Report on Bloody Fighting in the Gaza Strip from 7 to 14 June 2007," *Palestinian Centre for Human Rights*, October 2007. Available at: https://reliefweb.int/sites/reliefweb.int/files/resources/5510713891F8DB1FC125736F00462458-Full_Report.pdf

22   Beverly Milton-Edwards and Stephen Farrell, *Hamas: The Islamic Resistance Movement* (Cambridge, UK: Polity Press, 2010), page 225.

23   Bahram Khodabandeh, "Hamas Official Reveals Money Laundering by Ghasem Soleimani," *IranWire*, December 30, 2020. https://iranwire.com/en/features/8458

24   Beverly Milton-Edwards and Stephen Farrell, *Hamas: The Islamic Resistance Movement* (Cambridge, UK: Polity Press, 2010), page 132.

25   Zaki Chehab, *Inside Hamas: The Untold Story of the Militant Islamic Movement* (NYC: Nation Books, 2007), page 134.

26   Beverly Milton-Edwards and Stephen Farrell, *Hamas: The Islamic Resistance Movement* (Cambridge, UK: Polity Press, 2010), page 133.

27   U.S. Department of the Treasury, Press Release, "Twin Treasury Actions Take Aim at Hizballah's Support Network," July 24, 2007. https://www.treasury.gov/press-center/press-releases/Pages/hp503.aspx

28   "Iran Sanctions," *Congressional Research Service.* April 6, 2021. https://fas.org/sgp/crs/mideast/RS20871.pdf

29   "Hamas Has No Intention of Establishing an Islamic State in Gaza, Says Haniyeh," *Ma'an News Agency* (West Bank), August 20, 2007. http://www.maannews.net/en/index.php?opr=ShowDetails&ID=24848

30   Marie Colvin, "Defiant Hamas Rules By Fear in Isolated Gaza," *The Times* (UK), November 25, 2007. https://www.thetimes.co.uk/article/defiant-hamas-rules-by-fear-in-isolated-gaza-shmqbcnf8br

31   "Black Pages in the Absence of Justice: Report on Bloody Fighting in the Gaza Strip from 7 to 14 June 2007," *Palestinian Centre for Human Rights*, October 2007. Available at: https://reliefweb.int/sites/reliefweb.int/files/resources/5510713891F8DB1FC125736F00462458-Full_Report.pdf

32   Khaled Abu Toameh, "Gaza: Christian-Muslim tensions heat up," *The Jerusalem Post* (Israel), September 25, 2007. https://www.jpost.com/middle-east/gaza-christian-muslim-tensions-heat-up

33   Khaled Abu Toameh, "Hamas forced professor to convert," *The Jerusalem Post* (Israel), August 6, 2007. https://www.jpost.com/middle-east/hamas-forced-professor-to-convert

34   Khaled Abu Toameh, "Gaza: Christian-Muslim tensions heat up," *The Jerusalem Post* (Israel), August 5, 2007.https://www.jpost.com/middle-east/hamas-forced-professor-to-convert; "Corpse of Christian Resident of Gaza Discovered," *Ma'an News Agency* (West Bank), October 7, 2007. http://www.maannews.net/en/index.php?opr=ShowDetails&ID=25738

35   Shelley Neese, "Who Will Speak for Gaza's Christians," *The Jerusalem Connection*, September 18, 2008. https://thejerusalemconnection.us/blog/2008/09/18/who-will-speak-for-gazas-christians

36   "Occupied Palestinian Territories Torn Apart By Factional Strife," *Amnesty International*, October 23, 2007, pages 16 and 36. https://www.amnesty.org/en/documents/MDE21/020/2007/en/

37   Palestinian Centre for Human Rights, Press Release, "PCHR Calls for Investigation into Methods of Torture Practiced by Palestinian Police in the Gaza Strip," November 19, 2007.

38   "Hamas Frees Senior Fatah Sympathizer," *The Jerusalem Post* (Israel), December 25, 2007. https://www.jpost.com/Middle-East/Hamas-frees-senior-Fatah-sympathizer

39   Khaled Abu Toameh, "Hamas detains PA's A-G over cover-up," *The Jerusalem Post* (Israel), August 16, 2007. https://www.jpost.com/middle-east/hamas-detains-pas-a-g-over-cover-up

40   Taghreed El-Khodary and Isabel Kershner, "Gaza is Tense as it Tallies Casualties," *The New York Times,* January 2, 2008. https://www.nytimes.com/2008/01/02/world/middleeast/02mideast.html?ref=todayspaper

41   "Occupied Palestinian Territories Torn Apart By Factional Strife," *Amnesty International,* October 23, 2007, pages 14–15. https://www.amnesty.org/en/documents/MDE21/020/2007/en/

42   "Hamas bans unregistered protests," *Al Jazeera* (Qatar), August 13, 2007. https://www.aljazeera.com/news/2007/8/13/hamas-bans-unregistered-protests

43   "Hamas Widens Gaza Crackdown with New Press Restrictions," *The Jerusalem Post* (Israel), November 15, 2007. https://www.jpost.com/middle-east/hamas-widens-gaza-crackdown-with-new-press-restrictions

44   Khaled Abu Toameh, "Palestinian journalists say Hamas's decision to issue its own press cards is 'a dangerous step,'" *The Jerusalem Post* (Israel), October 17, 2007. https://www.jpost.com/Middle-East/Palestinian-journalists-say-Hamass-decision-to-issue-its-own-press-cards-is-a-dangerous-step

45   Steven Erlanger, "Promising Freedom, Hamas Pressures Journalists," *The New York Times*, September 10, 2007. https://www.nytimes.com/2007/09/10/world/middleeast/10gaza.html

46   Khaled Abu Toameh, "Hamas Sets Up new Security Force," *The Jerusalem Post* (Israel), July 31, 2007. https://www.jpost.com/middle-east/hamas-sets-up-new-security-force

47   Khaled Abu Toameh, "Palestinian journalists say Hamas's decision to issue its own press cards is 'a dangerous step,'" *The Jerusalem Post* (Israel), October 17, 2007. https://www.jpost.com/Middle-East/Palestinian-journalists-say-Hamass-decision-to-issue-its-own-press-cards-is-a-dangerous-step

48   Steven Weisman and Craig Smith, "U.S. and Europe Halt Aid to Palestinian Government," *The New York Times*, April 8, 2006. https://www.nytimes.com/2006/04/08/world/middleeast/us-and-europe-halt-aid-to-palestinian-government.html

49   Government of Canada, Press Release, "Update: Canadian Aid Programs in the West Bank and Gaza," April 1, 2006. https://www.canada.ca/en/news/archive/2006/04/update-canadian-aid-programs-west-bank-gaza.html

50   Ewen MacAskill, "US opens the door for Europe to save Palestinians from funding disaster," *The Guardian* (UK), May 10, 2006. https://www.theguardian.com/world/2006/may/10/israel.usa

51   Richard Boudreaux, "Israel OKs Gaza Electricity Cutoffs," *Los Angeles Times*, October 26, 2007. (Accessed via Lexis Nexis)

52   Scott Wilson, "Sealed Off by Israel, Gaza Reduced to Beggary," *The Washington Post*, December 15, 2007. https://www.washingtonpost.com/wp-dyn/content/article/2007/12/14/AR2007121402214.html

53   "The Occupied Palestinian Territories: Dignity Denied," *International Committee of the Red Cross*, December 13, 2007. http://www.icrc.org/Web/Eng/siteengo0.nsf/html/Palestine-report-131207

54   Paul Martin, "Hamas Carries Out Mass Arrests and Puts Down Gaza Schoolgirl Demo," *The Times* (UK), November 13, 2007.

CHAPTER EIGHT | A CANCELED VOTE

1   U.S. House of Representatives, Committee on Foreign Affairs, Subcommittee on the Middle East and South Asia, "Chronic Kleptocracy: Corruption Within the Palestinian Political Establishment," *Hearing Before the Subcommittee on the Middle East and South Asia*, July 10, 2012. https://www.govinfo.gov/content/pkg/CHRG-112hhrg74960/html/CHRG-112hhrg74960.htm

2   See polls conducted by Palestinian Center for Policy and Survey Research: http://pcpsr.org/en/node/154

3   "PA bars Hamas speaker of parliament from Ramallah, since dissolution 'in effect,'" *The Times of Israel* (Israel), December 26, 2018. https://www.timesofisrael.com/hamas-speaker-of-pa-parliament-barred-from-ramallah-as-dissolution-in-effect

4   Samer Anabtawi and Nathan J. Brown, "Why Mahmoud Abbas dissolved the Palestinian parliament — and what it means for the future," *The Washington Post*, January 18, 2019. https://www.washingtonpost.com/news/monkey-cage/wp/2019/01/18/heres-what-the-dissolution-of-the-legislative-council-means-for-the-future-of-palestinian-governance

5   Palestinian Council of Ministers, "Dr. Mohammad Shtayyeh," accessed July 2, 2021. http://www.palestinecabinet.gov.ps/portal/Government/PrimeMinisterEn

6   Grant Rumley and Evan Charney, "Meet Mahmoud al-Aloul, Abbas' New Deputy," *Foundation for Defense of Democracies*, February 15, 2017. https://www.fdd.org/analysis/2017/02/15/meet-mahmoud-al-aloul-abbas-new-deputy

7   "A Step Towards Peace: The 'New Normal' for the United Arab Emirates," *Event Hosted by the Foundation for Defense of Democracies*, October 8, 2020. https://www.fdd.org/events/2020/10/08/a-step-towards-peace-the-new-normal-for-the-united-arab-emirates/

8   U.S. Department of State, Bureau of Near Eastern Affairs, "The Abraham Accords," accessed July 2, 2021. https://www.state.gov/the-abraham-accords

9   Steve Holland, "Morocco joins other Arab nations agreeing to normalize Israel ties," *Reuters*, December 10, 2020. https://www.reuters.com/article/israel-usa-morocco-int/morocco-joins-other-arab-nations-agreeing-to-normalize-israel-ties-idUSKBN28K2CW

10   "Sudan signs pact with US on normalizing ties with Israel," *Deutsche Welle* (Germany), January 6, 2021. https://www.dw.com/en/sudan-signs-pact-with-us-on-normalizing-ties-with-israel/a-56148309

11   Salih al-Na'ami, "الانتخابات الفلسطينية 2021: السياق والتوقعات [Palestinian Elections 2021: Context and Prospects]," *Al Jazeera* (Qatar), January 29, 2021. https://studies.aljazeera.net/ar/article/4902

12   "Fatah, Hamas say deal reached on Palestinian elections," *Al Jazeera* (Qatar), September 24, 2020. https://www.aljazeera.com/news/2020/9/24/fatah-hamas-say-deal-reached-on-palestinian-elections

13   Interview with Egyptian official, Washington, DC, June 1, 2021.

14   Isabel Kershner and Adam Rasgon, "Abbas Announces Palestinian Elections After Years of Paralysis," *The New York Times*, January 15, 2021. https://www.nytimes.com/2021/01/15/world/middleeast/palestinian-elections-abbas.html

15   Ali Sawafta, Nidal al-Mughrabi, and Rami Ayyub, "Palestinians announce first elections in 15 years, on eve of Biden era," *Reuters*, January 15, 2021. https://www.reuters.com/article/us-palestinians-election/palestinians-announce-first-elections-in-15-years-on-eve-of-biden-era-idUSKBN29K2C9

16   "Jerusalem issue complicates Palestinian elections," *The Arab Weekly* (UK), December 22, 2019. https://thearabweekly.com/jerusalem-issue-complicates-palestinian-elections

17   Aaron Boxerman, "PA demands Israel allow East Jerusalemites to take part in Palestinian elections," *The Times of Israel* (Israel), January 18, 2021. https://www.timesofisrael.com/pa-demands-israel-allow-east-jerusalemites-to-take-part-in-palestinian-elections

18   Khaled Abu Toameh and Lahav Harkov, "PA: Jerusalem Arabs to participate in Palestinian elections," *The Jerusalem Post* (Israel), March 14, 2021. https://www.jpost.com/middle-east/pa-jerusalem-arabs-to-participate-in-palestinian-elections-661979

19   Phone interview with senior Israeli official, April 4, 2021.

20   Ibid.

21   "Public Opinion Poll No (77)," *Palestinian Center for Policy and Survey Research*, September 15, 2020. https://www.pcpsr.org/sites/default/files/Poll%2077%20English%20full%20text%20September2020.pdf

22   "[Public Opinion Poll No. (78)]," نتائج استطلاع الرأي العام رقم (87) *Palestinian Center for Policy and Survey Research*, December 8–11, 2020. https://www.pcpsr.org/ar/node/830

23   Edith M. Lederer, "US gives \$15 million to Palestinians to deal with COVID-19," *Associated Press*, March 25, 2021. https://abcnews.go.com/US/wireStory/us-15-million-palestinians-deal-covid-19-76684275

24   Matthew Lee, "Biden administration quietly ramping up aid to Palestinians," *Associated Press*, March 31, 2021. https://abcnews.go.com/Politics/wireStory/biden-administration-quietly-ramping-aid-palestinians-76790948

25   Cody Levine, "US memo details Biden Administration's Palestinian 'reset'-report," *The Jerusalem Post* (Israel), March 17, 2021. https://www.jpost.com/middle-east/us-memo-details-biden-administrations-palestinian-reset-report-662334

26   Khaled Abu Toameh, "Hamas presents list of candidates for parliamentary election," *The Jerusalem Post* (Israel), March 29, 2021. https://www.jpost.com/middle-east/hamas-presents-list-of-candidates-for-parliamentary-election-663540

27   "Biden Administration Requests Clarification on Hamas-Fatah Election Partnership," *Asharq Al-Awsat* (UK), February 17, 2021. https://english.aawsat.com/home/article/2810766/biden-administration-requests-clarification-hamas-fatah-election-partnership

28   Khaled Abu Toameh, "Israel, US asked Abbas to delay or cancel Palestinian elections – report," *The Jerusalem Post* (Israel), March 16, 2021. https://www.jpost.com/middle-east/israel-us-asked-abbas-to-delay-or-cancel-palestinian-elections-report-662195

29   "Report: Biden's teams asks PA's Abbas to hold elections," *Middle East Monitor*, January 13, 2021. https://www.middleeastmonitor.com/20210113-report-bidens-teams-asks-pas-abbas-to-hold-elections

30   Palestinian Anti-Terrorism Act of 2006, Pub. L. 109-446, 120 Stat. 3318, codified as amended at 22 U.S.C. §2378. https://www.govinfo.gov/content/pkg/PLAW-109publ446/html/PLAW-109publ446.htm

31   Salih al-Naʿami, "الانتخابات الفلسطينية ٢٠٢١: السياق والتوقعات" [Palestinian Elections 2021: Context and Prospects]," *Al Jazeera* (Qatar), January 29, 2021. https://studies.aljazeera.net/ar/article/4902

32   Jack Khoury, "Palestinian Court Sentences Abbas Rival Dahlan to Three Years in Jail," *Haaretz* (Israel), December 14, 2016. https://www.haaretz.com/middle-east-news/palestinians/palestinian-court-convicts-dahlan-of-theft-1.5473981

33   Aaron Boxerman, "Exiled Abbas rival Mohammad Dahlan hints he could run for PA president," *The Times of Israel* (Israel), March 18, 2021. https://www.timesofisrael.com/exiled-abbas-rival-mohammad-dahlan-hints-he-could-run-for-pa-president

34   Aaron Boxerman, "At request of Abbas foe, UAE will send another 40,000 Russian vaccines to Gaza," *The Times of Israel* (Israel), March 10, 2021. https://www.timesofisrael.com/at-behest-of-abbas-foe-uae-will-send-another-40000-russian-vaccines-to-gaza

35   Avi Issacharoff, "Barghouti calls for Palestinian leadership primaries as heat turns up for Israel," *The Times of Israel* (Israel), February 21, 2021. https://www.timesofisrael.com/barghouti-calls-for-palestinian-leadership-primaries-as-heat-turns-up-for-israel

36   "Poll: Barghouti to win Palestine presidential elections," *Middle East Monitor*, March 30, 2021. https://www.middleeastmonitor.com/20210330-poll-barghouti-to-win-palestine-presidential-elections

37   Aaron Boxerman, "In blow to Abbas, senior Fatah official to form separate bloc to run in election," *The Times of Israel* (Israel), March 4, 2021. https://www.timesofisrael.com/in-blow-to-abbas-senior-fatah-official-to-form-separate-bloc-to-run-in-election

38   Nidal al-Mughrabi and Ali Sawafta, "Fatah expels Arafat's nephew over election breakaway bid," *Reuters*, March 11, 2021. https://www.reuters.com/article/palestinians-election-abbas-int/fatah-expels-arafats-nephew-over-election-breakaway-bid-idUSKBN2B31AA

39   "Palestinians offered a Third Way," *Al Jazeera* (Qatar), January 17, 2006. https://www.aljazeera.com/news/2006/1/17/palestinians-offered-a-third-way

40   Joseph Massad, "Palestinian elections: The resurrection of Salam Fayyad," *Middle East Eye*, March 18, 2021. https://www.middleeasteye.net/opinion/palestine-elections-salam-fayyad-resurrection

41   Aaron Boxerman, "93% of Palestinians register to vote in election, amid claims of voter tampering," *The Times of Israel* (Israel), February 17, 2021. https://www.timesofisrael.com/93-of-palestinians-register-to-vote-in-election-amid-claims-of-voter-tampering

42   Nathan J. Brown, "The Benefits of a Ballot," *Carnegie Middle East Center*, March 24, 2021. https://carnegie-mec.org/diwan/84156

43   "Report: Shin Bet Chief Demanded President Abbas Cancel the Palestinian Elections," *Haaretz* (Israel), March 31, 2021. https://www.haaretz.com/israel-news/report-shin-bet-chief-demanded-president-abbas-cancel-the-palestinian-elections-1.9672299

44   Aaron Boxerman, "Abbas said to tell Shin Bet head he won't call off elections: 'You built Hamas,'" *The Times of Israel* (Israel), April 1, 2021. https://www.timesofisrael.com/abbas-said-to-tell-shin-bet-head-he-wont-call-off-elections-you-built-hamas

45   "Military liaison: Israel should end security ties with PA if Hamas wins election," *The Times of Israel* (Israel), April 1, 2021. https://www.timesofisrael.com/military-liaison-israel-should-end-security-ties-with-pa-if-hamas-wins-election

46   Phone interview with senior Israeli official, April 4, 2021.

47   World Health Organization, Regional Office for the Eastern Mediterranean, "Coronavirus disease 2019 (COVID-19 Situation Report 68)," March 18, 2021, page 2. Available at: https://www.un.org/unispal/document/coronavirus-disease-2019-covid-19-who-situation-report-68/

48   Oliver Holmes and Hazem Balousha, "Israel allows 2,000 Covid vaccine doses into Gaza after hold-up," *The Guardian* (UK), February 17, 2021. https://www.theguardian.com/world/2021/feb/17/israel-allows-1000-covid-vaccines-into-blockaded-gaza-after-hold-up

49   Ken Stein, "Analyses of Palestinian Community in 2021," *Center for Israel Education*, April 12, 2021, https://israeled.org/analyses-of-palestinian-community-in-2021-bibliography-and-references/

50   Palestinian Central Elections Commission, "Presidential decrees and Cabinet Decisions," accessed July 2, 2021. https://www.elections.ps/tabid/288/language/en-US/Default.aspx

51   Loveday Morris, "A U.S. law is about to end security aid to the Palestinians, and Israel is not happy," *The Washington Post*, January 31, 2019. https://www.washingtonpost.com/world/middle_east/a-us-law-is-about-to-end-security-aid-to-the-palestinians-and-israel-is-not-happy/2019/01/31/d5d8d750-2550-11e9-ad53-824486280311_story.html

52   "Palestinians ask Europe to send monitors for elections," *Associated Press*, January 24, 2021. https://apnews.com/article/legislature-europe-israel-elections-west-bank-24478d71e9b71270a7343d6c978d6d37

53   Email correspondence with Paloma Garron Carrillo De Albornoz, Project Manager, DT Global, April 13, 2021.

54   "US source to Palestinian paper: Washington will understand election postponement," *The Times of Israel* (Israel), April 17, 2021. https://www.timesofisrael.com/us-source-to-palestinian-paper-washington-will-understand-election-postponement

55   Ghaith al-Omari, "Preserving Israeli-Palestinian Security Cooperation," *The Washington Institute for Near East Policy*, April 10, 2015. https://www.washingtoninstitute.org/policy-analysis/preserving-israeli-palestinian-security-cooperation

56   Nidal al-Mughrabi, Ali Sawafta, and Rami Ayyub, "Palestinian leader
        delays parliamentary and presidential elections, blaming Israel," *Reuters*,
        April 30, 2021. https://www.reuters.com/world/middle-east/palestinian-
        elections-delayed-says-president-mahmoud-abbas-2021-04-29

CHAPTER NINE | THE WAR BETWEEN WARS

1   Yaakov Lappin, "'The War Between Wars': Israel vs Iran in Syria," *Fathom
        Journal*, October 2018. https://fathomjournal.org/the-war-between-wars-
        israel-vs-iran-in-syria. This is also known as the "campaign between wars."

2   Michal Shmulovich, "Israel's strike on Syria also hit biological weapons
        facility, says report," *The Times of Israel* (Israel), February 2, 2013. https://
        www.timesofisrael.com/extra-targets-hit-during-israels-strike-on-syria-
        western-sources-tell-time

3   Anne Barnard, Michael R. Gordon, and Jodi Rudoren, "Israel Targeted
        Iranian Missiles in Syria Attack," *The New York Times*, May 4, 2013. https://
        www.nytimes.com/2013/05/05/world/middleeast/israel-syria.html

4   Ariel Ben Solomon, "Syrian opposition: Israeli jets bomb missile launchers
        in Latakia," *The Jerusalem Post* (Israel), January 27, 2014. https://www.jpost.
        com/defense/syrian-opposition-israeli-jets-bomb-missile-launchers-in-
        latakia-339465

5   Ilan Ben Zion, "Israeli jets reportedly strike arms shipment en route to
        Hezbollah," *The Times of Israel* (Israel), February 24, 2014. https://www.
        timesofisrael.com/israeli-jets-reportedly-strike-targets-near-lebanon-syria-
        border

6   "Israeli air strikes in Golan 'kill Syrian soldier,'" *BBC News* (UK), March
        19, 2014. https://www.bbc.com/news/world-middle-east-26641815

7   Orlando Crowcroft, "Israeli Air Strikes Hit Syrian Military Targets," *The
        Guardian* (UK), June 22, 2014. https://www.theguardian.com/world/2014/
        jun/23/israel-air-strikes-syria

8   "Israeli Jets 'Strike Near Damascus' – Syrian Army," *BBC News*
        (UK), December 7, 2014. https://www.bbc.com/news/world-middle-
        east-30370670

9   Itamar Sharon, "Six Iranians, including a general, killed in Israeli strike,"
        The Times of Israel (Israel), January 19, 2015. https://www.timesofisrael.com/
        six-iranians-also-said-killed-in-alleged-israeli-strike

10   "Israel air force hits Syrian army after Golan rocket fire," *Yahoo News*,
        January 28, 2015. https://news.yahoo.com/israel-hits-syrian-military-
        targets-golan-rockets-075003685.html

11   Thomas Joscelyn, "Death by Car Bomb in Damascus," *The Washington Examiner*, February 25, 2008. https://www.washingtonexaminer.com/ weekly-standard/death-by-car-bomb-in-damascus

12   Avi Issacharoff, "Israel reportedly hits Hezbollah, Assad targets in Syria," *The Times of Israel* (Israel), April 25, 2015. https://www.timesofisrael.com/ israel-reportedly-hits-hezbollah-assad-targets-in-syria

13   Judah Ari Gross and Mitch Ginsburg, "Airstrike kills squad placing mine on northern border," *The Times of Israel* (Israel), April 26, 2015. https:// www.timesofisrael.com/israel-thwarts-attack-on-northern-border-kills-four-terrorists

14   "Pro-Syrian military source denies reports of Israeli strikes inside Syria," *Reuters*, February 17, 2016. https://uk.reuters.com/article/us-mideast-crisis-syria-israel/pro-syrian-military-source-denies-reports-of-israeli-strikes-inside-syria-idUKKCN0VQ2WA

15   "Report: Israeli fighter jets strike weapons convoy headed towards Hezbollah," *The Jerusalem Post* (Israel), May 10, 2016. https://www.jpost. com/arab-israeli-conflict/report-israeli-fighter-jets-strike-weapons-convoy-on-way-to-hezbollah-453649

16   "Top Hezbollah commander in Syria killed by Israel, Lebanese TV says," *The Times of Israel* (Israel), May 13, 2016. https://www.timesofisrael.com/ top-hezbollah-commander-in-syria-killed-by-israel-lebanese-media-says

17   Gili Cohen, "Israeli Airstrikes Target ISIS Facility in Syria, Hours after First Direct Clashes in Golan Heights," *Haaretz* (Israel), November 28, 2016. https://www.haaretz.com/israel-news/israeli-airstrikes-target-isis-facility-in-syria-after-direct-clashes-1.5466995

18   "Airbase near Damascus said bombed by Israel," *The Times of Israel* (Israel), January 13, 2017. https://www.timesofisrael.com/damascus-airbase-said-bombed-by-israeli-planes

19   "Judah Ari Gross, Israeli jets strike outside Damascus – Syrian media," *The Times of Israel* (Israel), February 22, 2017. https://www.timesofisrael.com/ israeli-jets-strike-outside-damascus-syrian-media

20   Jack Khoury, Noa Shpigel, and Gili Cohen, "Syrians Report Israeli Drone Strike Kills Commander of pro-Assad Militia," *Haaretz* (Israel), March 19, 2017. https://www.haaretz.com/israel-news/reports-israeli-drone-strike-kills-pro-assad-militia-commander-1.5450716

21   "Syria war: 'Israeli strike' hits military site near Damascus airport," *BBC News* (UK), April 27, 2017. https://www.bbc.com/news/world-middle-east-39728682

22   William Booth, "Israel hits Syrian military targets after errant fire reaches its side of the Golan Heights," *The Washington Post*, June 24, 2017. https://www.washingtonpost.com/world/middle_east/israel-hits-syrian-military-targets-after-errant-fire-reaches-its-side-of-the-golan-heights/2017/06/24/44d5aa98-5910-11e7-840b-512026319da7_story.html

23   "Israeli Air Strikes Hit Military Facility in Hama Province, Syrian Army Says," *France 24* (France), July 9, 2017. https://www.france24.com/en/20170907-israel-syria-air-strikes-hit-military-facility-hama-province-army

24   Peter Beaumont, "Israeli Jets Bombed Site Close to Damascus Airport, Reports Say," *The Guardian* (UK), September 22, 2017. https://www.theguardian.com/world/2017/sep/22/israeli-jets-bomb-site-close-to-damascus-airport-reports-say; Peter Beaumont, Israeli Jets Attack Anti-Aircraft Battery in Syria in Retaliatory Strike, *The Guardian* (UK), October 16, 2017. https://www.theguardian.com/world/2017/oct/16/israeli-jets-attack-anti-aircraft-battery-in-syria-in-retaliatory-strike; "Syrian groups report Israeli airstrikes near Damascus," *Deutsche Welle* (Germany), December 5, 2017. https://www.dw.com/en/syrian-groups-report-israeli-airstrikes-near-damascus/a-41650869

25   Tony Badran and Jonathan Schanzer, "The Iran-Israel War Flares Up," *The Wall Street Journal*, February 11, 2018. https://www.wsj.com/articles/the-iran-israel-war-flares-up-1518377530

26   Gili Cohen, "Israel Shoots Down Syrian Drone Over Golan Heights," *Haaretz* (Israel), April 27, 2017. https://www.haaretz.com/israel-news/israel-shoots-down-syrian-drone-over-golan-heights-1.5466014

27   "Israeli airstrikes against Syria 'biggest since 1982,'" *BBC News* (UK), February 10, 2018. https://www.bbc.com/news/world-middle-east-43019682

28   "Israel TV: Monday's strike on Syria targeted air base Iran was building," *The Times of Israel* (Israel), April 10, 2018. https://www.timesofisrael.com/israel-tv-mondays-strike-on-syria-targeted-air-base-iran-was-building

29   Judah Ari Gross, "Death toll from Syria strike rises to 15, including 8 Iranians — monitor," *The Times of Israel* (Israel), May 9, 2018. https://www.timesofisrael.com/death-toll-from-syria-strike-rises-to-15-including-8-iranians-monitor

30   Stuart Winer, "New images show damage at Damascus International Airport from Israeli strike," *The Times of Israel* (Israel), May 13, 2018. https://www.timesofisrael.com/new-images-show-damage-at-damascus-international-airport-from-israeli-strike

31   "Iraq denounces mysterious Syria airstrike attributed to Israel," *The Times of Israel* (Israel), June 19, 2018. https://www.timesofisrael.com/iraq-denounces-mysterious-syria-airstrike-attributed-to-israel

32   "Netanyahu confirms latest Israeli strike in Syria," *Reuters*, February 12, 2019. https://www.reuters.com/article/us-mideast-crisis-syria-israel/netanyahu-confirms-latest-israeli-strike-in-syria-idUSKCN1Q12PB

33   Tamar Pileggi, "Top minister: 'As far as Iran knows, it's Israel' that carried out Syria strike," *The Times of Israel* (Israel), March 28, 2019. https://www.timesofisrael.com/top-minister-as-far-as-iran-knows-its-israel-that-carried-out-syria-strike

34   Tamar Pileggi, "Netanyahu appears to hint Israel carried out latest Syria strike," *The Times of Israel* (Israel), April 14, 2019. https://www.timesofisrael.com/netanyahu-appears-to-hint-israel-carried-out-latest-syria-strike

35   Judah Ari Gross, "IDF says it bombed Syrian anti-aircraft battery that fired at Israeli jet," *The Times of Israel* (Israel), May 27, 2019. https://www.timesofisrael.com/idf-says-it-bombed-syrian-anti-aircraft-battery-that-fired-at-israeli-jet

36   "Israeli intel firm: Alleged IDF strike on Syrian base targeted Iranian drone," *The Times of Israel* (Israel), June 4, 2019. https://www.timesofisrael.com/israeli-intel-firm-alleged-idf-strike-on-syrian-base-targeted-iranian-drones

37   "Syrian State Media Claims Israeli Airstrikes Hit Sites Near Damascus," *The Guardian* (UK), July 1, 2019. https://www.theguardian.com/world/2019/jul/01/syria-state-media-claims-israeli-airstrikes-hit-sites-near-damascus

38   "Israel hits Iranian force in Syria to stop 'killer drones': military," *Reuters*, August 24, 2019. https://www.reuters.com/article/us-syria-security-explosions/israel-hits-iranian-force-in-syria-to-stop-killer-drones-military-idUSKCN1VE0SN

39   "Nearly 40 Strikes Hit Syrian Territories Since Early 2019, Killing 11 Civilians, and 225 Iranians, Regime Soldiers and Loyalists," *Syrian Observatory for Human Rights*, June 5, 2020. https://www.syriahr.com/en/?p=168371

40   Anna Ahronheim, "Senior defense official: Iran reducing presence in Syria," *The Jerusalem Post* (Israel), May 5, 2020. https://www.jpost.com/middle-east/senior-defense-official-iran-reducing-presence-in-syria-626985

41   "Israeli Strike in Syria Said to Hit Onion Factory Used by Iran to Store Weapons," *The Times of Israel* (Israel), June 26, 2020. https://www.timesofisrael.com/israeli-strike-in-syria-said-to-hit-onion-factory-used-by-iran-to-store-weapons

42   "Israel Attacks Weapon Truck Convoy in Syria Bound for Hezbollah – Report," *The Jerusalem Post* (Israel), July 6, 2020. https://www.jpost.com/breaking-news/israel-attacks-weapon-truck-convoy-in-syria-bound-for-hezbollah-report-633998

43   "Intel firm: Strikes on Syrian airfields halted Iran's ability to transport arms," *The Times of Israel* (Israel), September 3, 2020. https://www.timesofisrael.com/intel-firm-strikes-on-syrian-airfields-halted-irans-ability-to-transport-arms

44   "Iranian Revolutionary Guards commander reported killed in drone strike," *The Times of Israel* (Israel), December 1, 2020. https://www.timesofisrael.com/iranian-revolutionary-guards-commander-reported-killed-in-drone-strike

45   Suleiman al-Khalidi, "Israel intensifying air war in Syria against Iranian encroachment," *Reuters*, April 22, 2021. https://www.reuters.com/world/middle-east/israel-intensifying-air-war-syria-against-iranian-encroachment-2021-04-22; Anna Ahronheim, "Rise in Israeli strikes in Syria has led to decrease of Iranian activity," *The Jerusalem Post* (Israel), December 10, 2020. https://www.jpost.com/middle-east/rise-in-israeli-strikes-in-syria-has-led-to-decrease-of-iranian-activity-651716

46   ‫""תקפנו אלפי מטרות בסוריה ולבנון בלי לקחת אחריות :איזנקוט"‬ [Eizenkot: "We struck thousands of targets in Syria and Lebanon without claiming responsibility"]," *Mako* (Israel), January 12, 2019. https://www.mako.co.il/news-military/security-q1_2019/Article-c092baefba14861004.htm

47   "Israel Hits Iran-Backed Forces In Syria For First Time In Biden Presidency," *Syrian Observatory for Human Rights*, January 28, 2021. https://www.syriahr.com/en/202614

48   Suleiman al-Khalidi, "Israel intensifying air war in Syria against Iranian encroachment," *Reuters*, April 22, 2021. https://www.reuters.com/world/middle-east/israel-intensifying-air-war-syria-against-iranian-encroachment-2021-04-22

49   Amos Harel, "Airstrikes in Syria Shake up Israel's Détente with Russia," *Haaretz* (Israel), July 27, 2021, https://www.haaretz.com/israel-news/airstrikes-in-syria-shake-up-israel-s-detente-with-russia-1.10031383?

50   "Iranian ship damaged in Mediterranean, Iran alleges 'terrorist' attack," *Reuters*, March 12, 2021. https://www.jpost.com/breaking-news/iranian-ship-damaged-in-mediterranean-iran-alleges-terrorist-attack-661815

51   Gordon Lubold, Benoit Faucon, and Felicia Schwartz, "Israeli Strikes Target Iranian Oil Bound for Syria," *The Wall Street Journal*, March 11, 2021. https://www.wsj.com/articles/israel-strikes-target-iranian-oil-bound-for-syria-11615492789

52   "Iranian 'spy ship' damaged by explosion in Red Sea," *BBC News* (UK), April 7, 2021. https://www.bbc.com/news/world-middle-east-56661069

53   Seth J. Frantzman, "Iranian fuel tanker attacked by drone, Israel suspected," *The Jerusalem Post* (Israel), April 24, 2021. https://www.jpost.com/breaking-news/syrian-oil-tanker-damaged-after-being-hit-by-suspected-drone-attack-666224

54   Tzvi Joffre, "Mysterious explosion on oil tanker off coast of Syria – report," *The Jerusalem Post* (Israel), May 9, 2021. https://www.jpost.com/breaking-news/explosion-on-ship-off-coast-of-syria-report-667669

55   Steve Hendrix, "Israel blames Iran for attack on freighter near the Persian Gulf," *The Washington Post*, March 1, 2021. https://www.washingtonpost.com/world/middle_east/israel-freighter-strike-iran/2021/03/01/3b25fed6-7a71-11eb-8c5e-32e47b42b51b_story.html

56   Arie Egozi, "Israeli Cargo Ship Struck In Oman Gulf After US Air Strike," *Breaking Defense*, February 26, 2021. https://breakingdefense.com/2021/02/israeli-cargo-ship-struck-in-oman-gulf-after-us-air-strike

57   "Ship owned by Israeli firm attacked off UAE coast: media," *Reuters*, April 13, 2021. https://www.reuters.com/world/middle-east/ship-owned-by-israeli-firm-attacked-off-uae-coast-media-2021-04-13

58   Lolita C. Baldor and Frank Jordans, "US and G7 Blame Iran for Deadly Attack on Tanker Off Oman," *Associated Press,* August 6, 2021, https://apnews.com/article/europe-middle-east-business-iran-persian-gulf-tensions-c1f24a3744785bc0514697edf8f0887f

59   Stephen Farrell, "Iranian nuclear scientist killed by one-ton automatic gun in Israeli hit: Jewish Chronicle," *Reuters*, February 10, 2021. https://www.reuters.com/article/us-iran-nuclear-scientist/iranian-nuclear-scientist-killed-by-one-ton-automated-gun-in-israeli-hit-jewish-chronicle-idUSKBN2AA2RC

60   Mehdi Jedinia, "History of Assassinations of Iran's Top Nuclear Scientists," *Voice of America*, December 3, 2020. https://www.voanews.com/extremism-watch/history-assassinations-irans-top-nuclear-scientists

61   Adam Goldman, Eric Schmitt, Farnaz Fassihi, and Ronen Bergman, "Al Qaeda's No. 2, Accused in U.S. Embassy Attacks, Was Killed in Iran," *The New York Times*, November 13, 2020. https://www.nytimes.com/2020/11/13/world/middleeast/al-masri-abdullah-qaeda-dead.html

62   Thomas Joscelyn, *Iran's Proxy War Against America* (Upland, CA: The Claremont Institute, 2007). https://books.google.com/books/about/Iran_s_Proxy_War_Against_America.html?id=UoELTPp9r0QC

63   Yaakov Katz, "'Stuxnet virus set back Iran's nuclear program by 2 years,'" *The Jerusalem Post* (Israel), December 15, 2020. https://www.jpost.com/iranian-threat/news/stuxnet-virus-set-back-irans-nuclear-program-by-2-years

64   "Iran accuses Israel of failed cyber-attack," *Reuters*, November 5, 2018. https://www.reuters.com/article/us-iran-israel-cyber/iran-accuses-israel-of-failed-cyber-attack-idUSKCN1NA1LJ

65   "Iran reports 'large-scale' cyberattack on government institutions," *The Times of Israel* (Israel), October 14, 2020. https://www.timesofisrael.com/iran-reports-major-cyberattack-on-government-institutions

66   Joby Warrick and Ellen Nakashima, "Officials: Israel linked to a disruptive
      cyberattack on Iranian port facility," *The Washington Post*, May 18, 2020.
      https://www.washingtonpost.com/national-security/officials-israel-linked-
      to-a-disruptive-cyberattack-on-iranian-port-facility/2020/05/18/9d1da866-
      9942-11ea-89fd-28fb313d1886_story.html

67   Maggie Miller, "Iranian hackers targeting US, Israeli medical researchers:
      analysis," *The Hill*, March 31, 2021. https://thehill.com/policy/
      cybersecurity/545654-iranian-hackers-targeting-us-israeli-medical-
      researchers-analysis

68   Tim Starks, "Suspected Iranian hackers snooping on Middle Eastern
      targets anew," *CyberScoop*, March 5, 2021. https://www.cyberscoop.com/
      suspected-iranian-hackers-snooping-on-middle-eastern-targets-anew

69   Staurt Winer, "Cyberattack hits Israeli companies, with Iran reportedly the
      likely culprit," *The Times of Israel* (Israel), December 13 2020. https://www.
      timesofisrael.com/israels-supply-chain-targeted-in-massive-cyberattack

70   John Evans, "OTORIO confirms Iranian hackers gained access to ICS
      at an Israeli water reservoir," *Industrial Cyber*, December 7, 2020. https://
      industrialcyber.co/threats-attacks/industrial-cyber-attacks/otorio-confirms-
      iranian-hackers-gained-access-to-ics-at-an-israeli-water-reservoir

71   "Significant Cyber Incidents Since 2006," *Center for Strategic and
      International Studies*, May 15, 2021. https://www.csis.org/programs/
      strategic-technologies-program/significant-cyber-incidents

72   "Iran hackers came close to infiltrating Israel missile alarm system: report,"
      i24NEWS (Israel), February 25 2019. https://www.i24news.tv/en/news/
      middle-east/195968-190225-iran-hackers-came-close-to-infiltrating-
      israel-missile-alarm-system-report

73   David M. Halbfinger and Ronen Bergman, "Gantz, Netanyahu's
      Challenger, Faces Lurid Questions After Iran Hacked His Phone," *The New
      York Times*, March 15, 2019. https://www.nytimes.com/2019/03/15/world/
      middleeast/gantz-netanyahus-challenger-faces-lurid-questions-after-iran-
      hacked-his-phone.html

74   David E. Sanger and Ronen Bergman, "How Israel, in Dark of Night,
      Torched Its Way to Iran's Nuclear Secrets," *The New York Times*, July 15,
      2018. https://www.nytimes.com/2018/07/15/us/politics/iran-israel-mossad-
      nuclear.html

75   Aaron Arnold, Matthew Bunn, Caitlin Chase, Steven E. Miller, Rolf
      Mowatt-Larssen, and William H. Tobey, "The Iran Nuclear Archive:
      Impressions and Implications," *The Belfer Center for Science and International
      Affairs*, April 2019, pages 1–3. https://www.belfercenter.org/sites/default/
      files/files/publication/The%20Iran%20Nuclear%20Archive.pdf

76   "Satellite images show activity at Iran site exposed in Mossad-seized nuke files," *The Times of Israel* (Israel), June 9, 2021. https://www.timesofisrael.com/satellite-images-show-activity-at-iran-site-exposed-in-mossad-seized-nuke-files

77   "Iran's Top Commander: Zionists to Come to Senses by Resistance Front," *Fars News Agency* (Iran), April 25, 2021. https://www.farsnews.ir/en/news/14000205000407/Iran%E2%80%99s-Tp-Cmmander-Ziniss-Cme-Senses-by-Resisance-Frn

78   "IRGC chief: Recent incidents against Zionists may be repeated," *Tehran Times* (Iran), April 26, 2021. https://www.tehrantimes.com/news/460283/IRGC-chief-Recent-incidents-against-the-Zionists-may-be-repeated

79   Tom O'Connor, "Top Iranian General Says Israel Could Be Defeated With 'a Single Operation,'" *Newsweek*, May 5, 2021. https://www.newsweek.com/top-iranian-general-says-israel-could-defeated-single-operation-1589062

CHAPTER TEN | THE 2021 GAZA WAR

1   "Hamas fires rockets at Jerusalem after clashes at mosque," *Associated Press*, May 10, 2021. https://www.politico.com/news/2021/05/10/israeli-police-and-palestinians-clash-at-jerusalem-holy-site-486540

2   Sammy Westfall, "Indiscriminate Hamas Rocket Attacks on Israel Are War Crimes, Human Rights Watch Says," *The Washington Post*, August 12, 2021, https://www.washingtonpost.com/world/2021/08/12/hamas-rockets-war-crimes/

3   Amos Harel, "The Rockets Hamas Fired at Israel Reflect the Success of Gaza's Military Industry," *Haaretz* (Israel), May 26, 2021. https://www.haaretz.com/middle-east-news/palestinians/.premium.HIGHLIGHT-hamas-rockets-reflect-success-in-creating-gaza-military-industry-1.9843784?lts=1623093257392

4   Judah Ari Gross and Aaron Boxerman, "2 women killed by rockets in Ashkelon amid massive barrages from Gaza," *The Times of Israel* (Israel), May 11, 2021. https://www.timesofisrael.com/2-killed-by-rockets-in-ashkelon-amid-massive-barrages-from-gaza

5   @IDF, "Hamas and Islamic Jihad have fired 3,100 rockets from Gaza in the past 7 days. That's the highest daily rate of rocket fire that Israel has faced in the history of the country. The threat is real. Millions of Israelis are living under fire. We will continue to defend ourselves." *Twitter*, May 16, 2021. https://twitter.com/IDF/status/1393992449979260928

6   Judah Ari Gross, "Hamas says it beat Iron Dome with concentrated salvos. The IDF says it didn't," *The Times of Israel* (Israel), May 7, 2021. https://www.timesofisrael.com/hamas-boasts-it-overcame-iron-dome-with-concentrated-rocket-salvos-it-didnt

7   Phone briefing by IDF official, May 13, 2021.

8   Isabel Debre, "How Hamas amassed thousands of rockets to strike at
        Israel," *Los Angeles Times*, May 20, 2021. https://www.latimes.com/world-
        nation/story/2021-05-20/hamas-amass-arsenal-rockets-strike-israel

9   Seth J. Frantzman, "Iran: Hamas already rebuilding Iran-backed rocket
        arsenal," *The Jerusalem Post* (Israel), May 31, 2021. https://www.jpost.
        com/arab-israeli-conflict/gaza-news/iran-hamas-already-rebuilding-iran-
        backed-rocket-arsenal-669680

10   Patrick Kingsley and Ronen Bergman, "Israel's Military Inflicted a Heavy
        Toll. But Did It Achieve Its Aim?" *The New York Times*, May 21, 2021.
        https://www.nytimes.com/2021/05/21/world/middleeast/israel-gaza-war-
        ceasefire.html

11   Amos Harel, "The Rockets Hamas Fired at Israel Reflect the Success of
        Gaza's Military Industry," *Haaretz* (Israel), May 26, 2021. https://www.
        haaretz.com/middle-east-news/palestinians/.premium.HIGHLIGHT-
        hamas-rockets-reflect-success-in-creating-gaza-military-industry-
        1.9843784?lts=1623093257392

12   Michael J. Armstrong, "Gaza's enhanced rocket technology challenges
        Israel's defences," *The Conversation*, May 17, 2021. https://theconversation.
        com/gazas-enhanced-rocket-technology-challenges-israels-
        defences-160853

13   Amos Harel, "The Rockets Hamas Fired at Israel Reflect the Success of
        Gaza's Military Industry," *Haaretz* (Israel), May 26, 2021. https://www.
        haaretz.com/middle-east-news/palestinians/.premium.HIGHLIGHT-
        hamas-rockets-reflect-success-in-creating-gaza-military-industry-
        1.9843784?lts=1623093257392

14   Alex Safian, "How Many Gaza Palestinians Were Killed by Hamas Rockets
        in May? An Estimate," *The Begin-Sadat Center for Strategic Studies*, June 27,
        2021. https://besacenter.org/how-many-gaza-palestinians-were-killed-by-
        hamas-rockets-in-may-an-estimate

15   Claire Parker and Adam Taylor, "What weapons do Palestinian militants in
        the Gaza Strip have and how powerful are they?" *The Washington Post*, May
        13, 2021. https://www.washingtonpost.com/world/2021/05/13/faq-hamas-
        missiles

16   @IDF, "The IDF has successfully completed Operation Guardian
        of the Walls. This is what the 12-day-long operation looked like
        in numbers:" *Twitter*, May 22, 2021. https://twitter.com/IDF/
        status/1396170789305659402

17   Claire Parker and Adam Taylor, "What weapons do Palestinian militants in
        the Gaza Strip have and how powerful are they?" *The Washington Post*, May
        13, 2021. https://www.washingtonpost.com/world/2021/05/13/faq-hamas-
        missiles

18   Seth J. Frantzman, "Iran: Hamas already rebuilding Iran-backed rocket arsenal," *The Jerusalem Post* (Israel), May 31, 2021. https://www.jpost. com/arab-israeli-conflict/gaza-news/iran-hamas-already-rebuilding-iran-backed-rocket-arsenal-669680

19   Claire Parker and Adam Taylor, "What weapons do Palestinian militants in the Gaza Strip have and how powerful are they?" *The Washington Post*, May 13, 2021. https://www.washingtonpost.com/world/2021/05/13/faq-hamas-missiles; Fabian Hinz, "Iran's Rockets to Palestinian Groups," *United States Institute of Peace*, May 24, 2021. https://iranprimer.usip.org/blog/2021/may/19/irans-rockets-palestinian-groups

20   Fabian Hinz, "Iran Transfers Rockets to Palestinian Groups," *The Wilson Center*, May 19, 2021. https://www.wilsoncenter.org/article/irans-rockets-palestinian-groups

21   Amos Harel, "The Rockets Hamas Fired at Israel Reflect the Success of Gaza's Military Industry," *Haaretz* (Israel), May 26, 2021. https://www. haaretz.com/middle-east-news/palestinians/.premium.HIGHLIGHT-hamas-rockets-reflect-success-in-creating-gaza-military-industry-1.9843784?lts=1623093257392

22   Interview with IDF Southern Command, Mahaneh Ra'im, June 22, 2021.

23   Ibid.

24   Joseph Trevithick, "Palestinian Militants Are Now Launching Suicide Drones At Israel," *The Drive*, May 13, 2021. https://www.thedrive.com/the-war-zone/40601/palestinian-militants-are-now-launching-suicide-drones-at-israel

25   Dion Nissenbaum, Sune Engel Rasmussen, and Benoit Faucon, "With Iranian Help, Hamas Builds 'Made in Gaza' Rockets and Drones to Target Israel," *The Wall Street Journal*, May 20, 2021. https://www.wsj.com/articles/with-iranian-help-hamas-builds-made-in-gaza-rockets-and-drones-to-target-israel-11621535346

26   Joseph Trevithick, "Palestinian Militants Are Now Launching Suicide Drones At Israel," *The Drive*, May 13, 2021. https://www.thedrive.com/the-war-zone/40601/palestinian-militants-are-now-launching-suicide-drones-at-israel

27   Dion Nissenbaum, Sune Engel Rasmussen, and Benoit Faucon, "With Iranian Help, Hamas Builds 'Made in Gaza' Rockets and Drones to Target Israel," *The Wall Street Journal*, May 20, 2021. https://www.wsj.com/articles/with-iranian-help-hamas-builds-made-in-gaza-rockets-and-drones-to-target-israel-11621535346

28   Rye Rempfer, "Drones are biggest tactical concern since the rise of IEDs in Iraq, CENTCOM boss says," *Army Times*, February 8, 2021. https://www. armytimes.com/news/your-army/2021/02/08/drones-are-biggest-tactical-concern-since-ieds-rose-in-iraq-four-star-says

29   Dion Nissenbaum, Sune Engel Rasmussen, and Benoit Faucon, "With Iranian Help, Hamas Builds 'Made in Gaza' Rockets and Drones to Target Israel," *The Wall Street Journal*, May 20, 2021. https://www.wsj.com/articles/with-iranian-help-hamas-builds-made-in-gaza-rockets-and-drones-to-target-israel-11621535346

30   Joseph Trevithick, "Palestinian Militants Are Now Launching Suicide Drones At Israel," *The Drive*, May 13, 2021. https://www.thedrive.com/the-war-zone/40601/palestinian-militants-are-now-launching-suicide-drones-at-israel

31   Seth J. Frantzman, "Iran's hand seen in Hamas drone threat against Israel – analysis," *The Jerusalem Post* (Israel), May 15, 2021. https://www.jpost.com/middle-east/iran-news/irans-hand-seen-in-hamas-drone-threat-against-israel-analysis-668110

32   Bradley Bowman, Seth J. Frantzman, and Ryan Brobst, "Add Egypt and the UAE to the Noble Dina Exercise," *Foundation for Defense of Democracies*, July 2, 2021. https://www.fdd.org/analysis/2021/07/02/add-egypt-uae-to-noble-dina-exercise

33   Stephen Bryen, "Hamas' underwater drones a wake-up call for Israel," *Asia Times* (Hong Kong), May 21, 2021. https://asiatimes.com/2021/05/hamas-underwater-drones-a-wake-up-call-for-israel

34   Sebastien Roblin, "How Hamas' Arsenal Shaped The Gaza War Of May 2021," *Forbes*, May 25, 2021. https://www.forbes.com/sites/sebastienroblin/2021/05/25/how-hamass-arsenal-shaped-the-gaza-war-of-may-2021/?sh=23ebf37279df

35   Lenny Ben-David, "Hamas Obtains New Weaponry Any Way It Can," *Jerusalem Center for Public Affairs*, December 11, 2019. https://jcpa.org/where-and-how-does-hamas-get-its-weapons

36   Interview with IDF Southern Command, Mahaneh Ra'im, June 22, 2021.

37   Yaniv Kubovich, "Army Thwarts Hamas Underwater Drone Attack on Israeli Ships," *Haaretz* (Israel), May 17, 2021. https://www.haaretz.com/israel-news/.premium-army-thwarts-hamas-automated-submarine-attack-on-israeli-ships-1.9816526

38   Interview with IDF Southern Command, Mahaneh Ra'im, June 22, 2021.

39   Seth J. Frantzman, "Israel activated its David's Sling missile system for the first time. Will more sales start booming?" *Defense News*, July 27, 2018. https://www.defensenews.com/smr/space-missile-defense/2018/07/27/davids-sling-missile-system-used-for-first-time-by-israel; "Arrow 2 (Israel)," *Center for Strategic and International Studies*, April 14, 2016. https://missilethreat.csis.org/defsys/arrow-2; Jen Judson, "US, Israel's Arrow-3 missile put to the test in Alaska," *Defense News*, July 28, 2019. https://www.defensenews.com/pentagon/2019/07/28/us-israels-arrow-3-missile-put-to-the-test-in-alaska

40   Jacob Nagel and Jonathan Schanzer, "The Powerful Implications of Israel's Successful Missile Defense Test," *Newsweek*, December 28, 2020. https://www.newsweek.com/powerful-implications-israels-successful-missile-defense-test-opinion-1557212

41   Anshel Pfeffer and Yanir Yagna, "Iron Dome Successfully Intercepts Gaza Rocket for First Time," *Haaretz* (Israel), April 7, 2011. https://www.haaretz.com/1.5148599

42   William Booth, "Four rockets fired into Israel from Lebanon," *The Washington Post*, August 22, 2013. https://www.washingtonpost.com/world/middle_east/rockets-fired-at-israel-from-lebanon/2013/08/22/163d3154-0b55-11e3-89fe-abb4a5067014_story.html

43   Adam Chandler, "How Ben Gurion Airport Changes the Entire Gaza War," *The Atlantic*, July 23, 2014. https://www.theatlantic.com/international/archive/2014/07/flight-ban-wont-hurt-israeli-economy-for-now/374870

44   Bradley Bowman and Seth Frantzman, "Israel Confronts Tehran's Terror Proxies in Gaza," *The Dispatch*, May 20, 2021. https://thedispatch.com/p/israel-confronts-tehrans-terror-proxies

45   Jacob Nagel, Bradley Bowman, and Liane Zivitski, "Assessing Israel's tactical laser breakthrough," *Defense News*, January 17, 2020. https://www.defensenews.com/opinion/commentary/2020/01/17/how-realistic-is-israels-tactical-laser-breakthrough

46   Yuval Azulai, "Eight facts about Iron Dome," *Globes* (Israel), July 10, 2014. https://en.globes.co.il/en/article-everything-you-wanted-to-know-about-iron-dome-1000953706

47   Brett Tignley, "Israel Has Shot Down Drones With An Airborne High-Power Laser," *The Drive*, June 21, 2021. https://www.thedrive.com/the-war-zone/41192/israel-has-shot-down-drones-with-an-airborne-high-power-laser

48   Jacob Nagel and Jonathan Schanzer, "Assessing Israel's Iron Dome Missile Defense System," *Foundation for Defense of Democracies*, November 13, 2019. https://www.fdd.org/analysis/memos/2019/11/13/assessing-israels-iron-dome-missile-defense-system

49   "IDF completes underground anti-tunnel barrier surrounding Gaza," *The Times of Israel* (Israel), March 5, 2021. https://www.timesofisrael.com/idf-completes-underground-anti-tunnel-barrier-surrounding-gaza

50   Raphael S. Cohen and Gabriel Scheinmann, "The Grim Lessons of 'Protective Edge,'" *RAND Corporation*, September 3, 2014. https://www.rand.org/blog/2014/09/the-grim-lessons-of-protective-edge.html

51   Jacob Nagel and Jonathan Schanzer, "A Closer Look at Israel's New High-Tech Barrier," *Real Clear Defense*, April 10, 2021. https://www.realcleardefense.com/articles/2021/04/10/a_closer_look_at_israels_new_high-tech_barrier_772195.html

52   "IDF releases Navy footage of Zikim attack," *The Times of Israel* (Israel), July 9, 2014. https://www.timesofisrael.com/liveblog_entry/idf-releases-navy-footage-of-zikim-attack

53   Yaakov Lappin, "Full footage of Zikim terrorist infiltration leaked to Palestinian media," *The Jerusalem Post* (Israel), December 11, 2014. https://www.jpost.com/arab-israeli-conflict/full-film-of-zikim-terrorist-infiltration-leaked-to-palestinian-media-384432

54   Interviews with IDF Southern Command, Mahaneh Ra'im, June 22, 2021.

55   Zohar Palti, "Israel's Security Fence: Effective in Reducing Suicide Attacks from the Northern West Bank," *The Washington Institute for Near East Policy*, July 7, 2004. https://www.washingtoninstitute.org/policy-analysis/israels-security-fence-effective-reducing-suicide-attacks-northern-west-bank

56   "Egypt begins building concrete wall along Gaza border," *The Times of Israel* (Israel), February 19, 2020. https://www.timesofisrael.com/egypt-begins-building-concrete-wall-along-gaza-border

57   Interview with IDF official, Tel Aviv, June 20, 2021.

58   Bradley Bowman, "Securing technological superiority requires a joint US-Israel effort," *Defense News*, May 22, 2020. https://www.defensenews.com/opinion/commentary/2020/05/22/securing-technological-superiority-requires-a-joint-us-israel-effort

59   Seth J. Frantzman, "Israel is Leading the Way as Drone Swarms Come to the Middle East," *The Jerusalem Post* (Israel), July 13, 2021. https://www.jpost.com/middle-east/drone-swarms-are-coming-to-the-middle-east-and-israel-is-leading-the-way-673615?fbclid=IwAR2qGfd-xliFNWclkLx34UF5iVycJ_DZ3Vd1TtKVv_vCPHZBnSembossQu4

60   Anna Ahronheim, "Israel's operation against Hamas was the world's first AI war," *The Jerusalem Post* (Israel), May 27, 2021. https://www.jpost.com/arab-israeli-conflict/gaza-news/guardian-of-the-walls-the-first-ai-war-669371

CHAPTER ELEVEN | UNREST IN THE STREETS

1   "Israel loses control over riots with dozens wounded, detained," *Ynet* (Israel), May 13, 2021. https://www.ynetnews.com/article/SJpDrS9du

2   Isabel Kershner, "Israeli Police Round Up More Than 1,550 Suspects in Mob Violence," *The New York Times*, May 24, 2021. https://www.nytimes.com/2021/05/24/world/middleeast/israel-police-arrests.html

3   "Israel declares emergency in Lod as unrest spreads," *BBC News* (UK), May 12, 2021. https://www.bbc.com/news/world-middle-east-57081848

4   Jessica Steinberg, "In Acre, known for Arab-Jewish coexistence, residents grapple with recent unrest," *The Times of Israel* (Israel), June 3, 2021. https://www.timesofisrael.com/in-acre-known-for-arab-jewish-coexistence-residents-grapple-with-recent-unrest

5   Allison Kaplan Sommer, "This Hotel Was a Model of Jewish-Arab Coexistence – Until an Angry Mob Arrived," *Haaretz* (Israel), May 16, 2021. https://www.haaretz.com/israel-news/.premium.HIGHLIGHT-this-hotel-was-a-model-of-jewish-arab-coexistence-until-an-angry-mob-arrived-1.9813450

6   Isabel Kershner, "Israeli Police Round Up More Than 1,550 Suspects in Mob Violence," *The New York Times*, May 24, 2021. https://www.nytimes.com/2021/05/24/world/middleeast/israel-police-arrests.html

7   "Palestinian killed after ramming car into 6 Israeli police in Jerusalem - police," *Reuters*, May 16, 2021. https://www.reuters.com/world/middle-east/palestinian-killed-after-ramming-car-into-6-israeli-police-jerusalem-police-2021-05-16

8   Tzvi Joffre, "Israel is winning battles, Hamas is winning the war – analysis," *The Jerusalem Post* (Israel), May 17, 2021. https://www.jpost.com/arab-israeli-conflict/israel-is-winning-battles-hamas-is-winning-the-war-analysis-668280

9   "After riots, police chief pans 'terrorists from both sides,' enraging minister," *The Times of Israel* (Israel), May 19, 2021. https://www.timesofisrael.com/after-riots-police-chief-pans-terrorists-from-both-sides-irking-minister

10   Josh Breiner, "Border Police Redeployed From West Bank to Israel to Quell Rioting in Arab-Jewish Cities," *Haaretz* (Israel), May 18, 2021. https://www.haaretz.com/israel-news/.premium-border-police-redeployed-from-west-bank-to-israel-to-quell-rioting-in-mixed-cities-1.9817241

11   Idan Zonshine, "Israel in chaos: 10 Border Police units called up to quell Arab-Jewish violence," *The Jerusalem Post* (Israel), May 13, 2021. https://www.jpost.com/israel-news/right-wing-rioters-smash-windows-of-arab-owned-businesses-in-bat-yam-667993

12   "Police chief warns Jewish-Arab violence inside Israel could résumé — TV," *The Times of Israel* (Israel), May 22, 2021. https://www.timesofisrael.com/police-chief-says-potential-for-jewish-arab-violence-remains-tv

13   Isabel Kershner, "Israeli Police Round Up More Than 1,550 Suspects in Mob Violence," *The New York Times*, May 24, 2021. https://www.nytimes.com/2021/05/24/world/middleeast/israel-police-arrests.html

14   Josh Breiner and Ran Shimoni, "Imam of Lod's Great Mosque Charged with Intimidation, Incitement," *Haaretz* (Israel), July 8, 2021. https://www.haaretz.com/israel-news/.premium-imam-of-lod-s-great-mosque-charged-with-intimidation-incitement-1.9981906

15   Yaniv Kubovich, "Israel Detains 10 Arabs for Allegedly Throwing Fire Bombs at Jewish Family's Home," *Haaretz* (Israel), July 16, 2021. https://www.haaretz.com/israel-news/.premium-israel-detains-10-arabs-for-allegedly-throwing-fire-bombs-at-jewish-family-s-home-1.10004409

16   Doron Matza, "The May 2021 Riots and Their Implications," *The Begin-Sadat Center for Strategic Studies*, June 8, 2021. https://besacenter.org/israel-may-2021-riots

17   Danny Zaken, "Mansour Abbas doubles budget for Arab sector," *Globes* (Israel), June 10, 2021. https://en.globes.co.il/en/article-mansour-abbas-doubles-budget-for-arab-sector-1001374021

18   "Hamas instigated violence says American Jewish Committee," *BBC News* (UK), May 13, 2021. https://www.bbc.com/news/av/world-middle-east-57104680

19   Avi Mayer, "Why Are They Fighting in the Middle East? Because Hamas Is Dedicated to Killing Jews," *Newsweek*, May 14, 2021. https://www.newsweek.com/why-are-they-fighting-middle-east-because-hamas-dedicated-killing-jews-opinion-1591492

20   Aaron Klein, "Stop Spreading Hamas's Lies," *Newsweek*, May 13, 2021. https://www.newsweek.com/stop-spreading-hamass-lies-opinion-1590956

21   Avi Mayer, "Why Are They Fighting in the Middle East? Because Hamas Is Dedicated to Killing Jews," *Newsweek*, May 14, 2021. https://www.newsweek.com/why-are-they-fighting-middle-east-because-hamas-dedicated-killing-jews-opinion-1591492

22   "Erdogan: Turkey won't 'remain silent' over Israeli strikes in Gaza," *Al-Monitor*, May 14, 2021. https://www.al-monitor.com/originals/2021/05/erdogan-turkey-wont-remain-silent-over-israeli-strikes-gaza#ixzz6z6qJPBYk

23   "Turkey rejects US claim Erdogan made 'anti-Semitic' remarks about Gaza," *The Times of Israel* (Israel), May 19, 2021. https://www.timesofisrael.com/turkey-rejects-us-criticism-that-erdogan-made-anti-semitic-remarks-about-gaza

24   "Israel must be taught a 'lesson', Erdogan tells Putin," *Al Jazeera* (Qatar), May 12, 2021. https://www.aljazeera.com/news/2021/5/12/israel-must-be-taught-a-lesson-erdogan-tells-putin

25   Amir Tibon and Yaniv Kubovich, "Jordan, Saudis and Palestinians Warn Israel: Erdogan Operating in East Jerusalem Under Your Nose," *Haaretz* (Israel), July 1, 2018. https://www.haaretz.com/middle-east-news/.premium-jordan-saudis-and-pa-warn-israel-erdogan-operating-in-east-jerusalem-1.6220111

26   Yori Yalon, "In bid to buy influence, Turkey hands out money in East Jerusalem," *Israel Hayom* (Israel), May 22, 2018. https://www.israelhayom. com/2018/05/22/in-bid-to-buy-influence-turkey-hands-out-money-in-east-jerusalem

27   Yuri Yalon and Ariel Kahana, "התוכנית לעצירת הסולטן: ישראל נגד ארדואן [The plan to stop the Sultan: Israel v. Erdogan]," *Israel Hayom* (Israel), June 10, 2019. https://www.israelhayom.co.il/article/697467

28   Nadav Shragai, "מחקר: טורקיה ואירופה מממנות ארגוני חברה אזרחית במזרח ירושלים [Research: Turkey and Europe fund civil society organizations in East Jerusalem]," *Israel Hayom* (Israel), June 23, 2020. https://www.israelhayom. co.il/article/773583

29   Yossi Melman, "How Israel began seeing Turkey as a threat instead of a partner," *Middle East Eye* (UK), June 26, 2020. https://www.middleeasteye. net/news/how-israel-began-seeing-turkey-threat-instead-partner

30   Mohammad al-Kassim, "Battle for Control in East Jerusalem," *The Media Line*, December 12, 2020. https://themedialine.org/top-stories/battle-for-control-in-east-jerusalem

31   "In east Jerusalem, a battle over 'every inch' of land," *France 24* (France), December 12, 2020. https://www.france24.com/en/live-news/20201220-in-east-jerusalem-a-battle-over-every-inch-of-land

32   "Erdogan's Davos Outburst Is Nothing New," *Forbes*, January 20, 2009. https://www.forbes.com/2009/01/30/erdogan-turkey-davos-opinions-contributors_0130_asli_aydintasbas.html?sh=6545749a5451

33   Hassan Ghani, "Turkey orders arrest over Gaza flotilla raid," *Al Jazeera* (Qatar), August 15, 2014. https://www.aljazeera.com/news/2014/8/15/turkey-orders-arrests-over-gaza-flotilla-raid-2. One was a Turkish-American dual national.

34   "Turkey Commemorates Mavi Marmara Victims of 11th Anniversary," *Daily Sabah* (Turkey), May 31, 2021. https://www.dailysabah.com/politics/turkey-commemorates-mavi-marmara-victims-on-11th-anniversary/news

35   Orlando Crowcroft, "Hamas official: we were behind the kidnapping of three Israeli teenagers," *The Guardian* (UK), August 21, 2014. https://www. theguardian.com/world/2014/aug/21/hamas-kidnapping-three-israeli-teenagers-saleh-al-arouri-qassam-brigades

36   David Barnett, "Israel Indicts More Palestinian Terror Cells," *FDD's Long War Journal*, April 18, 2013. www.longwarjournal.org/threat-matrix/archives/2013/04/israel_indicts_more_palestinia.php

37   Israeli Security Agency, "מעורבות פעיל ששוחרר ב"עסקת שליט" בהכוונת טרור [Involvement of an operative released in the 'Shalit deal' for directing terrorism]," April 16, 2013. https://www.shabak.gov.il/publications/Pages/shotef170413.aspx

38   U.S. Department of the Treasury, Press Release, "Treasury Sanctions Major Hamas Leaders, Financial Facilitators and a Front Company," September 10, 2015. https://www.treasury.gov/press-center/press-releases/Pages/jl0159.aspx

39   Jonathan Schanzer, "Hamas Still Finds Harbor in Turkey," *The Washington Examiner*, June 8, 2016. https://www.washingtonexaminer.com/weekly-standard/hamas-still-finds-harbor-in-turkey

40   Israeli Ministry of Foreign Affairs, "Hamas is exploiting Turkish aid for military purposes," March 21, 2017. https://mfa.gov.il/MFA/ForeignPolicy/Terrorism/Pages/Hamas-is-exploiting-Turkish-aid-for-military-purposes-21-March-2017.aspx

41   "İsrail Gazze'ye tüm yardımları kesmeye çalışıyor [Israel tries to cut off all aid to Gaza]," *IHH Humanitarian Relief Foundation*, March 3, 2017. https://www.ihh.org.tr/haber/israil-gazzeye-tum-yardimlari-kesmeye-calisiyor

42   @tcbestepe, "Cumhurbaşkanı @RTEdogan, Hamas Siyasi Büro Başkanı İsmail Heniyye ve beraberindeki heyeti Vahdettin Köşkü'nde kabul etti. [President @RTErdogan received Hamas Political Bureau Head Ismail Haniyeh and his delegation at Vahdettin Mansion.]" *Twitter*, August 22, 2020. https://twitter.com/tcbestepe/status/1297183739592814593

43   Spokesperson Morgan Ortagus, U.S. Department of State, Press Statement, "President Erdogan's Meeting With Hamas Leadership," August 25, 2020. https://2017-2021.state.gov/president-erdogans-meeting-with-hamas-leadership/index.html

44   U.S. Department of the Treasury, Press Release, "Treasury Targets Wide Range of Terrorists and Their Supporters Using Enhanced Counterterrorism Sanctions Authorities," September 10, 2019. https://home.treasury.gov/news/press-releases/sm772

45   Lahav Harkov, "Netanyahu: We will bring rule of law to Israel's cities with an iron fist," *The Jerusalem Post* (Israel), May 12, 2021. https://www.jpost.com/arab-israeli-conflict/netanyahu-we-will-bring-rule-of-law-to-israels-cities-with-iron-fist-667964

CHAPTER TWELVE | THE OTHER GAZA WARS

1   Zaki Chehab, *Inside Hamas: The Untold Story of the Militant Islamic Movement* (NYC: Nation Books, 2007), page 139.

2   Sarah El Deeb, "Haniyeh: Iran Pledges 4250m in Aid," *The Associated Press*, December 11, 2006. https://www.washingtonpost.com/wp-dyn/content/article/2006/07/11/AR2006071100742.html

3   "Rice: Two-State Solution in Mideast in Jeopardy," *Associated Press*, October 24, 2007. https://www.nbcnews.com/id/wbna21457082

4   Dan Murphy, "Gaza Tunnel Smugglers Stay Busy," *The Christian Science Monitor*, January 14, 2008. http://www.csmonitor.com/2008/0114/p06s02-wome.html

5   Erica Silverman, "Goods smuggled in Gaza tunnels, taxed by Hamas," *The Washington Times*, January 9, 2008. https://www.washingtontimes.com/news/2008/jan/9/goods-smuggled-in-gaza-tunnels-taxed-by-hamas

6   Interview with senior Israeli official, Tel Aviv, November 2007.

7   David Bedein, "Tape Allegedly Shows Egyptian Guards Helping Smugglers," *The Philadelphia Bulletin*, December 27, 2007. http://www.thebulletin.us/site/news.cfm?newsid=19147921&BRD=2737&PAG=461&dept_id=618959&rfi=6

8   Yaakov Katz, Herb Keinon, and Hillary Krieger, "Israel Sends US Videos of Egypt Helping Hamas," *The Jerusalem Post* (Israel), December 18, 2007. https://www.jpost.com/israel/israel-sends-us-videos-of-egypt-helping-hamas

9   Yaakov Katz, "Egypt vows to end weapons smuggling," *The Jerusalem Post* (Israel), December 26, 2007. https://www.jpost.com/middle-east/egypt-vows-to-end-weapons-smuggling

10   Israeli Ministry of Foreign Affairs, Press Release, "IDF targets Hamas post in southern Gaza," November 28, 2007. https://mfa.gov.il/mfa/foreignpolicy/terrorism/palestinian/pages/idf%20targets%20hamas%20post%20in%20southern%20gaza%20%2028-nov-2007.aspx

11   Amos Harel, "Defense officials concerned as Hamas upgrades Qassam arsenal," *Haaretz* (Israel), December 7, 2007. Archived version available at: https://web.archive.org/web/20071208051907/http://www.haaretz.com/hasen/spages/932106.html

12   Hanan Greenberg, "Defense officials predict limited conflict in Gaza after summit," *Ynet* (Israel), November 18, 2007. http://www.ynetnews.com/articles/0,7340,L-3472673,00.html

13   Shahar Ilan, "Olmert rules out Gaza ground operation," *Haaretz* (Israel), January 14, 2008. Archived version available at: https://web.archive.org/web/20081007082327/http://www.haaretz.com:80/hasen/spages/944665.html

14   Nick Francona, "Hamas's Military Capabilities after the Gaza Takeover," *The Washington Institute for Near East Policy*, August 27, 2007. https://www.washingtoninstitute.org/pdf/view/7604/en

15   Steve Erlanger, "Israel Warns of Hamas Military Buildup in Gaza," *The New York Times*, April 1, 2007. https://www.nytimes.com/2007/04/01/world/middleeast/01gaza.html

16   Nick Francona, "Hamas's Military Capabilities after the Gaza Takeover," *The Washington Institute for Near East Policy*, August 27, 2007. https://www.washingtoninstitute.org/pdf/view/7604/en

17   Amos Harel, "IDF's tactical upper hand over Hamas in Gaza is diminishing," *Haaretz* (Israel), October 30, 2007. Archived version available at: https://web.archive.org/web/20091121121232/http://www.haaretz.com:80/hasen/spages/918243.html; Amos Harel, "Reservists: Hamas fights like an army," *Haaretz* (Israel), November 7, 2007. Archived version available at: https://web.archive.org/web/20081011045052/http://www.haaretz.com/hasen/spages/921630.html

18   Ibrahim Barzak, "Gazans Facing 8-Hour Daily Power Outages Because of Israeli Fuel Cutbacks," *Associated Press*, January 6, 2008. (Accessed via Lexis Nexis)

19   "Gaza's Power Plant Shuts Down as Israel Blocks Fuel and Food Shipments for Third Day," *Ma'an News Agency* (West Bank), January 20, 2008. http://www.maannews.net/en/index.php?opr=ShowDetails&ID=27329

20   Khaled Abu Toameh, "Arab editor blames Hamas for Gaza crisis," *The Jerusalem Post* (Israel), January 21, 2008. https://www.jpost.com/middle-east/arab-editor-blames-hamas-for-gaza-crisis

21   Ali Abunimah, Muslim Brotherhood, "Top EU official backs Israel's crimes in occupied Gaza," January 24, 2008. https://www.ikhwanweb.com/article.php?id=15624&ref=search.php

22   IV Geneva Convention Relative to the Protection of Civilian Persons in Time of War, Geneva, August 12, 1949. https://www.un.org/en/genocideprevention/documents/atrocity-crimes/Doc.33_GC-IV-EN.pdf

23   Interview with senior IDF official, Tel Aviv, June 20, 2021.

24   Rebecca Anna Stoil, "IDF completes first stage of Operation Hot Winter," *The Jerusalem Post* (Israel), March 3, 2008. https://www.jpost.com/israel/idf-completes-first-stage-of-operation-hot-winter

25   Ibid.

26   For more on human shields, see: Orde Kittrie, "Time to Act on Human Shields," *Foundation for Defense of Democracies*, October 15, 2020. https://www.fdd.org/wp-content/uploads/2020/10/fdd-memo-time-to-act-on-human-shields.pdf

27   Israeli Ministry of Foreign Affairs, "Operation Cast Lead (2008)," accessed July 14, 2021. https://mfa.gov.il/MFA/AboutIsrael/Maps/Pages/Operation-Cast-Lead.aspx

28   Ibid.

29   UN Human Rights Council, "Report of the United Nations Fact-Finding Mission on the Gaza Conflict," A/HRC/12/48, September 25, 2009. https://www2.ohchr.org/english/bodies/hrcouncil/docs/12session/A-HRC-12-48.pdf

30   Dore Gold, "The Dangerous Bias of the United Nations Goldstone Report," *US News & World Report*, March 24, 2010. https://www.usnews.com/opinion/articles/2010/03/24/the-dangerous-bias-of-the-united-nations-goldstone-report

31   Richard Goldstone, "Reconsidering the Goldstone Report on Israel and war crimes," *The Washington Post*, April 11, 2011. https://www.washingtonpost.com/opinions/reconsidering-the-goldstone-report-on-israel-and-war-crimes/2011/04/01/AFg111JC_story.html

32   "Follow-Up To Information Badr Airline Flights Information," 09STATE5567_a, *Wikileaks*, January 22, 2009. http://wikileaks.org/cable/2009/01/09STATE5567.html; "IDF Deputy Chief Of Staff Discusses Gaza Operation Cast Lead And U.S.-Egyptian Roles To Slow Smuggling To Hamas," 09TELAVIV422_a, *Wikileaks*, February 19, 2009. http://wikileaks.org/cable/2009/02/09TELAVIV422.html

33   "Sudan blames Israel for convoy attack," *The Irish Times* (Ireland), March 27, 2009. https://www.irishtimes.com/news/sudan-blames-israel-for-convoy-attack-1.838204

34   Israeli troops killed in Gaza border clashes," *BBC News* (UK), March 26, 2010. http://news.bbc.co.uk/2/hi/middle_east/8589529.stm

35   "Israeli airstrike targets Gaza after 7 killed in southern Israel," *CNN*, August 18, 2011. https://www.cnn.com/2011/WORLD/meast/08/18/israel.shooting/index.html

36   "Suspected hit squad in Mahmoud al-Mabhouth killing," *The Guardian* (UK), February 17, 2010. https://www.theguardian.com/world/gallery/2010/feb/16/palestinian-territories-hamas

37   U.S. Department of the Treasury, Press Release, "Fact Sheet: U.S. Treasury Department Targets Iran's Support for Terrorism Treasury Announces New Sanctions Against Iran's Islamic Revolutionary Guard Corps-Qods Force Leadership," August 3, 2010. http://www.treasury.gov/press-center/press-releases/Pages/tg810.aspx

38   Yaakov Katz, "Victoria's Secret: The inside story of an arms-laden ship," *The Jerusalem Post* (Israel), March 18, 2011. http://www.jpost.com/Defense/Article.aspx?id=212683

39   Yaakov Katz, "'Time': IDF official confirms strike in Sudan," *The Jerusalem Post* (Israel), April 7, 2011. https://www.jpost.com/defense/time-idf-official-confirms-strike-in-sudan

40   U.S. Department of State, Office of the Spokesperson, Media Note, "Terrorist Designation of HAMAS Operative Muhammad Hisham Muhammad Isma'il Abu Ghazala," September 22, 2011. https://2009-2017. state.gov/r/pa/prs/ps/2011/09/173352.htm

41   Nidal al-Mughrabi, "Foreign funds for Hamas hit by Syria unrest: diplomats," *Reuters*, August 21, 2011. https://www.jpost.com/middle-east/ iran-cuts-funding-for-hamas-due-to-syria-unrest

42   "Sudan blames Israel for Khartoum arms factory blast," *BBC News* (UK), October 24, 2012. https://www.bbc.com/news/world-africa-20050781

43   "Satellite pictures suggest Sudanese weapons factory hit by air strike," *Associated Press*, October 27, 2012. http://www.guardian.co.uk/world/2012/ oct/27/sudan-weapons-factory-airstrike-israel

44   Phone interview with Israeli intelligence official, October 24, 2012.

45   "US, Israel begin largest-ever joint military exercise," *France 24* (France), October 21, 2012. https://www.france24.com/en/20121021-usa-israel- begin-largest-ever-joint-missile-defence-exercise-austere-challenge-12

46   "Israeli Strike Kills Hamas Commander Ahmed Jabari," *The Wall Street Journal*, November 14, 2012. https://www.wsj.com/video/israeli-strike- kills-hamas-commander-ahmed-jabari/CD5FAFBE-F35E-49B5-9D7D- 36E0E4C4BD7F.html

47   Barak Ravid, "Israel's 2002 Hit of Hamas Leader Was Justified, Despite Civilian Casualties,'" *Haaretz* (Israel), February 27, 2011. https://www. haaretz.com/1.5128863

48   Joshua Nevett, "Mohammed Deif: The one-eyed Hamas chief in Israel's crosshairs," *BBC News* (UK), May 31, 2021. https://www.bbc.com/news/ world-middle-east-57253521

49   Amos Harel, "How Were Palestinian Militants Able to Abduct Gilad Shalit?" *Haaretz* (Israel), October 18, 2011. https://www.haaretz. com/1.5200670

50   David Trifunov, "Ahmed Jabari: Hamas leader took all efforts to remain hidden," *PRI*, November 14, 2012. https://www.pri.org/stories/2012-11-14/ ahmed-jabari-hamas-leader-took-all-efforts-remain-hidden

51   Jonathan Schanzer, "Why U.S.-Israel ties just got warmer," *CNN*, November 28, 2012. https://globalpublicsquare.blogs.cnn.com/2012/11/28/ why-u-s-israel-ties-just-got-warmer

52   "Cease-fire appears to be holding in Gaza," *CNN*, November 22, 2012. https://www.cnn.com/2012/11/21/world/meast/gaza-israel-strike/index. html?iref=allsearch

53   Jonathan Schanzer, "Hamas's Benefactors: A Network of Terror," *Testimony Before the House Committee on Foreign Affairs*, September 12, 2014. https://www.fdd.org/analysis/2014/09/12/hamass-benefactors-a-network-of-terror-2

54   "Iran's Ahmadinejad Meets Egypt's Morsi on Historic Visit to Cairo," *Associated Press*, February 5, 2013. https://www.haaretz.com/cairo-rolls-out-red-carpet-for-iran-prez-1.5228436

55   Israel Defense Forces, "Operation Pillar of Defense," accessed July 14, 2021. https://www.idf.il/en/minisites/wars-and-operations/operation-pillar-of-defense

56   David Barnett, "Israeli navy intercepts Iranian weapons shipment headed for Gaza," *FDD's Long War Journal*, March 5, 2014. http://www.longwarjournal.org/archives/2014/03/israeli_navy_interce.php

57   Orlando Crowcroft, "Hamas official: we were behind the kidnapping of three Israeli teenagers," *The Guardian* (UK), August 21, 2014. https://www.theguardian.com/world/2014/aug/21/hamas-kidnapping-three-israeli-teenagers-saleh-al-arouri-qassam-brigades

58   Raoul Wootliff, "Minors handed life sentence, 21 years for Abu Khdeir murder," *The Times of Israel* (Israel), February 4, 2016. https://www.timesofisrael.com/life-sentence-21-years-in-jail-handed-to-minors-for-abu-khdeir-murder

59   Ali Hashem, "Did Iran Train Gaza Rocket Makers?" *Al-Monitor*, July 17, 2014. http://www.al-monitor.com/pulse/originals/2014/07/gaza-rockets-palestine-iran-self-sufficient.html

60   Ali Akbar Dareini, "Iran says country has transferred missile technology to Hamas," *Associated Press*, August 4, 2014. http://www.usnews.com/news/world/articles/2014/08/04/iran-says-it-gave-missile-technology-to-hamas

61   Ruth Michaelson, "Kerry in Cairo to push for Gaza ceasefire," *Radio France Internationale* (France), July 23, 2014. https://www.rfi.fr/en/africa/20140723-kerry-cairo-push-gaza-ceasefire

62   "Implementation of the Joint Plan of Action," *Arms Control Association*, November 2020. https://www.armscontrol.org/Implementation-of-the-Joint-Plan-of-Action-At-A-Glance

63   "Larijani Says Iran Gave Hamas Its Rocket Know-How," *Naharnet* (Lebanon), July 24, 2014. http://www.naharnet.com/stories/en/140398

64   Raymond Tanter, "Iran's terror tunnels," *Foreign Policy*, December 23, 2014. https://foreignpolicy.com/2014/12/23/irans-terror-tunnels

65   Michael R. Gordon, "To Talk With Hamas, U.S. Needs Help From a Testy Trio of Nations," *The New York Times*, July 21, 2014. https://www.nytimes.com/2014/07/22/us/politics/to-talk-with-hamas-us-needs-help-from-a-testy-trio-of-nations.html

66   Sevil Erkus, "Turkey, Qatar propose cease-fire in parallel track with Egypt," *Hurriyet Daily News* (Turkey), July 17, 2014. https://www.hurriyetdailynews. com/turkey-qatar-propose-cease-fire-in-parallel-track-with-egypt-69283

67   Jacob Stoil, "Why a Gaza Ceasefire Is So Difficult," *War on the Rocks*, July 29, 2014. https://warontherocks.com/2014/07/why-a-gaza-ceasefire-is-so-difficult

68   Jodi Rudoren, "Qatar's Emir Visits Gaza, Pledging $400 Million to Hamas," *The New York Times*, October 23, 2012. https://www.nytimes. com/2012/10/24/world/middleeast/pledging-400-million-qatari-emir-makes-historic-visit-to-gaza-strip.html

69   "Hamas elects Doha-based Meshaal to head foreign policy outfit," *The Arab Weekly* (UK), April 13, 2021. https://thearabweekly.com/hamas-elects-doha-based-meshaal-head-foreign-policy-outfit

70   Ariel Ben Solomon, "Erdogan accuses Israel of 'using terrorism' in its operations against Hamas in Gaza," *The Jerusalem Post* (Israel), July 14, 2014. https://www.jpost.com/Operation-Protective-Edge/Erdogan-accuses-Israel-of-using-terrorism-in-its-operations-against-Hamas-in-Gaza-362759

71   Zvi Bar-el, "Turkey May Provide Hamas With $300 Million in Annual Aid," *Haaretz* (Israel), January 28, 2012. https://www.haaretz. com/1.5176983

72   Israeli Ministry of Foreign Affairs, "Iran provided most of Hamas' weapons," August 31, 2014. https://mfa.gov.il/MFA/ForeignPolicy/Iran/SupportTerror/Pages/Iran-provided-most-of-Hamas-weapons-31-Aug-2014.aspx

73   Niidal al-Mughrabi, "Hamas's deputy chief says it has patched ties with Iran," *Reuters*, December 17, 2014. https://www.reuters.com/article/uk-mideast-hamas-gaza-idAFKBN0JV1OH20141217

74   "Boosted by nuke deal, Iran ups funding to Hezbollah, Hamas," *The Times of Israel* (Israel), September 21, 2015. https://www.timesofisrael.com/boosted-by-nuke-deal-iran-ups-funding-to-hezbollah-hamas

75   Elior Levy, "Iran's $100 million aid to Hamas and Islamic Jihad," *Ynet* (Israel), August 3, 2018. https://www.ynetnews.com/articles/0,7340,L-5321985,00.html

76   Huthifa Fayyad, "Gaza's Great March of Return protests explained," *Al Jazeera* (Qatar), March 30, 2019. https://www.aljazeera.com/news/2019/3/30/gazas-great-march-of-return-protests-explained

77   Khaled Abu Toameh, "Israel warns Gaza bus companies ahead of 'March of Return,'" *The Times of Israel* (Israel), March 28, 2018. https://www.timesofisrael.com/israel-warns-gaza-bus-companies-ahead-of-march-of-return

78 "Hamas cancels school on Saturday so Gaza kids can join border protests," *The Times of Israel* (Israel), March 27, 2019. https://www.timesofisrael.com/liveblog_entry/hamas-cancels-school-on-saturday-so-gaza-kids-can-join-border-protests

79 "For 6th day straight, Israel strikes Gaza over balloon attacks," *Ynet* (Israel), August 17, 2020. https://www.ynetnews.com/article/HyrNI5PMP)

80 "Hundreds of Palestinians said to riot at Gaza border," *The Times of Israel* (Israel), August 15, 2020. https://www.timesofisrael.com/liveblog_entry/hundreds-of-palestinians-said-to-riot-at-gaza-border

81 "After rocket fire, Israel renews Gaza airstrikes, closes enclave's fishing zone," *The Times of Israel* (Israel), August 16, 2020. https://www.timesofisrael.com/after-rocket-fire-israeli-jets-strike-gaza-for-second-time-in-hours/

82 Interview with IDF Southern Command, Mahaneh Ra'im, June 22, 2021.

83 Michael Bachner, "Iran said increasing Hamas funding $30 million per month, wants intel on Israel," *The Times of Israel* (Israel), August 5, 2019. https://www.timesofisrael.com/iran-agrees-to-increase-hamas-funding-to-30-million-per-month-report/

CHAPTER THIRTEEN | NORTHERN EXPOSURE

1 James Rickards, "Crisis in Lebanon: Anatomy of a Financial Collapse," *Foundation for Defense of Democracies*, August 2020. https://www.fdd.org/analysis/2020/08/04/crisis-in-lebanon/

2 Greg Myre and Steven Erlanger, "Israeli Forces Enter Lebanon After 2 Soldiers are Seized," *The New York Times*, July 12, 2006. https://www.nytimes.com/2006/07/12/world/middleeast/12cnd-mideast.html

3 Brian Whitaker, "Reconstruction alone is estimated at $7bn in Lebanon," *The Guardian* (UK), August 16, 2006. https://www.theguardian.com/world/2006/aug/16/syria.lebanon

4 Najia Houssari, "Warning against dragging Lebanon into 'total chaos' amid hopes for economic recovery," *Arab News* (Saudi Arabia), May 16, 2021. https://www.arabnews.com/node/1859311/amp

5 "Three rockets launched at Israel from Lebanon, no damage, says Israeli military," *France 24* (France), May 13, 2021. https://www.france24.com/en/live-news/20210513-three-rockets-launched-at-israel-from-lebanon-no-damage-says-israeli-military

6   Anna Ahronheim and Tzvi Joffre, "Lebanon fires rockets at Israel, no injuries reported," *The Jerusalem Post* (Israel), May 14, 2021. https://www.jpost.com/breaking-news/three-rockets-fired-from-lebanon-initial-report-668129

7   Judah Ari Gross, "Six rockets fired from Lebanon, fall short of Israel border; IDF hits back," *The Times of Israel* (Israel), May 18, 2021. https://www.timesofisrael.com/six-rockets-fired-at-israel-from-lebanon-idf-responds-with-artillery-fire

8   Anna Ahromheim, "Rockets fired into northern Israel from Lebanon amid fighting in Gaza," *The Jerusalem Post* (Israel), May 19, 2021. https://www.jpost.com/israel-news/sirens-sound-in-israels-north-two-rockets-fall-in-open-areas-668526

9   "Israel fires at south Lebanon after cross-border rocket launches," *Reuters*, May 19, 2019. https://www.reuters.com/world/middle-east/rocket-sirens-sound-northern-israel-military-says-2021-05-19

10   "جوزف عون للفرنسيّين: أعيدوا النازحين... وادعمونا لئلّا ينهار الجيش" [Joseph Aoun to the French: Bring back the displaced... and support us so that the army does not fall apart]," *Al-Akhbar* (Lebanon), June 10, 2021. https://al-akhbar.com/Politics/308171/ جوزف-عون-للفرنسي-ين-أعيدوا-النازحين-وادعمونا-لئل-ا-ينهار-الجي

11   "سردار حاجى‌زاده: سپاه "پهپاد امکیو-نه" از آمریکا غنیمت گرفته/ ناو های آمریکا "سیبل" هستند [General Hajizadeh: The IRGC has obtained the 'MQ-9 drone' as booty from America/American vessels are 'targets']," *Tasnim News Agency* (Iran), November 21, 2019. https://tn.ai/1881618

12   "Hezbollah chief: We have enough precision-guided missiles for any confrontation," *Al Arabiya* (Saudi Arabia), August 31, 2019. https://english.alarabiya.net/News/middle-east/2019/08/31/Hezbollah-chief-We-have-enough-precision-guided-missiles-for-any-confrontation

13   Michael Crowley, Falih Hassan, and Eric Schmitt, "U.S. Strike in Iraq Kills Qassim Suleimani, Commander of Iranian Forces," *The New York Times*, January 2, 2020. https://www.nytimes.com/2020/01/02/world/middleeast/qassem-soleimani-iraq-iran-attack.html

14   Israel Defense Forces, "Hezbollah's Precision Guided Missile Project," September 1, 2019. https://www.idf.il/en/minisites/hezbollah/hezbollahs-precision-guided-missile-project

15   Jonathan Schanzer, "The New Rocket Threat to Israel," *Commentary Magazine*, January 2020. https://www.commentarymagazine.com/articles/jonathan-schanzer/the-new-rocket-threat-to-israel

16   Richard Spencer, "Israeli drone attack targeted Iranian missile makers in Beirut," *The Times* (UK), August 28, 2019. https://www.thetimes.co.uk/article/israeli-drone-attack-targeted-iranian-guided-missile-technology-5680836b9

17   Israel Defense Forces, "Exposed: Three Hezbollah Missile Sites in Beirut," October 2, 2020. https://www.idf.il/en/minisites/hezbollah/exposed-three-hezbollah-missile-sites-in-beirut

18   Judah Ari Gross, "IDF: Clip from Hezbollah tour of Beirut 'workshop' proves it's a missile factory," *The Times of Israel* (Israel), October 2, 2020. https://www.timesofisrael.com/idf-says-clip-from-hezbollah-tour-of-workshop-proves-it-is-a-missile-factory

19   "IOF Chief Warns of Iranian Threat, Acknowledged for First Time 'Israel' Attacked Iraq," *Al-Manar* (Lebanon), December 25, 2019. http://english.almanar.com.lb/897008

20   "Iron Dome (Israel)," *Center for Strategic and International Studies* (Israel, accessed July 2, 2021. https://missilethreat.csis.org/defsys/iron-dome

21   Yoav Zeitun, "מ2006 לראשונה, מוגבלות הסלמות ייזום חיזבאללה :אמ"ן מערכת [Assessment of the Military Intelligence Directorate: Hezbollah initiates limited escalations, for the first time since 2006]," *Ynet* (Israel), February 9, 2021. https://www.ynet.co.il/news/article/HyobjzyZd#autoplay

22   Bradley Bowman, "Lebanese Armed Forces must act against Hezbollah to retain America's military aid," *Defense News*, April 1, 2020. https://www.defensenews.com/opinion/commentary/2020/04/01/lebanon-must-act-against-hezbollah-to-retain-americas-military-aid

23   Colin Dwyer, "Israel's Army Says it Found Tunnels Dug By Hezbollah Beneath Border With Lebanon," *NPR*, December 4, 2018. https://www.npr.org/2018/12/04/673181288/israels-army-says-it-found-tunnels-dug-by-hezbollah-beneath-border-with-lebanon

24   Tony Badran and Jonathan Schanzer, "Lebanon, Hezbollah and Iran's Emerging Client State," *Foundation for Defense of Democracies*, September 18, 2019. https://www.fdd.org/analysis/2019/09/18/lebanon-hezbollah-and-irans-emerging-client-state; @AcrossTheBay, "The IDF reveals a Hezbollah facility in Nabi Sheet to manufacture/upgrade the precision of its missiles. A quick note on that location, which you can see here:," *Twitter*, September 3, 2019. https://twitter.com/AcrossTheBay/status/1168918989298380801

25   Tony Badran, "Terminate the UN Interim Force in Lebanon," *Newsweek*, August 24, 2020. https://www.newsweek.com/terminate-un-interim-force-lebanon-opinion-1526970

26   See Appendix 1.

27   Yossi Melman, "Inside Hamas's southern Lebanon strategy," *The Jerusalem Post* (Israel), March 17, 2018. https://www.jpost.com/jerusalem-report/intelligence-report-hamass-northern-front-544452

28 حماس تخطط سرّاً لبناء قدرات عسكرية في لبنان بعيداً عن أعين الجيش وحزب الله لضرب إسرائيل" [Hamas is secretly planning to build military capabilities in Lebanon, away from the eyes of the army and Hezbollah, to strike Israel]," *Beirut Observer*, January 20, 2018. https://www.beirutobserver.com/2018/01/hamas-lebanon-3

29 Judah Ari Gross, "With 1st Declared Rocket Attack in 15 years, Hezbollah Risks War to Test Israel," *The Times of Israel* (Israel), August 7, 2021. https://www.timesofisrael.com/with-first-rocket-attack-in-15-years-hezbollah-risks-war-to-test-israel/

CHAPTER FOURTEEN | FOREIGN FIGHTER

1 Joe Truzman, "Hamas fighter with American citizenship killed in recent Gaza conflict," *FDD's Long War Journal*, May 23, 2021. https://www.longwarjournal.org/archives/2021/05/hamas-fighter-with-american-citizenship-killed-in-recent-gaza-conflict.php

2 Ibid.

3 Joe Truzman, "IDF launches targeted killing operations against Gaza-based militants," *FDD's Long War Journal*, May 16, 2021. https://www.longwarjournal.org/archives/2021/05/idf-launches-targeted-killing-operations-against-gaza-based-militants.php

4 A.H Nayfeh, J.M. Elzebda, and D.T. Mook, "Analytical Study of the Subsonic Wing-Rock Phenomenon for Slender Delta Wings," *Aerospace Research Central*, Volume 26, Issue 9, May 22, 2012. https://arc.aiaa.org/doi/10.2514/3.45844

5 Yinon Shalom Yathach, Israel Defense Forces, "'שומר החומות' מגיע לצמרת החמאס:אלה בכירי 'פורום המטה הכללי' של חמאס שחוסלו במבצע המיוחד ['Guardian of the Walls' reaches the top of Hamas: These are senior members of the Hamas "General Staff Forum" who were killed in the special operation]," May 12, 2021. https://www.idf.il/132455

6 Nasser Atta, Hatem Maher, and Guy Davies, "US citizen working for Hamas killed in Israeli air strike," *ABC News*, May 25, 2021. https://abcnews.go.com/International/us-citizen-working-hamas-killed-israeli-air-strike/story?id=77890472

7 Ala Alzebda, *Facebook*, May 12, 2021. https://www.facebook.com/aya.alzibda/posts/3056461711303728

8 Osama Jamal, *Facebook*, May 19, 2021. https://www.longwarjournal.org/wp-content/uploads/2021/05/Facebook.jpg

9   Nasser Atta, Hatem Maher, and Guy Davies, "US citizen working for Hamas killed in Israeli air strike," *ABC News*, May 25, 2021. https://abcnews.go.com/International/us-citizen-working-hamas-killed-israeli-air-strike/story?id=77890472

10   Ibid.

11   «تدوينة نجل مسؤول في حماس ينتقد فيها أساليب وتصريحات القادة العسكريين تحدث «جدلا» [A post by the son of a Hamas official criticizing the methods and statements of the military leaders causes controversy]," *Amad* (West Bank), November 19, 2019. https://www.amad.ps/ar/post/324072

12   @Jtruzmah, "Al-Qassam Brigades officially announced the death of Osama Jamal al-Zebda, a field commander belonging to the militant group. FDD's Long War Journal confirmed w/ official that al-Zebda was a U.S. citizen & on a terrorist watch list in an article published Sunday. #Gaza #Israel," *Twitter*, May 24, 2021. https://twitter.com/Jtruzmah/status/1396793678908182538?s=20

13   مدينة خانيونس شامل 1, *Facebook*, May 22, 2021. https://www.facebook.com/knsamal20/posts/116775863906494

14   Nasser Atta, Hatem Maher, and Guy Davies, "US citizen working for Hamas killed in Israeli air strike," *ABC News*, May 25, 2021. https://abcnews.go.com/International/us-citizen-working-hamas-killed-israeli-air-strike/story?id=77890472

15   Ibid.

16   Agencies and Aaron Boxerman, "Hamas Gaza chief threatens new, heavier onslaught if Israel 'violates' Al-Aqsa," *The Times of Israel* (Israel), May 26, 2021. https://www.timesofisrael.com/hamas-gaza-chief-threatens-to-renew-fighting-if-israel-violates-al-aqsa

17   @PalInfoAr, "صور| السنوار يحمل طفل الشهـيد أسامة الزبدة ويقبل رأس نجل الشهـيد" جمال الزبدة في مهرجان تأبين شهـداء معركة سـيف القدس [Pictures| Al-Sinwar holds the child of martyr Osama Al-Zibdeh and kisses the head of the martyr›s son Jamal Al-Zibdah in the memorial festival for the martyrs of the Battle of the Sword of Jerusalem." *Twitter*, May 25, 2021, https://twitter.com/PalinfoAr/status/1396894558978457604

18   Anshel Pfeffer, "Revealed: why Israel gunned down an obscure engineer in Malaysia," *The Times* (UK), September 21, 2020. https://www.thetimes.co.uk/article/revealed-why-israel-gunned-down-an-obscure-engineer-in-malaysia-q8mcvx7f6

19   Hannah Beech and Ronen Bergman, "Behind a Roadside Hit in Malaysia, Israeli-Palestinian Intrigue," *The New York Times*, April 25, 2018. https://www.nytimes.com/2018/04/25/world/asia/hamas-mossad-malaysia.html

20   Adive Sterman, "Malyasia denies it trained Hamas operatives," *The Times*

of Israel (Israel), July 21, 2014. https://www.timesofisrael.com/malaysia-denies-it-trained-hamas-operatives

21   Mitch Ginsburg, "Abbas orders probe into Hamas coup plot revealed by Israel," *The Times of Israel* (Israel), August 19, 2014. https://www.timesofisrael.com/abbas-orders-investigation-into-hamas-coup-plot-revealed-by-israel

22   Shaul Shay, "Malaysia – Hamas Military Cooperation," *International Institute for Counter-Terrorism*, May 13, 2015. https://www.ict.org.il/Article/1394/Malaysia-Hamas-Cooperation

23   Matthew Grimson, "Adam Gadahn, al Qaeda Leader Killed in U.S. Drone Strike, Was a Wanted Man," *NBC News*, April 23, 2015. https://www.nbcnews.com/news/world/american-al-qaeda-leader-adam-gadahn-dead-drone-strke-state-n346891

24   Greg Miller, "Legal memo backing drone strike that killed American Anwar al-Awlaki is released," *The Washington Post*, June 23, 2014. https://www.washingtonpost.com/world/national-security/legal-memo-backing-drone-strike-is-released/2014/06/23/1f48dd16-faec-11e3-8176-f2c941cf35f1_story.html

25   Graeme Wood, "The American Climbing The Ranks of ISIS," *The Atlantic*, March 2017. https://www.theatlantic.com/magazine/archive/2017/03/the-american-leader-in-the-islamic-state/510872

26   Carol Rosenberg, "John Walker Lindh, Known as the 'American Taliban,' Is Set to Leave Federal Prison This Week," *The New York Times*, May 21, 2019. https://www.nytimes.com/2019/05/21/us/politics/american-taliban-john-walker-lindh.html

CHAPTER FIFTEEN | EGYPT'S THANKLESS CEASEFIRE

1   Phone interview with senior Israeli official, July 21, 2013.

2   "Hamas re-elects exiled leader Meshaal for a new term: official," *Al Arabiya* (Saudi Arabia), April 2, 2013. http://english.alarabiya.net/en/2013/04/02/Hamas-re-elects-exiled-leader-Meshaal-for-a-new-term-official.html

3   Aya Ibrahim, "Funds Of Qaradawi, 29 Other MB Frozen," *BBC* (UK), July14, 2014. https://www.bbc.com/news/world-middle-east-23308838

4   "Egypt Army Destroys 13 More Gaza Tunnels," *Agence France-Presse*, July 27, 2014. http://news.yahoo.com/egypt-army-destroys-13-more-gaza-tunnels-093712884.html

5   David Lev, "IDF: Hamas Makes a Million a Day in 'Taxes,'" *Arutz Sheva*

(Israel), February 11, 2013. http://www.israelnationalnews.com/News/News.aspx/165125#.VAnpC_mwJgl

6   Nidal al-Mughrabi, "Hamas reeling from Egyptian crackdown On Gaza tunnels," *Aswat Masriya* (Egypt), July 21, 2013. http://en.aswatmasriya.com/news/view.aspx?id=2c404781-4e17-412e-8e03-7e2804bf7417

7   Nidal al-Mughrabi, "Hamas quietly quits Syria as violence continues," *Reuters*, January 12, 2012. https://www.reuters.com/article/us-syria-hamas/hamas-quietly-quits-syria-as-violence-continues-idUSTRE80Q0QS20120127

8   Allison McManus, "ISIS in the Sinai: A Persistent Threat for Egypt," *Newslines Institute for Strategy and Policy*, June 23, 2020. https://newlinesinstitute.org/isis/isis-in-the-sinai-a-persistent-threat-for-egypt

9   Rina Bassist, "East-Med Gas Forum Evolves as Israel, Egypt Enhance Cooperation," *Al-Monitor*, September 22, 2020, https://www.al-monitor.com/originals/2020/09/israel-egypt-greece-cyprus-italy-france-natural-gas-fields.html

10 "Photos of a Beaming Sisi with Netanyahu Inspire Egyptian Satire," *Al Bawaba* (Jordan), September 19, 2017. https://www.albawaba.com/loop/photos-beaming-sisi-netanyahu-inspire-egyptian-satire-and-fury-1023832

11 Hillel Frisch, "The Strategic Genius Behind Allowing Qatar Suitcases of Cash into Gaza," *The Begin-Sadat Center for Strategic Studies* (Israel), May 27, 2021. https://besacenter.org/the-strategic-genius-behind-allowing-qatari-suitcases-of-cash-into-gaza

12 Haisam Hassanein, "What Egypt Wants In Gaza," *Mosaic*, June 14, 2021. https://mosaicmagazine.com/response/israel-zionism/2021/06/what-egypt-wants-in-gaza

13 Meeting with Egyptian official, Washington, DC, June 1, 2021.

14 "FM says to UN diplomat: Israel responsible for ensuring calm, security in Al-Quds," *Egypt Today* (Egypt), May 11, 2021. https://www.egypttoday.com/Article/1/103816/FM-says-to-UN-diplomat-Israel-responsible-for-ensuring-calm

15 Egyptian Ministry of Foreign Affairs, *Facebook*, May 10, 2021. https://www.facebook.com/MFAEgyptEnglish/posts/3000971800230389

16 Egyptian Ministry of Foreign Affairs, *Facebook*, May 10, 2021. https://www.facebook.com/MFAEgyptEnglish/posts/3001311113529791

17 "The Latest: Israeli aircraft strike another building in Gaza," *Associated Press*, May 11, 2021. https://apnews.com/article/israel-middle-east-gaza-government-and-politics-64aa822c846255008dcadc1fcb47d1d5; "Egypt Reached Out To Israel Over Tensions To No Avail: FM," *Agence France-Presse*, May 11, 2021. https://www.barrons.com/news/egypt-reached-out-to-israel-over-tensions-to-no-avail-fm-01620752116

18   Egyptian Ministry of Foreign Affairs, *Facebook*, May 12, 2021. https://www.facebook.com/MFAEgyptEnglish/posts/3002579773402925

19   Egyptian Ministry of Foreign Affairs, *Facebook*, May 12, 2021. https://www.facebook.com/MFAEgyptEnglish/posts/3002595386734697

20   Amr Kandil, "Egypt to send security delegations to Tel Aviv, Gaza to seek de-escalation: Sources tell Al-Arabiya," *Ahram Online* (Egypt), May 12, 2021. https://english.ahram.org.eg/NewsContent/1/64/411045/Egypt/Politics-/Egypt-to-send-security-delegations-to-Tel-Aviv,-Ga.aspx; "Israel rejects Egypt's ceasefire proposal for conflict with Gaza," *Middle East Monitor*, May 12, 2021. https://www.middleeastmonitor.com/20210512-israel-rejects-egypts-ceasefire-proposal-for-conflict-with-gaza

21   Josef Federman and Fares Akran, "Israel threatens Gaza ground invasion despite truce efforts," *Associated Press*, May 13, 2021. https://apnews.com/article/israel-palestinians-conflict-violence-spreads-1ad9613de6ad16c4d248da9934cf0412

22   Egyptian Ministry of Foreign Affairs, *Facebook*, May 12, 2021. https://www.facebook.com/MFAEgyptEnglish/posts/3003843699943199

23   Egyptian Ministry of Foreign Affairs, *Facebook*, May 14, 2021. https://www.facebook.com/MFAEgyptEnglish/posts/3005830626411173

24   Egyptian State Information Service, Readout, "Shoukry, Safadi probe means of reaching to immediate halt to Gaza clashes," May 14, 2021. https://www.sis.gov.eg/Story/155403/Shoukry%2c-Safadi-probe-means-of-reaching-to-immediate-halt-to-Gaza-clashes?lang=en-us

25   Shahar Klaiman, "Egyptian official: Israel refusing to consider ceasefire," *Israel Hayom* (Israel), May 14, 2021. https://www.israelhayom.com/2021/05/14/egyptian-official-israel-refusing-to-consider-ceasefire

26   Egyptian Ministry of Foreign Affairs, *Facebook*, May 15, 2021. https://www.facebook.com/MFAEgyptEnglish/posts/3005870369740532

27   Egyptian Ministry of Foreign Affairs, *Facebook*, May 15, 2021. https://www.facebook.com/MFAEgyptEnglish/posts/3005779393082963

28   "Egypt opens Rafah crossing early for Palestinian travelers – sources," *Reuters*, May 16, 2021. https://www.reuters.com/world/middle-east/egypt-opens-rafah-crossing-early-palestinian-travellers-sources-2021-05-16; "Egypt sends ambulances to evacuate Gaza wounded," *The New Arab* (UK), May 15, 2021. https://english.alaraby.co.uk/news/egypt-sends-ambulances-evacuate-gaza-wounded-0

29   Sami Hegazi, "Egyptian government conveys solidarity with Palestinians amid Gaza attack," *Daily News Egypt* (Egypt), May 16, 2021. https://dailynewsegypt.com/2021/05/16/egyptian-government-conveys-solidarity-with-palestinians-amid-gaza-attack

3

30   United Nations, Press Release, "Senseless Cycle of Bloodshed, Destruction between Israel, Palestinians in Gaza Must Stop Now, Secretary-General Tells Security Council," May 16, 2021. https://www.un.org/press/en/2021/sc14521.doc.htm

31   Ibid.

32   U.S. Department of State, Office of the Spokesperson, Readout, "Secretary Blinken's Call with Egyptian Foreign Minister Shoukry," May 16, 2021. https://www.state.gov/secretary-blinkens-call-with-egyptian-foreign-minister-shoukry-2; Egyptian Ministry of Foreign Affairs, *Facebook*, May 16, 2021. https://www.facebook.com/MFAEgyptEnglish/posts/3005760476418188

33   Egyptian Ministry of Foreign Affairs, *Facebook*, May 16, 2021. https://www.facebook.com/MFAEgyptEnglish/posts/3005788836415352

34   Egyptian Ministry of Foreign Affairs, *Facebook*, May 17, 2021. https://www.facebook.com/MFAEgyptEnglish/posts/3005909616403274

35   Bradley Bowman and Ryan Brobst, "The Iniochos military exercise in Greece is bad news for Iran," *Defense News*, April 30, 2021. https://www.defensenews.com/opinion/commentary/2021/04/30/the-iniochos-military-exercise-in-greece-is-bad-news-for-iran

36   "Egypt's Sisi, France's Macron discuss ongoing Palestine-Israel conflict, GERD issue," *Egypt Today* (Egypt), May 17, 2021. https://www.egypttoday.com/Article/1/104011/Egypt-s-Sisi-France-s-Macron-discuss-ongoing-Palestine-Israel

37   Egyptian State Information Service, Press Release, "President El-Sisi Pays Official Visit to Paris," May 19, 2021. https://www.sis.gov.eg/Story/155466/President-El-Sisi-Pays-Official-Visit-to-Paris?lang=en-us; Tovah Lazaroff and Lahav Harkov, "France, Egypt, Jordan call for ceasefire amid UNSC resolution push," *The Jerusalem Post* (Israel), May 19, 2021. https://www.jpost.com/arab-israeli-conflict/france-pushing-for-unsc-resolution-on-gaza-668495

38   Mohammed Abu Zaid, "Egypt sends medicines to Gaza, prepares hospitals for Palestinians," *Arab News* (Saudi Arabia), May 18, 2021. https://www.arabnews.com/node/1860786/middle-east

39   Egyptian State Information Service, Press Release, "President El-Sisi Pays Official Visit to Paris," May 19, 2021. https://www.sis.gov.eg/Story/155466/President-El-Sisi-Pays-Official-Visit-to-Paris?lang=en-us

40   Egyptian Ministry of Foreign Affairs, *Facebook*, May 19, 2021. https://www.facebook.com/MFAEgyptEnglish/posts/3007744639553105

41   Israeli Office of the Prime Minister, Press Statement, "Prime Minister's Office Statement," May 20, 2021. https://www.gov.il/en/departments/news/spoke_cabinet200521

42 Egyptian Ministry of Foreign Affairs, *Facebook*, May 20, 2021. https://www.facebook.com/MFAEgyptEnglish/posts/3008534929474076

43 Samy Magdy, "Mediating in Gaza conflict, Egypt seeks broader influence," *ABC News*, May 20, 2021. https://abcnews.go.com/International/wireStory/mediating-gaza-conflict-egypt-seeks-broader-influence-77803255; The White House, Readout, "Readout of President Joseph R. Biden, Jr. Call with President Abdel Fattah Al Sisi of Egypt," May 20, 2021. https://www.whitehouse.gov/briefing-room/statements-releases/2021/05/20/readout-of-president-joseph-r-biden-jr-call-with-president-abdel-fattah-al-sisi-of-egypt); Egyptian Presidency, Readout, "President El-Sisi Receives Phone Call from US President," May 2021. https://www.presidency.eg/en

44 Egyptian Presidency, Readout, "President El-Sisi Receives Phone Call from UN Secretary-General," May 20, 2021. https://www.presidency.eg/en

45 President Joe Biden, The White House, "Remarks by President Biden on the Middle East," May 20, 2021. https://www.whitehouse.gov/briefing-room/speeches-remarks/2021/05/20/remarks-by-president-biden-on-the-middle-east

46 "Biden's behind-the-scenes push for Israel-Hamas cease-fire," *Los Angeles Times*, May 21, 2021. https://www.latimes.com/politics/story/2021-05-21/bidens-behind-the-scenes-push-for-cease-fire-between-israel-and-hamas

47 The White House, Readout, "Readout of President Joseph R. Biden, Jr. Call with President Abdel Fattah Al Sisi of Egypt," May 24, 2021. https://www.whitehouse.gov/briefing-room/statements-releases/2021/05/24/readout-of-president-joseph-r-biden-jr-call-with-president-abdel-fattah-al-sisi-of-egypt-2; Egyptian Presidency, Readout, "President El-Sisi Receives Phone Call from US President Joe Biden," May 24, 2021. https://www.presidency.eg/en

48 President Joe Biden, The White House, Press Statement, "Statement by President Joe Biden on Secretary of State Antony Blinken's Visit to the Middle East," May 24, 2021. https://www.whitehouse.gov/briefing-room/statements-releases/2021/05/24/statement-by-president-joe-biden-on-secretary-of-state-antony-blinkens-visit-to-the-middle-east; U.S. Department of State, Office of the Spokesperson, Readout, "Secretary Blinken's Meeting with Egyptian President Al Sisi," May 26, 2021. https://www.state.gov/secretary-blinkens-meeting-with-egyptian-president-al-sisi; Secretary of State Antony J. Blinken, U.S. Department of State, "Secretary Antony J. Blinken at a Press Availability," May 26, 2021. https://www.state.gov/secretary-antony-j-blinken-at-a-press-availability-6

CHAPTER SIXTEEN | BIDEN'S TOUGH TALK

1   U.S. Department of State, Office of the Spokesperson, Readout, "Secretary Blinken's First Call with Israeli Foreign Minister Ashkenazi," January 27, 2021. https://www.state.gov/secretary-blinkens-first-call-with-israeli-foreign-minister-ashkenazi

2   National Security Council Spokesperson Emily Horne, The White House, Readout, "Statement by NSC Spokesperson Emily Horne on National Security Adviser Jake Sullivan's Call with National Security Advisor Meir Ben Shabbat of Israel," January 24, 2021. https://www.whitehouse. gov/briefing-room/statements-releases/2021/01/24/statement-by-nsc-spokesperson-emily-horne-on-national-security-advisor-jake-sullivans-call-with-national-security-advisor-meir-ben-shabbat-of-israel

3   Mark Dubowitz and Jonathan Schanzer, "Strengthen the Alliance with Israel to Contain China," *Foundation for Defense of Democracies*, December 15, 2020. https://www.fdd.org/analysis/2020/12/15/defending-forward-strengthen-the-alliance-with-israel-to-contain-china

4   Annie Fixler and Mark Dubowitz, "The Iran Deal's Fatal Flaws After One Year: Emboldened Iran and Diminished American Deterrence," *Foundation for Defense of Democracies*, July 14, 2016. https://www.fdd.org/analysis/2016/07/14/the-iran-deals-fatal-flaws-after-one-year-emboldened-iran-and-diminished-american-deterrence

5   Peter Baker, "For Obama and Netanyahu, A Final Clash After Years of Conflict," *The New York Times*, December 23, 2016. https://www.nytimes.com/2016/12/23/world/middleeast/israel-benjamin-netanyahu-barack-obama.html

6   "First 100 Days," *Clinton Digital Library*, accessed August 10, 2021. https://clinton.presidentiallibraries.us/items/show/22013; U.S. Department of State, Office of the Historian, "Visits By Foreign Leaders in 1993," accessed August 10, 2021. https://history.state.gov/departmenthistory/visits/1993

7   Press Secretary Ari Fleischer, The White House, Press Statement, "Statement by the Press Secretary: Election of Ariel Sharon as Prime Minister of Israel," February 6, 2001. https://georgewbush-whitehouse. archives.gov/news/releases/20010206-8.html

8   Roni Sofer, "Obama calls Abbas, Olmert on first day," *Ynet* (Israel), January 21, 2009. https://www.ynetnews.com/articles/0,7340,L-3659961,00.html

9   The White House, Readout, "Readout of the President's call with Israeli Prime Minister Netanyahu," April 1, 2009. https://obamawhitehouse. archives.gov/the-press-office/readout-president-s-call-with-israeli-prime-minister-netanyahu

10   Karen DeYoung, "Trump Speaks With Netanyahu," *The Washington Post*, January 22, 2017. https://www.washingtonpost.com/world/national-security/trump-speaks-with-israeli-prime-minister-benjamin-netanyahu/2017/01/22/ae06c3d2-e0d2-11e6-a453-19ec4b3d09ba_story.html

11   Ian Lee and James Masters, "Where Donald Trump and Benjamin Netanyahu Stand on Key Issues," *CNN*, February 15, 2017. https://www.cnn.com/2017/02/15/politics/trump-netanyahu-white-house-meeting/index.html

12   The White House, Readout, "Readout of President Joseph R. Biden, Jr. Call with President Vladimir Putin of Russia," January 26, 2021. https://www.whitehouse.gov/briefing-room/statements-releases/2021/01/26/readout-of-president-joseph-r-biden-jr-call-with-president-vladimir-putin-of-russia

13   The White House, Readout, "Readout of President Joseph R. Biden's call with President Xi Jinping of China," February 10, 2021. https://www.whitehouse.gov/briefing-room/statements-releases/2021/02/10/readout-of-president-joseph-r-biden-jr-call-with-president-xi-jinping-of-china

14   The White House, Readout, "Readout of President Joe Biden call with Prime Minister Justin Trudeau of Canada," January 22, 2021. https://www.whitehouse.gov/briefing-room/statements-releases/2021/01/22/readout-of-president-joe-biden-call-with-prime-minister-justin-trudeau-of-canada

15   The White House, Readout, "Readout of President Joe Biden call with President Andrés Manuel López Obrador of Mexico," January 23, 2021. https://www.whitehouse.gov/briefing-room/statements-releases/2021/01/23/readout-of-president-joe-biden-call-with-president-andres-manuel-lopez-obrador-of-mexico

16   The White House, Readout, "Readout of President Joseph R Biden call with Prime Minister Boris Johnson of the United Kingdom," January 23, 2021. https://www.whitehouse.gov/briefing-room/statements-releases/2021/01/23/readout-of-president-joe-biden-call-with-prime-minister-boris-johnson-of-the-united-kingdom

17   Press Secretary Jen Psaki, The White House, "Press Briefing by Press Secretary Jen Psaki and Council of Economic Advisers Member Jared Bernstein, February 5, 2021," February 5, 2021. https://www.whitehouse.gov/briefing-room/press-briefings/2021/02/05/press-briefing-by-press-secretary-jen-psaki-and-council-of-economic-advisers-member-jared-bernstein-february-5-2021; Secretary of State Anthony J. Blinken, U.S. Department of State, "Secretary Antony J. Blinken With Andrea Mitchell of MSNBC Andrea Mitchell Reports," February 1, 2021. https://www.state.gov/secretary-antony-j-blinken-with-andrea-mitchell-of-msnbc-andrea-mitchell-reports; National Security Advisor Jake Sullivan, The White House, "Press Briefing by Secretary Jen Psaki and National Security Advisor Jake Sullivan, February 4, 2021," February 4, 2021. https://www.whitehouse.gov/briefing-room/press-briefings/2021/02/04/press-briefing-by-press-secretary-jen-psaki-and-national-security-advisor-jake-sullivan-february-4-2021

18   Michael Crowley, "Why Biden's Pick for Iran Envoy Is 'a Proxy for Everything,'" *The New York Times*, February 26, 2021. https://www.nytimes.com/2021/02/13/us/politics/robert-malley-iran-middle-east.html

19   "Top Iran General Says Destroying Israel 'Achievable Goal,'" *Agence France-Presse*, September 30, 2019. https://www.voanews.com/middle-east/top-iran-general-says-destroying-israel-achievable-goal

20   Reuel Marc Gerecht, "The Iran Deal Is Strategically and Morally Absurd," *The Atlantic*, May 4, 2018. https://www.theatlantic.com/international/archive/2018/05/iran-nuclear-deal-flawed/559595

21   Jacob Nagel, "A return to the 2015 Iran deal is impossible," *The Jerusalem Post* (Israel), February 11, 2021. https://www.jpost.com/middle-east/a-return-to-the-2015-iran-deal-is-impossible-658707

22   Joby Warrick, "Stolen records show Iran overcoming key hurdles in 2003 quest for a nuclear bomb, book says," *The Washington Post*, May 14, 2021. https://www.washingtonpost.com/national-security/iran-nuclear-bomb-design-capability/2021/05/14/a47e75cc-b4f8-11eb-ab43-bebddc5a0f65_story.html

23   Amnon Lord, "Will Biden's presidency be Obama's third term?" *Israel Hayom* (Israel), January 20, 2021. https://www.israelhayom.com/opinions/will-bidens-presidency-be-obamas-third-term

24   Kevin Breuninger, "Biden and Israel leader Netanyahu talk for first time since inauguration," *CNBC*, February 17, 2021. https://www.cnbc.com/2021/02/17/israel-pm-netanyahu-says-he-had-an-hourlong-phone-call-with-biden.html

25   "Biden on Israel-Gaza Violence: 'Israel has a right to defend itself,'" *The Washington Post*, May 12, 2021, https://www.washingtonpost.com/video/politics/biden-on-israel-gaza-violence-israel-has-a-right-to-defend-itself/2021/05/12/50736d03-9c09-46fe-8b33-bb23dfc0bfb9_video.html

26   Laura Kelly, "Biden Sending Official on Israeli-Palestinian Affairs to Deescalate Tensions," *The Hill*, May 12, 2021. https://thehill.com/policy/international/middle-east-north-africa/553108-biden-sending-top-official-on-israeli-and

27   Amanda Macias, "Biden tells Netanyahu U.S. supports ceasefire as Israel, Hamas conflict escalates," *CNBC*, May 17, 2021. https://www.cnbc.com/2021/05/17/biden-tells-netanyahu-us-supports-ceasefire-as-israel-hamas-tensions-escalate.html

28   David E. Sanger and Isabel Kershner, "Biden Supports Israel-Gaza Cease-Fire, as Fighting Rages into Second Week," *The New York Times*, May 17, 2021. https://www.nytimes.com/2021/05/17/world/asia/biden-israel-gaza.html

29   "Israel-Palestine US blocks UN statement for third week," *Al Jazeera* (Qatar), May 17, 2021. https://www.aljazeera.com/news/2021/5/17/no-us-action-after-third-unsc-meeting-on-israel-palestine

30   Asma Khalid, "How The Gaza Violence Marked A Shift In The American Political Debate Over Israel," *NPR*, May 21, 2021. https://www.npr.org/2021/05/21/998955323/progressives-are-mostly-pleased-with-biden-that-deepened-frustration-over-israel

31   John Hlatiwanger, "Biden's refusal to criticize Israel killing civilians undermines his pledge to prioritize human rights," *Business Insider*, May 18, 2021. https://www.businessinsider.com/biden-refusal-to-criticize-israel-undermines-human-rights-pledge-2021-5

32   Alana Wise, "Rep. Tlaib Pushes Biden To Protect At-Risk Palestinians In Middle East Conflict," *NPR*, May 18, 2021. https://www.npr.org/2021/05/18/998038591/rep-tlaib-pushes-biden-to-protect-at-risk-palestinians-in-middle-east-conflict

33   Clara Hill, "Alexandria Ocasio-Cortex calls Israel an 'apartheid state,'" *The Independent* (UK), May 17, 2021. https://www.independent.co.uk/news/world/americas/us-politics/aoc-israel-palestine-gaza-apartheid-b1848703.html

34   Colby Itkowitz and Sean Sullivan, "Rep. Ilhan Ohmar clarifies tweet grouping U.S., Israel and Hamas, Taliban after criticism from Jewish democratic lawmakers," *The Washington* Post, June 10, 2021. https://www.washingtonpost.com/politics/jewish-democrats-omar-israel/2021/06/10/45d5db22-c9e9-11eb-a11b-6c6191ccd599_story.html

35   @RepCori, "The fight for Black lives and the fight for Palestinian liberation are interconnected. We oppose our money going to fund militarized policing, occupation, and systems of violent oppression and trauma. We are anti-war. We are anti-occupation. And we are anti-apartheid. Period." *Twitter,* May 13, 2021. https://twitter.com/RepCori/status/1392991612364591107

36   @BernieSanders, "The devastation in Gaza is unconscionable. We must urge an immediate ceasefire. The killing of Palestinians and Israelis must end. We must also take a hard look at nearly $4 billion a year in military aid to Israel. It is illegal for U.S. aid to support human rights violations." *Twitter*, May 16, 2021. https://twitter.com/berniesanders/status/1393972598237696007

37   Jonathan Schanzer, "The Congressman Who Hated Israel," *Commentary Magazine*, September 2019. https://www.commentarymagazine.com/articles/jonathan-schanzer/the-congressman-who-hated-israel

38   Celestine Bohlen, "The 1982 Elections: The Illinois 20th District," *The Washington Post*, October 31, 1982. https://www.washingtonpost.com/archive/politics/1982/10/31/the-1982-elections-the-illinois-20th-district-race/76e5660e-4e40-4615-88b0-f012ad57000a

39   Paul Findley, *They Dare to Speak Out: People and Institutions Confront Israel's Lobby* (Chicago: Chicago Review Press, 2003).

40   Brittney De Lea, "GOP Rep. Waltz battles Pelosi over renaming 'Squad' the 'Hamas caucus,'" *Fox News*, June 14, 2021. https://www.foxnews.com/politics/gop-rep-waltz-battles-pelosi-renaming-squad-hamas-caucus

41   "Israel-Gaza: Biden tells Netanyahu he wants 'path to ceasefire,'" *BBC News* (UK), May 19, 2021. https://www.bbc.com/news/world-middle-east-57168051

42   Barak Ravid, "Biden presses Netanyahu on Gaza ceasefire," *Axios*, May 19, 2021. https://www.axios.com/biden-presses-netanyahu-for-gaza-ceasefire-call-75909b5e-c38b-428d-8994-4f19675e865d.html

43   Aamer Madhani, "Biden's pattern with Israel: public support, private scolds," *Associated Press*, May 20, 2021. https://apnews.com/article/middle-east-israel-government-and-politics-8865a9b89162df255c6707736610a7af

44   Bradley Bowman and Seth J. Frantzman, "Israel Confronts Tehran's Terror Proxies in Gaza," *The Dispatch*, May 20, 2021. https://thedispatch.com/p/israel-confronts-tehrans-terror-proxies

45   Eliza Collins, "Bernie Sanders Drops Effort to Stop Weapons Sales to Israel," *The Wall Street Journal*, May 25, 2021. https://www.wsj.com/articles/bernie-sanders-drops-effort-to-stop-weapons-sales-to-israel-11621985228

46   Senator James E. Risch and Congressman Michael T. McCaul, *Letter to President Joseph R. Biden*, May 20, 2021. https://gop-foreignaffairs.house.gov/wp-content/uploads/2021/05/210520-TO-POTUS-RE-Israel.pdf

47   Eliza Collins and Siobhan Hughes, "Progressives Pressure Top Democrats on Israel Arms Deal, Policing," *The Wall Street Journal*, May 22, 2021. https://www.wsj.com/articles/progressives-pressure-top-democrats-on-israel-arms-deal-policing-11621697400

48   Grace Segers, "11 House Democrats object to Ilhan Omar's comments on Hamas and Israel," *CBS News*, June 10, 2021. https://www.cbsnews.com/news/ilhan-omar-hamas-israel-democrats-objection

49   Congresswoman Ilhan Omar, Press Statement, "Rep. Ilhan Omar Statement on Questions During the House Foreign Affairs Committee," June 10, 2021. https://omar.house.gov/media/press-releases/rep-ilhan-omar-statement-questions-during-house-foreign-affairs-committee

50   Jonathan Weisman, "Showdown Over Omar's Comments Exposes Sharp Divisions Among Democrats," *The New York Times*, June 10, 2021. https://www.nytimes.com/2021/06/10/us/politics/ilhan-omar-israel.html

51   @RepLeeZeldin, "Ilhan Omar must be removed from the House Foreign Affairs Committee. She should have never been appointed to this Committee in the first place." *Twitter*, June 9, 2021. https://twitter.com/RepLeeZeldin/status/1402827823497236481

CHAPTER SEVENTEEN | UNRWA COMES CLEAN

1   For more on the process that led to UNRWA's establishment, see: Asaf Romirowsky and Alexander H. Joffe, *Religion, Politics, and the Origins of Palestine Refugee Relief* (NYC: Palgrave Macmillan, 2013).

2   Gilad Erdan, "UN must recognize Jewish refugees from Arab countries – opinion," *The Jerusalem Post* (Israel), November 30, 2021. https://www.jpost.com/opinion/un-must-recognize-jewish-refugees-from-arab-countries-opinion-650645

3   Adam Entous, "Gaza headmaster was Islamic Jihad 'rocket maker,'" *Reuters*, May 5, 2008. https://www.reuters.com/article/idINIndia-33413620080505

4   Ilan Ben Zion, "Rockets found in UNRWA school, for third time," *The Times of Israel* (Israel), July 30, 2014. https://www.timesofisrael.com/rockets-found-in-unrwa-school-for-third-time; "UN admits Palestinians fired rockets from UNRWA schools," *UN Watch*, April 7, 2015. https://unwatch.org/un-admits-palestinians-fired-rockets-unrwa-schools

5   Ian Williams, "Ethics report accuses UNRWA leadership of abuse of power," *Al Jazeera* (Qatar), July 29, 2021. https://www.aljazeera.com/news/2019/7/29/ethics-report-accuses-unrwa-leadership-of-abuse-of-power

6   Jackson Richman, "Declassified report on UNRWA accuses US State Department of misleading Congress on Palestinian textbooks," *Jewish News Syndicate*, February 8, 2019. https://www.jns.org/declassified-report-on-unrwa-accuses-state-department-of-misleading-congress-on-palestinian-textbooks

7   "US ends aid to Palestinian refugee agency UNRWA," *BBC News* (UK), September 1, 2018. https://www.bbc.com/news/world-us-canada-45377336

8   Melissa Weiss, "U.N. agency head admits printing 'inappropriate' content in Palestinian classroom content," *Jewish Insider*, January 14, 2021. https://jewishinsider.com/2021/01/unrwa-textbooks-gaza-west-bank

9   "Review of UNRWA-Produced Study Materials in the Palestinian Territories November 2020 – January 2021," *IMPACT-se*, February 2021, pages 1–2. https://www.impact-se.org/wp-content/uploads/UNRWA-Produced-Study-Materials_Post-November-2020.pdf

10   For more, see: Adi Schwartz and Einat Wilf, *The War of Return: How Western Indulgence of the Palestinian Dream has Obstructed the Path to Peace* (NYC: All Points Books, 2020).

11   Alexander H. Joffee "UNRWA Resists Resettlement," *Middle East Quarterly*, Fall 2012, https://www.meforum.org/3350/unrwa-resettlement

12   Jonathan Schanzer, "Status Update," *Foreign Policy*, May 21, 2012. https://foreignpolicy.com/2012/05/21/status-update

13   Aaron Bandler, "Haley calls on administration to release classified reports on Palestinian Refugees," *Jewish News Syndicate*, November 26, 2020. https://www.jns.org/haley-calls-on-trump-administration-to-release-classified-report-on-palestinian-refugees

14   @SecPompeo, "We suspended funding to UNRWA, which is riddled with waste, fraud & concerns of support to terrorism. UNRWA is not a refugee agency; it's estimated <200,000 Arabs displaced in 1948 are still alive and most others are not refugees by any rational criteria." *Twitter*, January 14, 2021. https://twitter.com/secpompeo/status/1349832113923780610

15   @SecPompeo, "Taxpayers deserve basic truths: most Palestinians under UNRWA's jurisdiction aren't refugees, and UNRWA is a hurdle to peace. America supports peace and Palestinian human rights; UNRWA supports neither. It's time to end UNRWA's mandate." *Twitter*, January 14, 2021. https://twitter.com/SecPompeo/status/1349832119829233664

16   "What is a Refugee?" *USA for UNHCR The UN Refugee Agency*, accessed July 1, 2021. https://www.unrefugees.org/refugee-facts/what-is-a-refugee

17   UN Relief and Works Agency for Palestinian Refugees in the Near East, "Frequently Asked Questions," accessed August 11, 2021. https://www.unrwa.org/who-we-are/frequently-asked-questions

18   Richard Goldberg, "United Nations Relief and Works Agency," *A Better Blueprint for International Organizations Advancing American Interests on the Global Stage*," Ed. Richard Goldberg (Washington, DC: Foundation for Defense of Democracies, 2021), pages 40–42. https://www.fdd.org/wp-content/uploads/2021/06/fdd-monograph-a-better-blueprint-for-international-organizations-advancing-american-interests-on-the-global-stage.pdf

19   Adiv Sterman, "'Abbas was ready to compromise on right of return,'" *The Times of Israel* (Israel), March 11, 2013. https://www.timesofisrael.com/abbas-was-willing-to-compromise-on-right-of-return)

20   "Biden administration to restore $235m in US aid to Palestinians," *BBC News* (UK), April 7, 2021. https://www.bbc.com/news/world-middle-east-56665199

21   Jonathan Schanzer and Richard Goldberg, "The U.N. Refugee Agency With Few Actual Refugees," *The Wall Street Journal*, February 3, 2021. https://www.wsj.com/articles/the-u-n-refugee-agency-with-few-actual-refugees-11612378415

22   Ibid.

23   "UNRWA director in Gaza apologizes after saying IDF strikes were 'precise,'" *The Jerusalem Post* (Israel), May 26, 2021. https://www.jpost.com/arab-israeli-conflict/gazans-outraged-after-unrwa-director-says-idf-strikes-were-precise-669090?_ga=2.37611552.1008525341.1621743173-449294072.1564573179

24   Ruthie Blum, "Did UNRWA's Gaza director lose the plot?" *The Jerusalem Post* (Israel), May 27, 2021. https://www.jpost.com/opinion/did-unrwas-gaza-director-lose-the-plot-opinion-669433

25   "Gaza Declares Matthias Persona Non Grata Overpraise UN Say. Neutrality & Inviolability of UNRWA Installations Must Be Respected," *Palestine News Network* (West Bank), June 5, 2021. http://english.pnn.ps/2021/06/05/the-neutrality-and-inviolability-of-unrwa-installations-must-be-respected-at-all-times

26   UN Relief and Works Agency for Palestine Refugees in the Near East, Press Release, "The neutrality and inviolability of UNRWA installations must be respected at all times," June 4, 2021. https://reliefweb.int/report/occupied-palestinian-territory/neutrality-and-inviolability-unrwa-installations-must-be

27   United Nations Relief and Works Agency for Palestine Refugees in the Near East, Press Release, "UNRWA Statement on UN Watch Allegations," August 5, 2021, https://www.unrwa.org/newsroom/official-statements/unrwa-statement-un-watch-allegations

28   "Hamas Said to Block UN Team from Inspecting School Where Tunnel was Found," *Times of Israel* (Israel), August 11, 2021, https://www.timesofisrael.com/hamas-said-to-block-un-team-from-inspecting-school-where-tunnel-was-found/

29   Jessica Donati, "Gaza Relief Plan Tests U.S. Ability to Bypass Hamas," *The Wall Street Journal*, June 4, 2021. https://www.wsj.com/articles/u-s-relief-plan-for-gaza-seeks-to-bypass-hamas-11622804401?page=1

30   Julia Schulman, "Why Cutting off Aid to Hamas Is Insufficient," *The National Interest*, June 8, 2021. https://nationalinterest.org/feature/why-cutting-aid-hamas-insufficient-187174

CHAPTER EIGHTEEN | REGIONAL PEACE BECKONS

1   David Daoud and Varsha Koduvayur, "Welcome to a Brand-New Middle East," *Foreign Policy*, September 30, 2020. https://foreignpolicy.com/2020/09/30/israel-uae-bahrain-palestinians-peace

2   Jonathan Schanzer, "Israel's next peace deal will be with Sudan," *New York Post*, September 22, 2021. https://nypost.com/2020/09/22/israels-next-peace-deal-will-be-with-sudan

3   "Hamas diaspora director: 'To hell with the worthless scum who normalized relations with Israel,'" *Jewish News Syndicate*, May 3, 2021. https://www.jns.org/hamas-diaspora-director-to-hell-with-the-worthless-scum-that-normalized-relations-with-israel

4   "Dubai official: Hamas can go to hell," *Israel Hayom* (Israel), September 6, 2021. https://www.israelhayom.com/2020/09/06/dubai-official-hamas-can-go-to-hell

5   Briefing by Emirati official, Washington, DC, July 13, 2021.

6   "Arab Nations Hit out at Israel over Jerusalem Violence," *Agence France-Presse*, May 9, 2021. https://www.voanews.com/middle-east/arab-nations-hit-out-israel-over-jerusalem-violence

7   "Saudi Arabia condemns Israel for 'flagrant violations' in Gaza," *Al Jazeera* (Qatar), May 16, 2021. https://www.aljazeera.com/news/2021/5/16/saudi-arabia-condemns-israel-over-flagrant-violations-in-gaza

8   "Israeli PM Netanyahu makes rare visit to Oman," *Reuters*, October 26, 2018. https://www.reuters.com/article/us-israel-oman/israeli-pm-netanyahu-makes-rare-visit-to-oman-idUSKCN1N01WN

9   "Oman's Foreign Minister expresses support to Palestinians," *Times of Oman* (Oman), May 12, 2021. https://timesofoman.com/article/101203-omans-foreign-minister-expresses-support-to-palestinians

10   "الكويت تدين اقتحام الاحتلال الاسرائيلي لباحة المسجد الأقصى واستهداف أبناء الشعب الفلسطيني [Kuwait condemns the Israeli occupation's storming of the Al-Aqsa Mosque and the targeting of the sons of the Palestinian people]," *Kuwait News Agency* (Kuwait), May 8, 2021. https://www.kuna.net.kw/ArticleDetails.aspx?id=2976464

11   "The Latest: Israeli aircraft strike another building in Gaza," *Associated Press*, May 11, 2021. https://apnews.com/article/israel-middle-east-gaza-government-and-politics-64aa822c846255008dcadc1fcb47d1d5

12   Shafik Mandhai, "Israel use of Quran verses to justify Gaza bombardment sparks anger," *Middle East Eye*, May 18, 2021. https://www.middleeasteye.net/news/israel-use-quran-verses-justify-gaza-bombardment-sparks-anger

13   "Explainer: Who is targeting the Muslim Brotherhood?" *Reuters*, May 3, 2019. https://www.reuters.com/article/us-usa-trump-muslimbrotherhood-explainer/explainer-who-is-targeting-the-muslim-brotherhood-idUSKCN1S90YX

14   "Saudi Arabia declares Muslim Brotherhood 'terrorist group,'" *BBC News* (UK), March 7, 2014. https://www.bbc.com/news/world-middle-east-26487092; "UAE lists Muslim Brotherhood as terrorist group," *Reuters*, November 15, 2014. https://www.reuters.com/article/us-emirates-politics-brotherhood/uae-lists-muslim-brotherhood-as-terrorist-group-idUSKCN0IZ0OM20141115

15   "Qatar crisis: What you need to know," *BBC News* (UK), July 19, 2017. https://www.bbc.com/news/world-middle-east-40173757

16   Jared Malsin and Nazih Osserian, "Israel's Conflict in Gaza Tests Limits of New Détente With Arab World," *The Wall Street Journal*, May 13, 2021. https://www.wsj.com/articles/israels-conflict-in-gaza-tests-limits-of-new-detente-with-arab-world-11620918769

17   "'Jerusalem Is My Cause': Social Media in Morocco, World Condemns Israel's Violent Attacks," *Morocco World News* (Morocco), accessed July 2, 2021. https://www.moroccoworldnews.com/2021/05/341764/jerusalem-is-my-cause-social-media-in-morocco-world-condemns-israels-violent-attacks

18   @marcowenjones, "I should add 'Palestine is not our cause' is also trending in United Arab Emirates," *Twitter*, May 12, 2021. https://twitter.com/marcowenjones/status/1392492224189931520

19   Ali Al Nuami, "I worked on the Abraham Accords. It's Time to Free the Palestinians from Hamas—and Iran," *Newsweek*, June 7, 2021. https://www.newsweek.com/i-helped-broker-abraham-accords-its-time-free-palestinians-hamas-iran-opinion-1598198

20   American Jewish Committee, Press Release, "Bahrain Foreign Minister Addresses AJC Global Forum on Arab-Israel Peace, Iran Threat," June 8, 2021. https://www.prnewswire.com/news-releases/bahrain-foreign-minister-addresses-ajc-global-forum-on-arab-israel-peace-iran-threat-301308437.html

21   "Morocco's PJD Receives Hamas Leader in Rabat," *Morocco World News* (Morocco), June 16, 2021. https://www.moroccoworldnews.com/2021/06/342940/moroccos-political-parties-receive-senior-hamas-leader-in-rabat

22   Interview with Moroccan official, Washington, DC, June 4, 2021.

23   "Moroccan PM congratulates Hamas on 'victory' over Israel in recent fighting," *The Times of Israel* (Israel), May 24, 2021. https://www.timesofisrael.com/moroccan-pm-congratulates-hamas-on-victory-over-israel-in-recent-fighting

24   "Israel Sends Top Official to Morocco For First Time Since Ties Were Normalized," *France 24* (France), August 11, 2021. https://www.france24.com/en/middle-east/20210811-yair-lapid-lands-in-morocco-on-first-visit-by-an-israeli-foreign-minister

25   "Sudan welcomes ceasefire between Israelis and Palestinians," *Reuters*, May 21, 2021. https://www.reuters.com/world/middle-east/sudan-welcomes-ceasefire-between-israelis-palestinians-2021-05-21

26   "Sudan's Burhan defends Israel normalization move amid violence with Palestine," *Agence France-Presse*, May 17, 2021. https://english.alarabiya.net/News/middle-east/2021/05/17/Sudan-s-Burhan-defends-Israel-normalization-move-amid-violence-with-Palestine

27   @wasilalitaha, "BREAKING: #Sudan @TSC_SUDAN chaiman @ aftaburhan rules out any resumption of ties with #Iran which he called a 'security threat' in the region & a threat to stability in many Arab countries," *Twitter*, June 9, 2021. https://twitter.com/wasilalitaha/ status/1402683871607590915?s=20

CHAPTER NINETEEN | IRAN LOOMS

1   U.S. Department of the Treasury, Press Release, "Treasury Sanctions Major Hamas Leaders, Financial Facilitators and a Front Company," September 10, 2015. https://www.treasury.gov/press-center/press-releases/Pages/ jl0159.aspx

2   Ibid.

3   Kelsey Davenport, "Implementation of the Joint Plan of Action at a Glance," *Arms Control Association*, November 2020. https://www. armscontrol.org/Implementation-of-the-Joint-Plan-of-Action-At-A- Glance

4   "Iran Always Ready To Assist Palestinian Fighters: Majlis Speaker," *Press TV* (Iran), January 17, 2013. Archived version available at: https://web.archive.org/web/20130119090201/https://www.presstv.ir/ detail/2013/01/17/284036/iran-always-ready-to-help-palestinians

5   Ibid.

6   U.S. Department of the Treasury, Press Release, "U.S. Designates Five Charities Funding Hamas and Six Senior Hamas Leaders as Terrorist Entities," August 22, 2003. https://www.treasury.gov/press-center/press- releases/pages/js672.aspx

7   Behnam Ben Taleblu, "Analysis: What The Gaza War Means For Iran," *FDD's Long War Journal*, August 1, 2014. http://www.longwarjournal.org/ archives/2014/08/what_the_gaza_war_me.php

8   Carol E. Lee and Jay Solomon, "U.S. Transferred $1.3 Billion More in Cash to Iran After Initial Payment," *The Wall Street Journal*, September 6, 2016. https://www.wsj.com/articles/u-s-sent-two-more-planeloads-of-cash- to-iran-after-initial-payment-1473208256

9   Jonathan Schanzer and Mark Dubowitz, "It Just Got Easier for Iran to Fund Terrorism," *Foreign Policy*, July 17, 2015. https://foreignpolicy. com/2015/07/17/it-just-got-easier-for-iran-to-fund-terrorism-swift-bank

10   Email correspondence with Mark Dubowitz, June 8, 2021.

11   Interview with U.S. government official, Washington, DC, March 15, 2016.

12   Mark Lander, "Trump Abandons Iran Nuclear Deal He Long Scorned," *The New York Times*, May 8, 2018. https://www.nytimes.com/2018/05/08/world/middleeast/trump-iran-nuclear-deal.html

13   U.S. Department of the Treasury, Press Release, "Treasury Targets Facilitators Moving Millions to Hamas in Gaza," August 29, 2019. https://home.treasury.gov/news/press-releases/sm761

14   Parisa Hafezi, "Iran lauds arms supply to Palestinians against 'tumor' Israel," *Reuters*, May 22, 2020. https://www.reuters.com/article/us-iran-israel-khamenei/iran-lauds-arms-supply-to-palestinians-against-tumor-israel-idUSKBN22Y10L

15   "Defense minister orders seizure of $4million sent by Iran to Hamas," *The Times of Israel* (Israel), December 22, 2020. https://www.timesofisrael.com/defense-minister-orders-seizure-of-4-million-sent-by-iran-to-hamas

16   Conor Skelding, "Talks underway to restore Iran nuclear deal," *New York Post*, May 1, 2021. https://nypost.com/2021/05/01/talks-underway-to-restore-iran-nuclear-deal

17   Arshad Mohammed and Daphne Psaledakis, "U.S. tiptoes through sanctions minefield toward Iran nuclear deal," *Reuters*, May 17, 2021. https://www.reuters.com/world/middle-east/us-tiptoes-through-sanctions-minefield-toward-iran-nuclear-deal-2021-05-17

18   Michael Crowley, "Iran Talks Loom as a New Test of Biden's Israel Ties," *The New York Times*, May 25, 2021. https://www.nytimes.com/2021/05/25/us/politics/biden-israel-iran.html

19   Kenneth Garger, "Iran's Khamenei says Palestinians must 'confront the enemy' amid Israel-Hamas conflict," *New York Post*, May 12, 2021. https://nypost.com/2021/05/12/khamenei-says-palestinians-must-confront-the-enemy-amid-israel-hamas-conflict

20   Dion Nissenbaum, Sune Engel Rasmussen, and Benoit Faucon, "With Iranian Help, Hamas Builds 'Made in Gaza' Rockets and Drones to Target Israel," *The Wall Street Journal*, May 20, 2021. https://www.wsj.com/articles/with-iranian-help-hamas-builds-made-in-gaza-rockets-and-drones-to-target-israel-11621535346

21   Seth J. Frantzman, "IRGC head praises Hamas commander Deif as 'living martyr' – analysis," *The Jerusalem Post* (Israel), May 20, 2021. https://www.jpost.com/arab-israeli-conflict/irgc-head-praises-hamas-commander-deif-as-living-martyr-analysis-668656

22   Tobias Siegal, "Hamas' Haniyeh vows to destabilize Jerusalem, thanks Iran for support," *The Jerusalem Post* (Israel), May 22, 2021. https://www.jpost.com/middle-east/hamas-haniyeh-vows-to-destabilize-jerusalem-thanks-iran-for-support-668791

23   "Iran leader urges Muslim states to back Palestinians militarily, financially," *Reuters*, May 21, 2021. https://www.reuters.com/world/middle-east/iran-hails-palestinian-victory-warns-deadly-blows-against-israel-2021-05-21

24   "Spokesman Of Palestinian Al-Quds Brigades (AQB): Missiles Fired On Ashkelon Today Were Badr 3; Iran Provided 'Generous' Support To Palestinian Factions," *Middle East Media Research Institute*, May 11, 2021. https://www.memri.org/jttm/spokesman-palestinian-al-quds-brigades-aqb-missiles-fired-ashkelon-today-were-badr-3-iran

25   Seth J. Frantzman, "Iran's hand seen in Hamas drone threat against Israel – analysis," *The Jerusalem Post* (Israel), May 15, 2011. https://www.jpost.com/middle-east/iran-news/irans-hand-seen-in-hamas-drone-threat-against-israel-analysis-668110

26   Stephen Bryen, "Hamas' underwater drones a wake-up call for Israel," *Asia Times* (Hong Kong), May 21, 2021. https://asiatimes.com/2021/05/hamas-underwater-drones-a-wake-up-call-for-israel

27   Con Coughlin, "Iran 'is intensifying efforts to support Hamas in Gaza,'" *The Telegraph* (UK), April 4, 2015. https://www.telegraph.co.uk/news/worldnews/middleeast/iran/11515603/Iran-is-intensifying-efforts-to-support-Hamas-in-Gaza.html

28   "Blinken: Tehran could build a nuclear bomb 'in a matter of weeks," *Reuters*, June 8, 2021. https://www.arabnews.com/node/1872141/middle-east

29   "Haniyeh Arrives in Iran to Attend President's Swearing-In Ceremony," *Middle East Monitor*, August 5, 2021. https://www.middleeastmonitor.com/20210805-haniyeh-arrives-in-iran-to-attend-presidents-swearing-in-ceremony/

30   "Raisi Hosts Palestinian Terror Chiefs, Vows to Keep Cause and Top of the Agenda," *The Times of Israel* (Israel), August 8, 2021. https://www.timesofisrael.com/raisi-meets-with-palestinian-terror-chiefs-vows-to-keep-cause-at-top-of-agenda/

CONCLUSION

1   Interview with senior IDF official, Tel Aviv, June 20, 2021.

2   Ibid.

3   Ibid.

4   Ibid.

5   Interview with IDF officer, Southern Command, June 22, 2021.

6   Interview with Eliezer Toledano, Southern Command, June 22, 2021.

7   Ibid.

ACKNOWLEDGMENTS

While my name appears as the only author, I must acknowledge the work of numerous colleagues at the Foundation for Defense of Democracies who co-authored previous articles with me, provided me with feedback, or generally informed my work. They include David Adesnik, Bradley Bowman, Mark Dubowitz, Aykan Erdemir, Richard Goldberg, Hussain Abdul Hussain, Clifford May, David May, Shany Mor, Jacob Nagel, Brenda Shaffer, and Joe Truzman. External reviewers included Sharon Schanzer, Julia Schulman, Kenneth Stein, and Boris Zilberman. I am incredibly grateful for their comments and feedback. Research Manager John Hardie went above and beyond in keeping this project remarkably organized while providing important edits, suggestions, and fact checks along the way. Tzvi Kahn and Gabrielle Chishinsky also served as reliable proofreaders. The dynamic production duo of Erin Blumenthal and Daniel Ackerman were creative, flexible, professional and on top of their game. Maryann Karinch, a longtime friend and colleague, helped us all navigate a new era in publishing, and Emily Fritz for formatting and design. My wife, Elana, once again helped support my writing habit, this time without the bribe of gourmet pizza. Even with all this assistance, I recognize that this book may still contain errors. They are not intentional, and they are entirely my own.

ABOUT THE AUTHOR

JONATHAN SCHANZER is a veteran writer and speaker on Middle East affairs.

Jonathan is senior vice president for research at FDD, a nonpartisan think tank that analyzes national security and foreign policy. For 11 years, he has overseen the work of the organization's experts and scholars. Jonathan previously worked as a terrorism finance analyst at the US Department of the Treasury, where he played an integral role in the designation of numerous terrorist financiers. He has held previous think tank research positions at the Washington Institute for Near East Policy and the Middle East Forum.

Jonathan has written hundreds of articles on the Middle East, along with more than a dozen monographs and chapters for edited volumes. His three previous books have made unique contributions to the field of Middle Eastern studies. *State of Failure: Yasser Arafat, Mahmoud Abbas, and the Unmaking of the Palestinian State* (Palgrave Macmillan, 2013) argues the main roadblock to Palestinian statehood is the Palestinian Authority's political dysfunction and mismanagement. *Hamas vs. Fatah: The Struggle for Palestine* (Palgrave Macmillan, 2008) is still the only book on the market that analyzes the ongoing Palestinian civil war. *Al-Qaeda's Armies: Middle East Affiliate Groups and the Next Generation of Terror* (Washington Institute for Near East Policy, 2004) was the first to explore the al-Qaeda franchises in the Middle East.

Jonathan has testified often before Congress. He has appeared on television channels such as Fox News, BBC, and CNN and on Arabic-language television channels such as *Al Arabiya* and *Al Hurra*. Jonathan has traveled widely throughout the Middle East, including to Saudi Arabia, Bahrain, the United Arab Emirates, Iraq, Yemen, Egypt, Morocco, Kuwait, Qatar, Oman, Turkey, Jordan, Israel, and the Palestinian territories.

Jonathan studied Middle East history in four countries. He earned his Ph.D. from King's College London, where he wrote his dissertation on the US Congress and its efforts to combat terrorism in the 20th century. He speaks Arabic and Hebrew.

The author in Gaza in 1998.